Educational Technology

Sunil Kumar

UGC NET, M.Ed, MA
(Education, Philosophy, Sociology, Hindi)
Assistant Professor
Pujya Bhaurao Devras Mahavidyalaya, Kanpur Dehat
Chhatrapati Shahu Ji Maharaj University, Kanpur

KUMAR PUBLICATION

Kumar Publication, Kanpur

Book Title: Educational Technology

Publisher:

Kumar Publication
(Self-Published)
Kanpur, Uttar Pradesh, India

ISBN:
978-93-344-0108-0

Edition:
First Edition – September 2025

Design and Layout:
Sunil Kumar

Published via:
Amazon Kindle Direct Publishing (KDP)
www.kdp.amazon.com

For Permissions or Inquiries:
Email: rohansinghsunil52@gmail.com

Preface

In the rapidly evolving world of education, technology has become an indispensable part of teaching and learning. From traditional classrooms to online platforms, the integration of digital tools has transformed the ways in which knowledge is imparted and acquired. This book, **Educational Technology**, aims to provide a comprehensive understanding of how technology can enhance educational practices and foster meaningful learning experiences.

The primary objective of this book is to equip B.Ed. and M.Ed. students, teachers, and education professionals with the theoretical knowledge and practical skills necessary for effectively using technology in educational settings. It covers a wide range of topics, including instructional design, multimedia integration, ICT tools, online learning platforms, assessment techniques, inclusive education, artificial intelligence, and emerging trends in EdTech.

Each chapter is designed to offer a balance between conceptual understanding and practical application. Case studies, examples, exercises, and references to authentic resources have been included to ensure that readers can relate the content to real-world educational scenarios. Special attention has been given to ethical considerations, accessibility, and student-centered approaches, which are essential for contemporary classrooms.

This book also emphasizes the role of teachers as facilitators, guiding learners through technology-enhanced environments while maintaining pedagogical effectiveness. By integrating research findings, policy frameworks, and innovative tools, it serves as a guide for educators who aspire to create engaging, inclusive, and effective learning experiences.

It is my sincere hope that this book will not only serve as an academic resource but also inspire educators to embrace technology thoughtfully, ethically, and creatively. I am confident that readers will find it both informative and practically useful for their professional development and classroom practice.

I extend my gratitude to all the scholars, researchers, and practitioners whose work has contributed to the knowledge compiled in this book. I also thank my teachers, colleagues and students whose experiences and insights have enriched this work.

Sunil Kumar

Table of Contents

Chapter 1

Introduction to Educational Technology

1.1 Definition and Scope of Educational Technology

Definition of Educational Technology Educational technology refers to the systematic application of scientific knowledge, tools, techniques, and processes to improve teaching, learning, and educational management. It integrates both hardware, such as computers, projectors, and smart devices, and software, such as learning management systems (LMS), educational apps, and multimedia resources, to create effective and engaging learning experiences. The primary goal of educational technology is to enhance the efficiency, accessibility, and quality of education by using modern communication tools and instructional strategies.

According to various scholars, educational technology is defined as "the application of scientific knowledge in educational settings to facilitate learning and improve performance." It is not limited to the use of gadgets or devices but also includes instructional designs, teaching models, assessment techniques, and educational research that support learners' development. In teacher education, educational technology plays a vital role by providing methods, materials, and support that guide teachers to plan lessons effectively, deliver content, and assess learning outcomes.

Scope of Educational Technology The scope of educational technology is wide and expanding rapidly with advances in science and communication. It covers various areas including teaching methods, learning strategies, instructional materials, educational tools, and assessment techniques. Below are key areas that define its scope:

1. **Teaching and Learning** Educational technology assists teachers in designing instructional activities, presentations, and digital content. It supports differentiated learning by offering personalized learning experiences that cater to diverse learners, including those with special needs. Students benefit from interactive lessons, videos, animations, and simulations that make abstract concepts easier to understand.
2. **Educational Management** Technology is also applied in educational administration. Schools and colleges use management software for attendance tracking, timetable scheduling, resource planning, and communication with students and parents. This streamlines operations and enhances accountability.
3. **Training and Professional Development** Teacher training programs increasingly use digital platforms for webinars, workshops, and online certifications. These help educators stay updated with modern teaching methodologies and technological tools.
4. **Assessment and Evaluation** Technology enables effective assessment through online quizzes, tests, and feedback mechanisms. Data analytics help educators monitor students' progress, identify learning gaps, and provide targeted interventions.
5. **Inclusive Education** Assistive technologies, such as screen readers, hearing aids, and learning apps, expand access to education for learners with disabilities. Technology ensures that learning resources are adaptable and accessible to all students.

6. **Research and Innovation** Educational technology promotes innovation by encouraging teachers and researchers to explore new methods of teaching, learning, and assessment. It facilitates action research and helps in analyzing educational challenges through data-driven insights.
7. **Global Collaboration** Technology enables communication and collaboration across geographical boundaries. Teachers and learners can participate in international forums, share resources, and learn from global best practices.

1.2 Importance and Objectives of Educational Technology

Importance of Educational Technology Educational technology has become an essential component of modern education. It plays a significant role in enhancing the quality, efficiency, and accessibility of teaching and learning. With the rapid growth of information and communication technologies, education systems across the world are transforming to meet the needs of diverse learners, changing societal expectations, and global developments.

1. **Improves Teaching and Learning** One of the most important aspects of educational technology is that it helps teachers present information in more interactive and engaging ways. Multimedia tools such as videos, animations, and simulations make learning easier and more understandable. Complex concepts are simplified, and learners can experiment with ideas in virtual environments, which fosters deeper understanding.
2. **Promotes Individualized Learning** Every student learns at their own pace and has unique learning styles. Educational technology provides adaptive learning systems that allow

learners to access customized content according to their strengths and weaknesses. Assistive technologies further ensure that students with disabilities can participate fully in educational activities.

3. **Enhances Accessibility and Flexibility** Technology breaks geographical barriers by offering online courses, e-learning platforms, and virtual classrooms. Students from remote areas can access high-quality education without the need to travel. Similarly, working professionals and adult learners can study at their convenience.
4. **Supports Teacher Training and Professional Growth** Through online workshops, webinars, and certification courses, teachers can enhance their professional skills. Technology helps educators stay updated with new teaching methods and classroom strategies, improving their confidence and competence.
5. **Encourages Collaborative Learning** Digital platforms enable students and teachers to collaborate on projects, share ideas, and learn from peers. Group discussions, forums, and cloud-based tools create opportunities for teamwork, enhancing communication and problem-solving skills.
6. **Facilitates Effective Assessment and Feedback** Educational technology enables real-time assessment through quizzes, tests, and assignments. Teachers can instantly analyze results, provide feedback, and plan remedial teaching accordingly. This data-driven approach helps improve learning outcomes.
7. **Promotes Research and Innovation** Technology supports educational research by providing tools for data collection and analysis. It encourages experimentation and creative thinking, allowing teachers and students to explore new methods of learning and teaching.

8. **Prepares Students for Future Careers** In a world dominated by technology, students need digital literacy and problem-solving skills. Educational technology equips learners with these competencies, making them ready for the workforce and life-long learning.

Objectives of Educational Technology The primary objectives of educational technology are designed to improve teaching methods, enhance learning outcomes, and ensure equitable access to education. Key objectives include:

1. **To facilitate effective teaching and learning** by using modern tools and techniques that enhance understanding and engagement.
2. **To individualize education** by adapting teaching methods and content to meet the diverse needs of learners.
3. **To make education more accessible** to learners regardless of location, socio-economic background, or disabilities.
4. **To improve teacher training** by providing resources for professional development, skill enhancement, and classroom management.
5. **To enhance assessment and feedback** by using digital tools for evaluating student performance, tracking progress, and guiding improvement.
6. **To encourage collaboration and communication** among students, teachers, and educational institutions across the world.
7. **To promote research and innovation** in teaching methodologies and educational content.
8. **To prepare learners for the demands of the modern workforce** by developing digital skills, critical thinking, and problem-solving abilities.

1.3 Historical Development of Educational Technology

Introduction

The history of educational technology is closely linked with the development of human communication, learning methods, and instructional tools. Over time, technology has evolved from simple aids to sophisticated digital platforms that support teaching, learning, assessment, and administration. Understanding this historical journey helps B.Ed. and M.Ed. students appreciate how education has adapted to societal, scientific, and technological changes.

Early Beginnings: Oral Tradition and Visual Aids

Education began with oral communication, storytelling, and memorization. Teachers used simple tools such as slates, chalk, and diagrams to explain lessons. Visual aids like charts, maps, and models helped learners understand subjects better. These early tools laid the foundation for structured learning and classroom interaction.

Printing Press and Mass Education (15th – 18th Century)

The invention of the printing press by Johannes Gutenberg in the 15th century marked a major turning point in education. Books became widely available, and formal education spread across societies. Printed textbooks enabled standardization of curriculum and improved access to learning materials. Literacy rates increased, and schools began to adopt systematic teaching methods.

The Industrial Revolution and Scientific Learning (19th Century)

During the Industrial Revolution, there was a growing demand for skilled workers and educated individuals. Scientific thinking and experimentation became important in education. Teaching tools expanded to include laboratory equipment, maps, and globes. The focus shifted from rote memorization to understanding concepts through observation and experimentation. Education technology in this period emphasized practical learning and vocational training.

Radio, Television, and Mass Communication (20th Century)

The 20th century witnessed a revolution in communication tools that transformed education. The radio became a popular medium for distance learning and educational broadcasts. Television brought visual instruction into homes and schools, helping students grasp abstract concepts with audio-visual support. Educational films and documentaries further enriched classroom teaching.

In addition, programmed instruction emerged as a new teaching approach, where learning was divided into small steps and students could progress at their own pace. Teaching machines and early computers began to supplement classroom activities.

The Digital Age and Computers (Late 20th Century)

With the rise of computers in the 1970s and 1980s, educational technology entered a new phase. Computer-assisted instruction (CAI) allowed students to interact with software programs for practice, simulations, and tutorials. Schools began adopting computers for record-keeping, learning management, and research.

The internet, introduced in the 1990s, expanded access to information and online learning platforms. Emails, websites, and online forums enabled global collaboration between educators and learners. Multimedia tools such as PowerPoint presentations and educational videos became commonplace in classrooms.

21st Century: Mobile Learning, Artificial Intelligence, and Virtual Platforms

The 21st century has seen rapid advancements in technology that are reshaping education. Smartphones, tablets, and apps provide learning resources anytime and anywhere. Learning management systems, digital classrooms, and video conferencing platforms such as Zoom and Google Classroom have become essential tools, especially during situations like the COVID-19 pandemic.

Artificial Intelligence (AI), adaptive learning platforms, virtual reality (VR), and augmented reality (AR) are further enhancing personalized learning experiences. Data analytics is being used to track progress and recommend customized learning pathways. Open educational resources (OER) and MOOCs are making education accessible across the globe.

1.4 Role of Educational Technology in Teaching and Learning

Introduction

Educational technology plays a vital role in modern teaching and learning. It helps teachers deliver lessons more effectively and assists students in understanding and applying knowledge in practical ways. By integrating technology into the learning process, education becomes more engaging, flexible, inclusive, and efficient. For B.Ed. and M.Ed. students, understanding this role is essential for improving classroom practices and preparing for future educational challenges.

Role in Teaching

1. **Enhancing Instructional Delivery** Technology provides teachers with various tools such as multimedia presentations, videos, animations, and interactive simulations. These tools help explain complex ideas clearly and keep students interested. For example, a science teacher can use videos to demonstrate experiments that may be difficult to perform in a classroom.
2. **Facilitating Lesson Planning and Organization** Digital platforms and learning management systems assist teachers in planning lessons, organizing content, and scheduling activities. Online resources offer ready-made lesson plans, worksheets, and teaching aids that reduce preparation time and increase effectiveness.
3. **Supporting Differentiated Instruction** Every student learns differently. Educational technology helps teachers design personalized lessons that cater to diverse learning styles and paces. Tools such as quizzes, adaptive learning software, and feedback systems allow teachers to adjust their teaching based on student performance.
4. **Providing Real-Time Assessment and Feedback** Technology enables teachers to assess student learning instantly through online quizzes, polls, and assignments. Immediate feedback helps learners correct mistakes and improve understanding while allowing teachers to track progress and plan remedial support.

5. **Encouraging Collaborative Teaching** Online forums, video conferencing tools, and group projects allow teachers to collaborate with other educators and share best practices. This interaction broadens teachers' perspectives and brings innovation into classroom strategies.

Role in Learning

1. **Making Learning Engaging and Interactive** Educational technology offers a variety of multimedia tools that make learning enjoyable. Interactive apps, educational games, and simulations encourage active participation, increasing motivation and retention.
2. **Promoting Self-Learning and Exploration** Digital platforms allow students to explore topics beyond the textbook. E-libraries, educational videos, and online courses enable learners to access information independently, fostering curiosity and critical thinking.
3. **Improving Accessibility and Inclusion** Students from remote areas or those with disabilities benefit from assistive technologies and online learning platforms. Audio books, screen readers, and subtitles ensure that every learner can participate fully in education.
4. **Developing 21st Century Skills** Technology helps students build essential skills such as digital literacy, communication, collaboration, and problem-solving. These skills are important for future careers and lifelong learning.
5. **Encouraging Continuous Learning** With access to online resources and learning apps, students can learn at their own pace and anytime they wish. This flexibility supports lifelong learning and helps students stay updated with new knowledge and skills.

1.5 Impact on Educational Practices

Introduction

The impact of educational technology on teaching and learning practices has been profound and far-reaching. It has transformed the way lessons are delivered, how students engage with content, and how teachers assess learning. Technology has not only improved efficiency and access but also reshaped educational philosophies and classroom environments. For B.Ed. and M.Ed. students, understanding this impact helps them design more effective and inclusive learning experiences.

Impact on Teaching Practices

1. **Shift from Teacher-Centered to Learner-Centered Approaches** Earlier, teaching was mostly teacher-centered, where the instructor delivered information and students passively listened. Educational technology has shifted this model towards learner-centered education. Teachers now encourage interactive learning, discussions, and exploration, allowing students to actively participate and engage in the learning process.
2. **Use of Multimedia and Visual Aids** Modern classrooms now integrate multimedia tools such as videos, animations, and presentations. These resources help teachers explain abstract concepts, maintain student attention, and cater to different learning styles. The use of visual aids makes learning more effective and enjoyable.
3. **Blended and Online Learning** Educational practices have expanded beyond physical classrooms. Online learning platforms and blended approaches (a combination of face-to-

face and online teaching) offer flexibility and allow teachers to reach students in remote areas. This practice is especially useful during emergencies, like the COVID-19 pandemic, where virtual classrooms ensured continuity in education.

4. **Improved Assessment and Feedback Mechanisms** Technology-enabled assessments like online quizzes and instant feedback systems help teachers track student progress in real-time. This data-driven approach allows educators to identify learning gaps, personalize instruction, and offer timely support.
5. **Professional Development** Technology has created opportunities for teachers to enhance their skills through online courses, webinars, and communities of practice. Teachers can now collaborate globally, share resources, and learn innovative teaching methods.

Impact on Learning Practices

1. **Greater Access to Educational Resources** Students now have access to a vast range of educational content through e-books, videos, podcasts, and online libraries. This access supports self-learning, exploration, and the ability to study at one's own pace.
2. **Development of Digital Skills** Learning practices now include digital literacy, which is essential for solving problems, communicating effectively, and collaborating in modern environments. Students learn how to navigate technology, critically analyze information, and use digital tools productively.
3. **Enhanced Motivation and Engagement** Interactive tools like educational games, simulations, and quizzes make learning fun and challenge students to think critically. These

practices help maintain attention and encourage active participation.

4. **Personalized Learning Paths** Technology allows students to learn according to their individual needs. Adaptive learning platforms recommend exercises, content, and feedback tailored to each learner, helping them progress without feeling overwhelmed.
5. **Inclusive Learning Opportunities** Assistive technologies such as screen readers, subtitles, and learning apps ensure that students with disabilities or learning difficulties can access educational content. This has made classrooms more inclusive and equitable.

Chapter 2

Information and Communication Technology (ICT) in Education

2.1 Understanding ICT (Information and Communication Technology)

Introduction

Information and Communication Technology (ICT) refers to the use of technological tools and resources to create, store, exchange, and manage information. In education, ICT plays a crucial role in facilitating teaching, learning, administration, and communication. It includes devices such as computers, smartphones, tablets, and software applications, along with networks like the internet, intranet, and wireless systems that enable seamless access to educational content.

Understanding ICT is essential for B.Ed. and M.Ed. students because it equips them to effectively integrate technology into classrooms, support learners' diverse needs, and improve learning outcomes. This section explains the components, functions, and relevance of ICT in educational settings.

What is ICT?

ICT stands for Information and Communication Technology. It is an umbrella term that includes all forms of technology used to handle information and facilitate communication. It goes beyond just computers and includes tools like telecommunication networks, digital platforms, broadcasting systems, and software that support educational activities.

In education, ICT refers to technologies that help in accessing, storing, delivering, and managing learning resources. It assists in creating interactive learning environments, connecting teachers and students, and providing opportunities for self-paced learning.

Components of ICT in Education

1. **Hardware** This includes devices such as computers, projectors, interactive whiteboards, scanners, printers, and mobile devices. These tools are used to display content, record information, and support various teaching-learning activities.
2. **Software** Educational software, learning management systems (LMS), apps, and digital platforms help in planning lessons, delivering content, and assessing student performance. Examples include Google Classroom, Moodle, Microsoft Teams, and Zoom.
3. **Networks and Connectivity** The internet, intranet, Wi-Fi networks, and broadband services enable access to online resources, virtual classrooms, and global collaboration platforms.
4. **Multimedia Tools** Audio, video, graphics, and animations are used to create engaging content that simplifies learning and enhances understanding.

Functions of ICT in Education

1. **Access to Information** ICT provides students and teachers access to educational content from across the globe. E-

books, online lectures, and educational videos enrich classroom instruction.

2. **Communication** Teachers, students, and parents can easily communicate through emails, messaging apps, and video conferencing platforms, ensuring timely exchange of information.
3. **Content Delivery** Digital tools allow teachers to present lessons in a visually appealing manner. Interactive lessons, animations, and simulations make learning more engaging.
4. **Assessment and Feedback** ICT tools help in conducting tests, tracking performance, and providing feedback. Learning analytics support teachers in planning interventions and improving instructional strategies.
5. **Collaboration and Creativity** Online platforms encourage group projects, peer learning, and idea-sharing, fostering creativity and problem-solving skills.

Importance of Understanding ICT

1. **Empowering Teachers** Understanding ICT helps teachers use technology to enhance their teaching methods, save time, and focus on student learning outcomes.
2. **Supporting Learners** Students benefit from personalized learning experiences, improved motivation, and better access to educational resources.
3. **Preparing for the Future** Digital skills are essential for students' future careers. Understanding ICT equips learners with the competencies needed in a technology-driven world.
4. **Promoting Inclusive Education** Assistive technologies and online platforms ensure that education is accessible to all, including students with special needs.

2.2 Tools and Devices in Education

Introduction

In today's educational environment, various tools and devices are used to support teaching, learning, communication, and administration. These tools not only help in delivering information but also make learning interactive, engaging, and accessible. Understanding these tools is essential for B.Ed. and M.Ed. students, as it enables them to integrate technology effectively into classrooms and enhance students' learning experiences.

This section explains the key tools and devices used in education, their functions, and how they contribute to modern teaching and learning practices.

Key Tools and Devices in Education

1. **Computers and Laptops** Computers are among the most common educational tools. They help teachers prepare lessons, present content through multimedia presentations, access information, and communicate with students. Laptops offer portability and flexibility, enabling teachers and students to access digital resources anytime and anywhere.
2. **Projectors and Interactive Whiteboards** Projectors are widely used to display presentations, videos, and animations on large screens, making it easier for students to visualize concepts. Interactive whiteboards allow teachers and students to write, draw, and interact with content in real-time, making learning more dynamic.
3. **Tablets and Smartphones** These handheld devices are increasingly popular for mobile learning. Educational apps,

e-books, online quizzes, and virtual classrooms can be accessed easily, allowing students to learn at their own pace. Teachers can also use tablets and smartphones for instant communication and classroom management.

4. **Audio-Visual Equipment** Devices like microphones, speakers, and headphones support audio learning. Educational videos, podcasts, and recorded lectures help students understand lessons through multiple senses, improving retention and comprehension.
5. **Learning Management Systems (LMS)** Platforms such as Moodle, Google Classroom, and Edmodo enable teachers to upload study materials, assign homework, conduct tests, and interact with students online. LMS tools facilitate blended learning and remote education.
6. **Internet and Wi-Fi Connectivity** A reliable internet connection is essential for accessing online resources, virtual classrooms, webinars, and collaborative tools. Schools and colleges use Wi-Fi networks to ensure students and teachers can connect to educational platforms seamlessly.
7. **Digital Libraries and E-Resources** Online libraries and databases provide access to a vast amount of information including books, journals, articles, and videos. These resources help students conduct research and improve their understanding of various subjects.
8. **Assistive Technologies** For inclusive education, devices like screen readers, speech recognition software, Braille displays, and hearing aids support students with disabilities. These tools ensure that every learner has equal access to education.
9. **Simulation Tools and Virtual Labs** Simulations and virtual laboratories provide a safe and interactive environment for practical learning. Students can experiment, test theories, and observe outcomes without the constraints of a physical lab.

10. **Communication Tools** Applications like Zoom, Microsoft Teams, and Google Meet allow teachers and students to connect virtually. Messaging apps and email platforms ensure continuous communication and collaboration.

Benefits of Using Educational Tools and Devices

Interactive Learning – Students engage more deeply when lessons are presented with visual and audio aids.
Flexible Access – Learning is no longer confined to classroom walls; students can learn anytime and anywhere.
Inclusive Education – Assistive technologies ensure students with disabilities can participate equally.
Improved Assessment – Online tests and feedback tools allow teachers to track progress in real time.
Teacher Support – Technology helps teachers save time, organize lessons, and focus on student development.

2.3 Internet Connectivity and Digital Infrastructure

Introduction

Internet connectivity and digital infrastructure form the backbone of modern educational technology. Without proper access to the internet and supporting infrastructure, it becomes difficult to implement online learning, access educational resources, or communicate effectively. For B.Ed. and M.Ed. students, understanding how internet connectivity and infrastructure support education is essential to ensuring that technology is used efficiently and equitably in classrooms.

What is Internet Connectivity and Digital Infrastructure?

Internet connectivity refers to the ability to access the internet through networks such as broadband, Wi-Fi, 4G/5G, or satellite connections. It enables users to connect devices like computers, tablets, and smartphones to educational platforms, websites, and communication tools.

Digital infrastructure includes the physical and organizational structures needed to support digital education. This encompasses devices (computers, servers), networking equipment (routers, switches), software platforms, data centers, and power supply systems. Together, internet connectivity and digital infrastructure create the environment where technology can be effectively used for learning.

Importance of Internet Connectivity in Education

1. **Access to Online Learning Platforms** A strong internet connection enables students and teachers to access educational websites, learning management systems, and virtual classrooms without interruption.
2. **Facilitating Real-Time Communication** Teachers can interact with students through video calls, webinars, and chat forums. Parents can also stay informed about their children's progress through online communication tools.
3. **Supporting Research and Self-Learning** The internet provides vast information in the form of e-books, academic journals, video tutorials, and databases. Students can explore topics beyond textbooks, encouraging independent learning and research.

4. **Encouraging Collaboration** Digital tools allow students and teachers to work together on projects, share resources, and participate in online discussions, irrespective of geographical boundaries.
5. **Enabling Inclusive Education** Online tools and content can be customized to meet the needs of diverse learners. Students with disabilities can benefit from assistive devices, ensuring equitable access.

Digital Infrastructure: The Foundation for Effective Learning

1. **Hardware Support** Digital infrastructure includes computers, tablets, projectors, routers, servers, and networking cables. Adequate hardware is essential for classrooms, libraries, and laboratories to function efficiently.
2. **Software Applications** Applications like Google Classroom, Zoom, and educational apps support lesson planning, content delivery, and evaluation. These platforms need proper installation, updates, and technical support.
3. **Power Supply and Backup Systems** Reliable electricity is critical for uninterrupted online learning. Backup solutions like generators and uninterrupted power supply (UPS) systems ensure that classes continue even during power outages.
4. **Data Security and Privacy** A robust digital infrastructure includes firewalls, secure networks, and encryption tools that protect sensitive information and ensure safe usage of online platforms.
5. **Maintenance and Technical Support** Regular maintenance of equipment and availability of technical support teams

ensure that classrooms and institutions remain functional and secure.

Challenges in Internet Connectivity and Infrastructure

- ✔ Poor network coverage in rural areas
- ✔ High cost of devices and internet services
- ✔ Lack of trained personnel to manage digital tools
- ✔ Cybersecurity threats and data misuse
- ✔ Power shortages affecting uninterrupted learning

2.4 Mobile Learning and Educational Apps

Introduction

Mobile learning and educational apps have revolutionized the way education is delivered and received. With the widespread availability of smartphones and tablets, learning is no longer confined to classrooms or textbooks. Students and teachers can access educational resources anytime and anywhere, making learning more flexible, engaging, and personalized. For B.Ed. and M.Ed. students, understanding mobile learning and the use of educational apps is essential for creating innovative, learner-centered teaching strategies.

What is Mobile Learning?

Mobile learning, often called m-learning, refers to the use of mobile devices such as smartphones, tablets, and e-readers to access educational content and participate in learning activities. It enables learners to study, practice, and collaborate through wireless internet connections, educational apps, and cloud-based platforms.

Unlike traditional learning methods, mobile learning allows learners to engage with content at their convenience, thereby supporting self-paced and lifelong learning. It also encourages creativity, critical thinking, and problem-solving skills.

What are Educational Apps?

Educational apps are software applications designed to support learning and teaching. These apps can include interactive lessons, quizzes, games, simulations, videos, and e-books that help learners understand and retain information. Some apps are subject-specific, such as language learning tools or math practice apps, while others focus on general learning skills like time management, note-taking, and collaborative projects.

Examples of popular educational apps include:
✔ Duolingo (language learning)
✔ Khan Academy (math, science, and other subjects)
✔ Quizlet (flashcards and practice tests)
✔ Google Classroom (lesson management)
✔ Byju's (interactive video lessons)

Benefits of Mobile Learning and Educational Apps

1. **Accessibility and Flexibility** Students can learn from anywhere, at any time, without the need for physical classrooms. This helps working professionals, distance learners, and students in rural areas access education more easily.
2. **Personalized Learning Experience** Apps offer adaptive learning paths, where content adjusts according to the

learner's pace and performance. This approach helps students focus on areas where they need more practice.

3. **Interactive and Engaging Content** Gamified quizzes, animations, and simulations make learning fun and encourage participation. Learners stay motivated and are more likely to retain information.
4. **Instant Feedback and Assessment** Many apps offer quizzes and exercises with instant feedback, helping students identify their strengths and areas for improvement.
5. **Promotes Self-Learning and Autonomy** Mobile learning encourages students to explore topics independently. Educational apps often provide supplementary resources that allow learners to go beyond the curriculum.
6. **Supports Collaborative Learning** Some apps include discussion forums, group projects, and peer review features that encourage students to collaborate, share knowledge, and learn from each other.

Challenges of Mobile Learning

✔ Unequal access to smartphones and internet connectivity

✔ Distractions from entertainment apps and social media

✔ Data privacy and cybersecurity concerns

✔ Lack of training for teachers and students in using apps effectively

✔ Over-reliance on technology may reduce interpersonal communication skills

2.5 Challenges and Solutions in Using ICT

Introduction

The use of Information and Communication Technology (ICT) in education has brought many benefits, but it also comes with challenges that can affect its effective implementation. Understanding these challenges and identifying possible solutions is essential for B.Ed. and M.Ed. students, as it prepares them to address obstacles in classrooms and educational institutions. This section explores common issues faced while using ICT and offers practical solutions to overcome them.

Challenges in Using ICT

1. **Lack of Infrastructure** Many schools and colleges, especially in rural areas, do not have adequate infrastructure like computers, internet access, or electricity. Without these basic facilities, the use of ICT becomes difficult.
2. **Digital Divide** There is often unequal access to digital devices and internet connectivity among students from different socio-economic backgrounds. This digital divide creates disparities in learning opportunities.
3. **Lack of Teacher Training** Some teachers are not familiar with how to use ICT tools effectively. Without proper training, technology remains underutilized, and teaching methods do not benefit from new tools.
4. **High Costs** Purchasing devices, software, and internet connections can be expensive. Budget constraints often prevent institutions from providing sufficient ICT facilities.
5. **Technical Issues** Frequent power cuts, slow internet speeds, and software glitches disrupt the learning process and cause frustration among teachers and students.
6. **Distractions and Misuse** Students may use devices for entertainment or social media, which distracts them from

learning. Misuse of technology can also lead to privacy concerns and cyberbullying.

7. **Language and Content Barriers** Most educational content available online is in English or other major languages. Students from different linguistic backgrounds may struggle to access or understand resources.

Solutions to Overcome ICT Challenges

1. **Improving Infrastructure** Governments and educational institutions should invest in basic infrastructure such as reliable internet connections, solar-powered devices, and smart classrooms. Public-private partnerships can help fund such initiatives.
2. **Bridging the Digital Divide** Schools can provide subsidized or loaned devices to students from disadvantaged backgrounds. Community centers and libraries can also serve as shared learning spaces with internet access.
3. **Teacher Training and Capacity Building** Regular workshops, webinars, and certification programs should be conducted to train teachers in the use of ICT tools. Peer learning and mentoring can help teachers build confidence.
4. **Cost-Effective Solutions** Open-source software, free educational apps, and government-sponsored platforms can reduce costs. Schools can prioritize purchasing essential tools that serve multiple purposes.
5. **Technical Support and Maintenance** Schools should have a dedicated technical support team to resolve issues quickly. Regular maintenance schedules and backup systems like generators can minimize disruptions.
6. **Promoting Responsible Use of Technology** Teachers should guide students on using technology responsibly by

establishing digital etiquette rules. Monitoring apps and parental controls can prevent misuse and distractions.

7. **Providing Multilingual and Accessible Content** Developing content in local languages and using voice-assisted tools can help learners from diverse backgrounds. Collaborations with content creators and educational organizations can enrich available resources.

Chapter 3

Multimedia and E-Learning

3.1 Components of Multimedia

Introduction

Multimedia plays a significant role in educational technology by combining different types of content to create an interactive and engaging learning experience. It integrates text, graphics, audio, video, animation, and interactivity to present information in ways that are easy to understand and remember. For B.Ed. and M.Ed. students, learning about the components of multimedia is essential for designing effective teaching materials and delivering lessons that cater to various learning styles.

What is Multimedia?

Multimedia refers to the integration of multiple forms of content—such as text, images, sound, video, and animation—into a single platform or application. It enhances learning by appealing to different senses and making educational content more engaging and interactive. Multimedia is widely used in presentations, e-learning platforms, simulations, and digital classrooms.

Key Components of Multimedia

1. **Text**
   Text is the most basic component of multimedia. It is used to convey information, instructions, definitions, or explanations. Text can be formatted with different fonts,

sizes, and colors to highlight key points and guide the learner through the content.

Uses:

✔ Titles and headings

✔ Explanations and definitions

✔ Instructions or descriptions

2. **Graphics**

   Graphics include still images such as photographs, charts, diagrams, and drawings. They help explain concepts visually, making it easier for students to understand complex ideas.

Uses:

✔ Illustrations of processes or structures

✔ Visual aids like charts and graphs

✔ Icons and symbols to represent ideas

3. **Audio**

   Audio includes sounds, music, or voice recordings. It enhances the learning experience by explaining content or adding emphasis to important points. It also supports learners with different needs, such as those with reading difficulties.

Uses:

✔ Narration of lessons

✔ Sound effects to highlight actions

✔ Background music to create a learning atmosphere

4. **Video**

   Video integrates moving images with sound, making it a

powerful tool for explaining processes, demonstrating experiments, or storytelling. It keeps learners engaged and helps in visualizing real-life scenarios.

Uses:

✔ Recorded lectures or tutorials

✔ Educational documentaries

✔ Simulations and case studies

5. **Animation**

   Animation refers to moving graphics or illustrations that show changes, actions, or transformations over time. Animations make abstract or difficult concepts easier to grasp.

Uses:

✔ Simulating processes like the water cycle

✔ Demonstrating scientific experiments

✔ Visualizing mathematical concepts

6. **Interactivity**

   Interactivity allows learners to participate actively in the learning process by responding to quizzes, selecting options, or exploring content. It promotes engagement and deeper understanding.

Uses:

✔ Interactive quizzes and assignments

✔ Virtual experiments or labs

✔ Simulations where learners control actions

Benefits of Using Multimedia in Education

✔ **Enhances Understanding** – Complex topics are broken down using visuals, audio, and animations.
✔ **Improves Retention** – Multisensory learning helps learners remember information better.
✔ **Encourages Active Participation** – Interactive elements promote engagement and curiosity.
✔ **Supports Diverse Learning Styles** – Visual, auditory, and kinesthetic learners benefit equally.
✔ **Makes Learning Enjoyable** – Multimedia keeps learners motivated and interested.

3.2 Designing Effective E-Learning Content

Introduction

With the increasing use of technology in education, e-learning has become a powerful tool for delivering knowledge beyond traditional classrooms. Designing effective e-learning content is crucial to ensure that learners stay motivated, understand concepts clearly, and achieve the desired learning outcomes. For B.Ed. and M.Ed. students, learning how to create structured, interactive, and learner-centered content is essential to prepare them for teaching in modern educational environments.

Key Principles for Designing Effective E-Learning Content

1. **Define Clear Learning Objectives** E-learning content must begin with well-defined learning objectives. These should state what learners are expected to know or do after

completing the course or module. Objectives should be specific, measurable, and aligned with the curriculum.

Example:
"Students will be able to identify different types of ecosystems and explain their characteristics using diagrams and examples."

2. **Understand the Learners' Needs** Analyze the learners' age, background, learning preferences, and prior knowledge. This helps in designing content that is age-appropriate, culturally relevant, and aligned with their learning styles.
3. **Organize Content Logically** Content should follow a structured sequence, starting from simple concepts and progressing toward complex topics. Use headings, bullet points, and summaries to make content easier to follow.
4. **Use Multimedia for Better Engagement** Integrating text with images, videos, animations, and audio enriches the learning experience. Multimedia helps explain abstract ideas and appeals to different senses, thereby improving understanding and retention.

Example:
A video demonstration of a science experiment combined with step-by-step instructions and quizzes to test comprehension.

5. **Encourage Interaction** Interactive elements such as quizzes, drag-and-drop exercises, forums, and simulations engage learners actively. Interaction promotes problem-solving, critical thinking, and collaborative learning.
6. **Ensure Accessibility and Inclusivity** E-learning content should be designed so that it is accessible to all learners, including those with disabilities. Use captions, screen-reader-friendly text, and adjustable fonts. Multilingual

content or translation features can support learners from various backgrounds.

7. **Provide Regular Feedback** Instant feedback through quizzes and assignments helps learners understand their strengths and areas for improvement. Teachers can track performance and offer targeted guidance to enhance learning.
8. **Maintain Visual Appeal and Consistency** A clean layout, consistent fonts, and appropriate colors improve readability and prevent cognitive overload. A visually appealing design keeps learners engaged and focused.
9. **Support Self-Paced Learning** Learners should be able to control the pace of their learning. Content should offer optional resources, additional readings, and flexible schedules to accommodate individual learning speeds.

Steps in Designing E-Learning Content

1. Identify learning goals and outcomes.
2. Conduct a learner analysis.
3. Outline the structure and sequence of lessons.
4. Select multimedia tools and software platforms.
5. Create interactive activities and assessments.
6. Ensure content accessibility and inclusivity.
7. Pilot the content and gather feedback.
8. Revise based on feedback and learner data.

3.3 Learning Management Systems (LMS)

Introduction

Learning Management Systems (LMS) are software platforms that help in the planning, delivery, tracking, and evaluation of educational courses or training programs. LMS has become an essential tool in modern education, especially in e-learning environments. It allows teachers and learners to access content anytime and from anywhere, thus supporting flexible, interactive, and learner-centered education. For B.Ed. and M.Ed. students, understanding LMS is critical to designing and managing effective teaching strategies in both traditional and online classrooms.

What is a Learning Management System (LMS)?

A Learning Management System (LMS) is an integrated platform that helps educators create, manage, and deliver courses digitally. It also enables learners to access course materials, submit assignments, take tests, and track their progress. LMS streamlines administrative tasks and improves communication between teachers and students.

Popular LMS platforms include:

✔ Moodle

✔ Google Classroom

✔ Blackboard

✔ Canvas

✔ Edmodo

Key Features of LMS

1. **Content Management** LMS allows teachers to upload study materials such as notes, videos, presentations, and assignments in various formats. It ensures that content is well-organized and easily accessible.
2. **Assessment and Evaluation** Teachers can create quizzes, assignments, and exams, and provide instant feedback. LMS

helps in tracking students' progress and identifying areas where they need additional support.

3. **Communication Tools** LMS offers forums, chats, and messaging features that help teachers and students interact in real time or asynchronously. This promotes discussion and collaboration.
4. **Personalized Learning Paths** LMS can track learners' progress and performance, offering customized learning paths and resources that suit their individual needs.
5. **Scheduling and Notifications** Teachers can schedule classes, exams, and assignments, and send reminders or announcements. Notifications keep learners informed and engaged.
6. **Reports and Analytics** LMS provides reports on attendance, assignment submissions, quiz scores, and learning patterns. These insights help teachers make data-driven decisions to enhance learning outcomes.
7. **Accessibility and Mobile Compatibility** Most LMS platforms are compatible with mobile devices, allowing learners to access content on the go. Features like captions, transcripts, and adjustable fonts make content accessible to all learners.

Benefits of Using LMS in Education

✔ **Flexibility** – Students can learn at their own pace and time.

✔ **Efficiency** – Teachers can easily manage content, assignments, and evaluations.

✔ **Engagement** – Interactive tools and multimedia keep learners motivated.

✔ **Accessibility** – LMS helps students from remote areas and those with disabilities to participate fully.

✔ **Data-Driven Instruction** – Performance analytics help teachers personalize instruction.

Challenges of LMS Implementation

✔ Lack of digital literacy among teachers and students
✔ Internet connectivity issues in rural areas
✔ High cost of implementation and maintenance
✔ Resistance to change from traditional teaching methods
✔ Data security and privacy concerns

3.4 Video Lectures, Podcasts, and Interactive Sessions

Introduction

In modern education, video lectures, podcasts, and interactive sessions have emerged as powerful tools for enhancing teaching and learning. These methods offer flexibility, engagement, and accessibility, making education more learner-centered and effective. For B.Ed. and M.Ed. students, understanding how to use these tools is crucial for designing instructional strategies that cater to diverse learning needs and preferences.

Video Lectures

Video lectures are recorded or live presentations delivered by teachers or subject experts. They combine audio, visual, and textual elements to explain concepts, demonstrate procedures, or share insights. Video lectures allow learners to study at their own pace, pause and rewind content, and revisit complex topics.

Benefits:

1. **Flexibility** – Students can access lectures anytime and anywhere.
2. **Visual and Auditory Learning** – Combines visual aids, demonstrations, and narration to enhance understanding.
3. **Reinforcement of Learning** – Allows repeated viewing for better retention.
4. **Support for Distance Learning** – Essential for learners who cannot attend physical classrooms.

Examples:

✔ Recorded lectures on YouTube or institutional platforms

✔ MOOCs (Massive Open Online Courses)

✔ Subject-specific tutorials with animations and demonstrations

Podcasts

Podcasts are audio recordings on educational topics that learners can listen to on smartphones, tablets, or computers. They offer a convenient way to deliver content outside the classroom, allowing students to learn while commuting, exercising, or performing other activities.

Benefits:

1. **Convenience** – Learners can access content on the go.
2. **Focus on Listening Skills** – Improves comprehension, pronunciation, and auditory learning.
3. **Supplementary Learning** – Supports classroom learning by providing additional explanations and insights.
4. **Cost-Effective** – Requires minimal technology and resources compared to video production.

Examples:

✔ Subject-specific podcasts for science, history, or language learning

✔ Expert interviews and panel discussions

✔ Educational storytelling for younger learners

Interactive Sessions

Interactive sessions involve live or virtual engagements between teachers and students, promoting active participation. This includes online discussions, webinars, group activities, polls, and Q&A sessions.

Benefits:

1. **Active Learning** – Encourages students to ask questions, solve problems, and discuss ideas.
2. **Immediate Feedback** – Teachers can address doubts and clarify concepts instantly.
3. **Collaboration** – Students learn to work in groups, share knowledge, and develop communication skills.
4. **Motivation and Engagement** – Interaction keeps learners interested and focused.

Examples:

✔ Zoom or Microsoft Teams webinars

✔ Virtual labs and simulations

✔ Interactive polls, quizzes, and discussion forums

Integrating These Tools in Education

- **Blended Learning:** Combine video lectures, podcasts, and interactive sessions with classroom instruction.
- **Flipped Classroom:** Students watch video lectures or listen to podcasts before class, allowing in-class time for discussion and activities.
- **Personalized Learning:** Use these tools to provide tailored content according to individual learning needs.
- **Assessment and Feedback:** Interactive sessions and quizzes can be integrated to evaluate comprehension.

3.5 Accessibility, Engagement, and Retention Strategies

Introduction

In modern education, technology offers opportunities to enhance accessibility, increase learner engagement, and improve retention of knowledge. Effective teaching goes beyond delivering content; it ensures that all students, regardless of their abilities or backgrounds, can access learning materials, stay motivated, and retain what they learn. For B.Ed. and M.Ed. students, understanding strategies to achieve accessibility, engagement, and retention is crucial for designing inclusive and impactful learning experiences.

Accessibility Strategies

Accessibility ensures that all learners, including those with disabilities or language barriers, can access educational resources. Key strategies include:

1. **Use of Assistive Technologies** Screen readers, speech-to-text tools, magnifiers, and Braille devices help learners with visual or auditory impairments participate fully.

2. **Multilingual Content** Providing content in multiple languages or using translation tools ensures students from diverse linguistic backgrounds can understand lessons.
3. **Flexible Formats** Offering materials in text, audio, video, and interactive formats caters to different learning preferences and needs.
4. **Mobile-Friendly and Offline Access** Making resources accessible on smartphones and tablets, as well as providing downloadable content for offline use, increases access for students in areas with limited connectivity.

Engagement Strategies

Engagement strategies keep learners motivated, attentive, and actively involved in the learning process. Key approaches include:

1. **Interactive Multimedia** Incorporating videos, animations, simulations, and interactive quizzes makes lessons more stimulating and enjoyable.
2. **Collaborative Learning** Group discussions, projects, forums, and peer-to-peer interactions promote active participation and social learning.
3. **Gamification** Applying game elements such as points, badges, leaderboards, and challenges motivates learners and encourages competition in a fun way.
4. **Personalized Learning Paths** Adaptive content that aligns with learners' progress and interests keeps them engaged and prevents boredom or frustration.
5. **Real-World Applications** Using case studies, practical examples, and problem-solving activities connects theoretical knowledge to real-life contexts, enhancing relevance and interest.

Retention Strategies

Retention strategies help learners remember and apply knowledge effectively. Key methods include:

1. **Repetition and Reinforcement** Periodic reviews, quizzes, and practice exercises reinforce learning and aid long-term retention.
2. **Chunking Content** Breaking down content into small, manageable units reduces cognitive overload and helps learners absorb information better.
3. **Active Learning Techniques** Encouraging note-taking, summarizing, teaching peers, and engaging in hands-on activities strengthens memory and understanding.
4. **Feedback and Assessment** Providing timely feedback on assignments, quizzes, and projects helps learners identify mistakes, correct them, and consolidate knowledge.
5. **Multisensory Learning** Combining visual, auditory, and kinesthetic activities ensures learners encode information through multiple senses, enhancing recall.

Integrating Accessibility, Engagement, and Retention

- **Blended Learning Models**: Combine online resources, interactive sessions, and in-person instruction.
- **Inclusive Content Design**: Ensure lessons are accessible to all learners and include elements that actively involve them.
- **Continuous Assessment**: Use formative and summative assessments to monitor learning and retention.
- **Technology-Enhanced Strategies**: Use apps, LMS, and digital tools to create adaptive, interactive, and inclusive learning experiences.

Chapter 4

Models of Teaching and Instructional Aids

4.1 Instructional Design Models

Introduction

Instructional Design (ID) refers to the systematic process of designing, developing, and delivering instructional materials and learning experiences in a way that ensures effective learning. Instructional design models provide structured frameworks that guide educators in planning, creating, and evaluating teaching and learning activities. For B.Ed. and M.Ed. students, understanding these models is essential for developing lessons that are organized, goal-oriented, and tailored to learners' needs.

What is an Instructional Design Model?

An instructional design model is a blueprint for creating effective instructional experiences. It provides a step-by-step methodology to ensure that content, teaching strategies, and assessments align with learning objectives. Models differ in their approach, complexity, and focus, but all aim to enhance the quality and efficiency of instruction.

Key Instructional Design Models

1. ADDIE Model

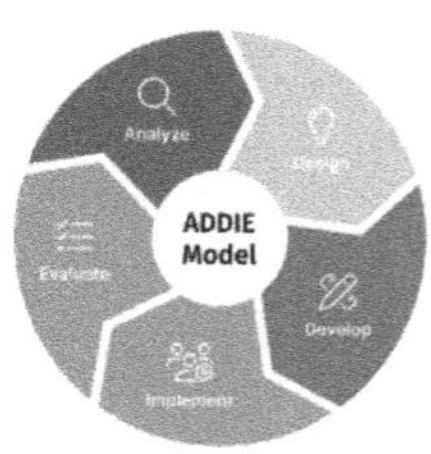

The **ADDIE Model** is one of the most widely recognized and applied instructional design models. It provides a systematic, step-by-step framework for designing, developing, implementing, and evaluating instructional materials and learning experiences. It is highly adaptable, applicable to various educational contexts, and ensures that teaching and learning processes are aligned with clearly defined goals. The model consists of five phases: Analysis, Design, Development, Implementation, and Evaluation.

1. Analysis Phase

Purpose: To understand the learning needs, identify the gaps, and define the goals of instruction.

Key Activities:

- **Learner Analysis:** Assess learners' prior knowledge, skills, learning styles, and motivational levels.
- **Needs Assessment:** Identify what learners need to achieve the learning objectives.
- **Context Analysis:** Consider the learning environment, available resources, technology, and constraints.
- **Goal Setting:** Define clear, measurable learning outcomes that guide the rest of the instructional process.

Example:
In a teacher-training program, analysis may reveal that student-teachers are unfamiliar with educational technology tools like LMS or multimedia resources, so the program's objective is to develop these skills.

Importance:
This phase ensures that instruction is relevant, learner-centered, and aligned with educational goals.

2. Design Phase

Purpose: To plan the structure and strategy of the instructional materials.

Key Activities:

- **Define Learning Objectives:** Specify what learners will know or be able to do after the instruction.
- **Content Sequencing:** Organize content logically from simple to complex concepts.
- **Instructional Strategies:** Choose appropriate teaching methods (lecture, discussion, multimedia, simulations, etc.).
- **Assessment Planning:** Determine formative and summative assessments to measure learning outcomes.
- **Storyboard or Blueprint Creation:** Design the course layout, including media elements, modules, and interactions.

Example:
A lesson plan for teaching "Classroom Management" may include interactive videos, role-playing activities, and quizzes to reinforce learning.

Importance:
The design phase ensures that the instruction is organized, engaging, and aligned with learners' needs and objectives.

3. Development Phase

Purpose: To create and assemble the instructional materials and resources based on the design plan.

Key Activities:

- **Content Creation:** Develop text, images, videos, animations, simulations, and other multimedia materials.
- **Integration of Technology:** Incorporate LMS platforms, apps, or software tools for delivery.
- **Prototype Development:** Prepare a draft version of the course to test usability and effectiveness.
- **Review and Revision:** Ensure accuracy, clarity, and engagement before implementation.

Example:
Creating e-learning modules, interactive PowerPoint presentations, and assessment quizzes for online teacher training.

Importance:
This phase transforms plans into tangible instructional resources ready for use by learners.

4. Implementation Phase

Purpose: To deliver the instructional materials to learners and facilitate learning.

Key Activities:

- **Training Instructors:** Ensure teachers are prepared to deliver content effectively.
- **Technology Setup:** Verify that required tools, software, and hardware are functional.
- **Learner Orientation:** Introduce learners to the course structure, tools, and expectations.
- **Instruction Delivery:** Conduct lessons, workshops, or online modules as planned.

Example:
Conducting live webinars, virtual classroom sessions, or face-to-face training sessions for student-teachers.

Importance:
Effective implementation ensures that learners engage with the content and achieve the intended learning outcomes.

5. Evaluation Phase

Purpose: To assess the effectiveness of instruction and improve it continuously.

Key Activities:

- **Formative Evaluation:** Gather feedback during the course to make real-time improvements.
- **Summative Evaluation:** Assess learners' performance at the end of the instruction.
- **Learner Feedback:** Collect feedback on the quality, clarity, and usability of instructional materials.
- **Revision:** Modify instructional strategies, content, or delivery methods based on evaluation results.

Example:
Using pre-tests and post-tests, surveys, and performance assessments to determine whether student-teachers have acquired the skills in educational technology.

Importance:
Evaluation ensures continuous improvement and validates the effectiveness of the instructional design process.

Advantages of the ADDIE Model

1. **Systematic Approach:** Provides a structured and logical framework for designing instruction.
2. **Flexibility:** Adaptable to any educational setting, subject, or learner group.
3. **Alignment:** Ensures that learning objectives, instructional strategies, content, and assessments are coherent.
4. **Continuous Improvement:** Evaluation allows for refinement and enhancement of teaching materials.
5. **Learner-Centered:** Focuses on analyzing learner needs to create meaningful learning experiences.

The ADDIE Model is a comprehensive framework that guides educators in creating effective, learner-centered instructional programs. Its systematic approach—from analyzing learner needs to evaluating outcomes—ensures that instructional design is purposeful, engaging, and aligned with educational objectives. For B.Ed. and M.Ed. students, mastering the ADDIE model equips them to plan, develop, and deliver high-quality teaching that fosters active learning and enhances student outcomes.

2. Dick and Carey Model

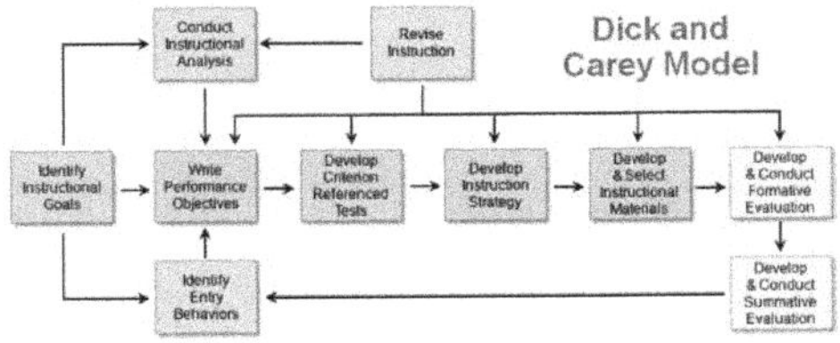

The **Dick and Carey Model** is a widely recognized instructional design framework that emphasizes a systematic, step-by-step approach to curriculum and lesson planning. Unlike linear models, it views instruction as an interrelated system where each component—

from goals to assessment—is connected and influences the others. This model is particularly useful for creating structured, measurable, and effective learning experiences. For B.Ed. and M.Ed. students, understanding this model is essential for designing lessons that are learner-centered, goal-oriented, and evidence-based.

Key Steps of the Dick and Carey Model

1. **Identifying Instructional Goals** The first step involves determining what learners should be able to achieve at the end of the instruction. Goals are broad statements that define the desired outcomes of learning.

   Example:
   In a teacher-training program, a goal might be: "Student-teachers will be able to integrate educational technology effectively into lesson planning."

   Importance:
   Clear goals provide direction for all subsequent instructional activities.

2. **Conducting Instructional Analysis** Instructional analysis involves breaking down the goals into smaller, teachable components or skills. It identifies the sequence of knowledge and skills that learners must acquire to achieve the instructional goals.

   Example:
   To achieve the goal of using educational technology, sub-skills might include: operating an LMS, creating multimedia content, and conducting online assessments.

Importance:
This ensures that all necessary skills and knowledge are addressed systematically.

3. **Specifying Entry Behaviors and Learner Characteristics**
In this step, the model assesses what learners already know (entry behaviors) and identifies characteristics that may affect learning, such as prior knowledge, learning styles, motivation, and cognitive abilities.

Example:
Student-teachers may already be familiar with basic computer operations but may need guidance on using interactive apps in teaching.

Importance:
Understanding learners' backgrounds helps tailor instruction to their needs and ensures it is appropriate and effective.

4. **Designing Performance-Based Assessments**
Assessments are designed to measure whether learners have achieved the instructional goals. These are often performance-based, requiring learners to demonstrate their knowledge or skills in practical tasks.

Example:
An assessment might involve designing a lesson plan that incorporates multimedia tools and evaluating its effectiveness.

Importance:
Performance-based assessments provide concrete evidence of learning outcomes and skill acquisition.

5. **Developing Instructional Strategies and Materials** Based on the analysis and assessments, educators plan instructional methods and create learning materials. This includes selecting teaching techniques, multimedia resources, interactive activities, and content organization.

   Example:
   Using video tutorials, hands-on workshops, group discussions, and e-learning modules for teaching educational technology.

   Importance:
   Effective strategies and materials ensure that learning objectives are achievable and engaging.

6. **Conducting Formative and Summative Evaluations** Evaluation occurs at two levels:
   - **Formative Evaluation:** Conducted during instruction to monitor progress and make adjustments.
   - **Summative Evaluation:** Conducted after instruction to assess overall effectiveness and learning outcomes.

   Example:
   Formative evaluation might include quizzes or peer feedback during training; summative evaluation could involve a final project or lesson demonstration.

   Importance:
   Continuous evaluation helps improve instruction and ensures that learning goals are met.

Advantages of the Dick and Carey Model

1. **Focus on Measurable Objectives:** Ensures learning outcomes are clear and assessable.
2. **Detailed Analysis:** Breaks down goals into specific skills and knowledge, providing a structured approach.
3. **Continuous Evaluation:** Incorporates feedback loops to improve instruction iteratively.
4. **Systematic Approach:** Treats instruction as an interconnected system, aligning goals, strategies, and assessments.
5. **Learner-Centered:** Considers entry behaviors and characteristics, tailoring instruction to learner needs.

The Dick and Carey Model provides a systematic and structured framework for instructional design. By connecting goals, learner analysis, instructional strategies, assessments, and evaluation, it ensures that learning is effective, measurable, and targeted. For B.Ed. and M.Ed. students, mastering this model enables the creation of organized, learner-centered, and evidence-based educational experiences. Its emphasis on performance-based outcomes and continuous evaluation makes it highly relevant for both traditional and technology-enhanced learning environments.

3. Kemp Model

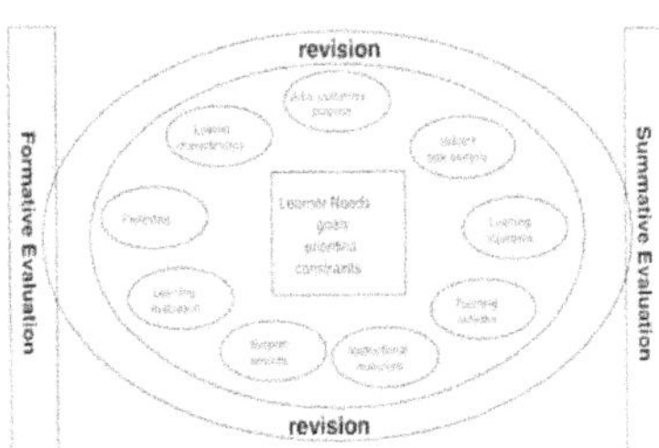

The **Kemp Model** is a flexible, non-linear instructional design framework that emphasizes a holistic, learner-centered approach. Unlike linear models like ADDIE or Dick and Carey, the Kemp Model allows designers to consider multiple elements of instruction simultaneously, making it highly adaptable to diverse educational contexts. For B.Ed. and M.Ed. students, understanding this model is essential for designing instruction that is both comprehensive and tailored to learners' needs.

Key Elements of the Kemp Model

1. **Goals and Objectives** Instruction begins with defining clear goals and objectives, which outline what learners should achieve. Objectives are specific, measurable, and guide the design and evaluation of instruction.

   Example:
   "Student-teachers will be able to create interactive lesson plans using multimedia tools."

2. **Learner Characteristics** Understanding learners' prior knowledge, skills, learning styles, motivation, and special needs is crucial. This ensures that instruction is personalized and appropriate for all learners.

   Example:
   Some learners may be comfortable with technology, while others require foundational support in using digital tools.

3. **Subject Content** Determine what content is essential for achieving the instructional goals. Content should be accurate, relevant, and organized logically.

   Example:
   Topics may include e-learning strategies, instructional technology tools, and classroom management techniques.

4. **Instructional Strategies** Select teaching methods that actively engage learners and facilitate effective learning. This may include lectures, demonstrations, discussions, simulations, and interactive activities.

   Example:
   Using flipped classrooms or blended learning approaches for teacher training.

5. **Resource Needs** Identify the materials, technologies, and human resources required to implement instruction effectively.

   Example:
   Computers, projectors, educational software, and access to online learning platforms.

6. **Support Services** Consider additional support required by learners, such as technical assistance, mentoring, counseling, or language support.

   Example:
   Providing online tutorials or help desks for learners using a new LMS platform.

7. **Timeline and Scheduling** Plan the sequence, duration, and pacing of instruction to ensure content is delivered efficiently and within the available time frame.

   Example:
   Scheduling online modules, live sessions, and assessments over a semester.

8. **Evaluation Strategies** Design both formative and summative assessments to monitor learner progress and the effectiveness of instruction. Feedback mechanisms should be built in for continuous improvement.

   Example:
   Quizzes, assignments, peer feedback, and project evaluations to measure learning outcomes.

9. **Continuous Revision** Use evaluation data to revise and improve instructional content, strategies, and delivery. Continuous revision ensures that learning remains effective, relevant, and engaging.

   Example:
   Updating multimedia lessons based on learner feedback and technological advancements.

Advantages of the Kemp Model

1. **Learner-Centered:** Focuses on the needs, characteristics, and learning styles of students.
2. **Non-Linear and Flexible:** Designers can work on multiple elements simultaneously rather than following a strict sequence.
3. **Comprehensive:** Considers all components of instruction, including goals, content, strategies, resources, and evaluation.
4. **Continuous Improvement:** Encourages ongoing revision and enhancement based on feedback and evaluation.
5. **Adaptable:** Suitable for both traditional classrooms and technology-driven learning environments.

The Kemp Model offers a holistic and flexible approach to instructional design, emphasizing learner-centered planning and the simultaneous consideration of multiple instructional elements. For B.Ed. and M.Ed. students, mastering the Kemp Model equips them to design comprehensive, adaptable, and effective learning experiences. By integrating goals, content, strategies, resources, support, evaluation, and continuous improvement, educators can create instruction that meets diverse learner needs, enhances engagement, and ensures meaningful learning outcomes in both conventional and technology-mediated educational contexts.

4. Gagne's Nine Events of Instruction

Introduction

Robert Gagne, a renowned educational psychologist, developed the **Nine Events of Instruction** to create a systematic approach to teaching that aligns with how humans learn. His model is grounded in cognitive psychology and focuses on engaging learners, facilitating understanding, and promoting retention and transfer of knowledge. For B.Ed. and M.Ed. students, applying Gagne's framework helps design lessons that are structured, interactive, and effective for diverse learners.

The Nine Events of Instruction

1. **Gain Attention** The first step is to capture learners' attention, motivating them to focus on the lesson. This can be achieved through questions, stories, videos, or surprising facts.

   Example:
   Starting a lesson on ecosystems with a short, dramatic video showing deforestation's impact.

   Importance:
   Attention is critical for activating the brain and preparing learners to receive new information.

2. **Inform Learners of Objectives** Clearly state what learners are expected to achieve by the end of the lesson. This sets expectations and provides direction for learning.

   Example:
   "By the end of this session, you will be able to design a lesson plan integrating ICT tools for primary education."

3. **Stimulate Recall of Prior Knowledge** Connect new content to learners' existing knowledge or experiences. This helps in building meaningful understanding.

   Example:
   Asking students to discuss previous experiences using educational technology before introducing new e-learning tools.

   Importance:
   Activating prior knowledge facilitates cognitive connections and better comprehension.

4. **Present Content** Deliver the instructional material using appropriate methods such as lectures, multimedia, demonstrations, or reading materials.

   Example:
   Using a combination of slides, videos, and animations to teach concepts of classroom management.

   Importance:
   Presentation should be clear, organized, and aligned with learning objectives.

5. **Provide Learning Guidance** Support learners in understanding and applying content. Use examples, analogies, hints, or scaffolding to guide learning.

   Example:
   Demonstrating step-by-step how to create an interactive quiz on a learning platform.

   Importance:
   Guidance helps learners process information effectively and reduces cognitive load.

6. **Elicit Performance (Practice)** Encourage learners to actively apply what they have learned through exercises, discussions, or practical activities.

   Example:
   Students practice designing a multimedia lesson plan in small groups.

Importance:
Practice consolidates learning and builds skills through application.

7. **Provide Feedback** Give immediate, constructive feedback on learners' performance to reinforce correct understanding and correct errors.

   Example:
   Reviewing students' lesson plans and providing suggestions for improvement.

   Importance:
   Feedback strengthens learning and motivates learners to improve.

8. **Assess Performance** Conduct formal or informal assessments to evaluate whether learners have achieved the learning objectives.

   Example:
   Using quizzes, projects, presentations, or peer assessments to measure comprehension and skill acquisition.

   Importance:
   Assessment validates learning and identifies areas needing further attention.

9. **Enhance Retention and Transfer** Design activities that help learners retain knowledge long-term and apply it in different contexts.

Example:
Assigning a project where students apply classroom technology skills in a simulated teaching environment.

Importance:
Encourages learners to transfer knowledge and skills to real-life situations, promoting deeper learning.

Advantages of Gagne's Nine Events

1. **Cognitive Focus:** Aligns instruction with the way humans process information.
2. **Systematic Engagement:** Provides a structured framework for engaging learners at each step.
3. **Skill Development:** Encourages practice, feedback, and application for mastery.
4. **Retention and Transfer:** Enhances long-term learning and practical use of knowledge.
5. **Versatility:** Applicable to face-to-face, online, or blended learning environments.

Gagne's Nine Events of Instruction provide a clear, structured approach to teaching that ensures learners are actively engaged, supported, and able to apply new knowledge effectively. For B.Ed. and M.Ed. students, mastering this model equips them to design lessons that are cognitively aligned, interactive, and outcome-oriented. By systematically incorporating attention, guidance, practice, feedback, and assessment, educators can maximize learning effectiveness and promote long-term retention and transfer of skills in diverse educational settings.

6. Rapid Prototyping Model

Introduction

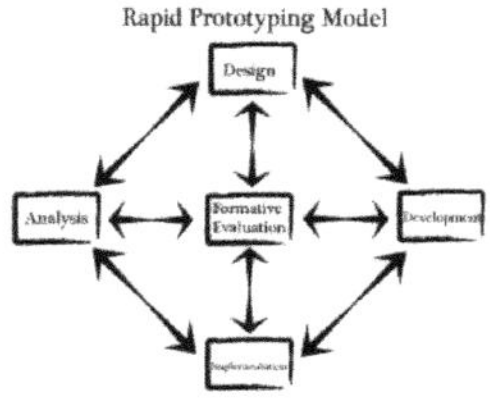

Rapid Prototyping Model

The **Rapid Prototyping Model** is an instructional design approach that emphasizes **iterative development and continuous refinement** of learning materials. Unlike traditional linear models, rapid prototyping allows educators to quickly create initial versions of instructional content, test them with learners, and make improvements based on feedback. This model is especially effective in **e-learning environments**, where technology enables fast development and deployment of interactive educational resources. For B.Ed. and M.Ed. students, understanding this model is valuable for designing flexible, responsive, and learner-centered instructional experiences.

Key Features of the Rapid Prototyping Model

1. **Iterative Development**
   - Instructional content is developed in cycles, allowing multiple iterations.
   - Each prototype version is tested with learners and refined based on observations and feedback. **Example:** Creating a preliminary e-learning module on classroom management, testing it with a small group of student-teachers, and updating it based on their responses.
2. **Early Testing with Learners**
   - Learners interact with the instructional materials early in the design process.

- Their feedback helps identify unclear content, usability issues, and areas for improvement. **Importance:** Early testing ensures that the final product meets learners' needs effectively.

3. **Flexibility and Adaptability**
    - Designers can modify content, design, and instructional strategies at any stage.
    - Allows adaptation to different learning styles, technological changes, or evolving course objectives.
4. **Focus on Learner-Centered Design**
    - Emphasizes meeting learners' needs rather than strictly following a pre-planned sequence.
    - Instruction is tailored based on learner performance and feedback.
5. **Integration with Technology**
    - Particularly suitable for online courses, multimedia lessons, and interactive simulations.
    - Software tools and Learning Management Systems (LMS) facilitate quick development and revision.

Steps in Rapid Prototyping

1. **Planning** – Identify instructional goals, learner characteristics, and content requirements.
2. **Initial Prototype Development** – Create a preliminary version of the instructional material, including multimedia elements if needed.
3. **Testing** – Deploy the prototype to a small group of learners and collect feedback on clarity, usability, and engagement.
4. **Analysis of Feedback** – Review learners' responses to identify strengths, weaknesses, and improvement areas.

5. **Revision** – Modify the content, structure, or instructional strategies based on feedback.
6. **Final Deployment** – Implement the revised version to the broader learner group.
7. **Continuous Improvement** – Periodically update and enhance content to keep it relevant and effective.

Advantages of Rapid Prototyping

1. **Continuous Improvement:** Iterative cycles allow ongoing refinement of instructional materials.
2. **Time-Efficient:** Quick prototyping reduces the time needed to develop fully polished content initially.
3. **Learner-Centered:** Feedback from real users ensures that instruction meets learners' needs and expectations.
4. **Error Reduction:** Early testing identifies problems before large-scale implementation, preventing costly mistakes.
5. **Adaptable to Technology:** Works well in e-learning, blended learning, and interactive multimedia environments.

The Rapid Prototyping Model offers a **flexible, iterative, and learner-centered approach** to instructional design. By creating preliminary versions of instructional materials, testing them with learners, and refining them continuously, educators can ensure that content is engaging, effective, and aligned with learners' needs. For B.Ed. and M.Ed. students, mastering this model equips them to design e-learning modules, multimedia lessons, and interactive educational experiences that are adaptive, efficient, and responsive. The model's emphasis on rapid development, feedback, and continuous improvement makes it particularly suitable for modern, technology-driven teaching and learning environments.

Benefits of Using Instructional Design Models

✔ Provides a systematic and structured approach to lesson planning
✔ Aligns content, objectives, and assessment
✔ Enhances learner engagement and retention
✔ Facilitates evaluation and improvement of instruction
✔ Supports effective integration of educational technology

4.2 Teaching Strategies Supported by Technology

Introduction

Technology has transformed the landscape of education, offering diverse tools that enhance teaching and learning. For B.Ed. and M.Ed. students, understanding **technology-supported teaching strategies** is essential to design engaging, effective, and learner-centered instruction. These strategies enable educators to address varied learning styles, promote active participation, and improve knowledge retention.

1. Blended Learning

Blended learning combines **face-to-face instruction with online learning**. Students interact with digital content (videos, quizzes, simulations) outside the classroom and engage in discussions, projects, and activities during in-person sessions.

Benefits:

- Flexible learning pace

- Enhanced engagement through multimedia
- Effective use of classroom time for problem-solving and collaboration

Example:
Student-teachers watch video lectures on educational psychology at home and apply concepts in classroom workshops.

2. Flipped Classroom

In a flipped classroom, traditional teaching is inverted: learners study instructional content **before class**, allowing classroom time for interactive exercises, discussions, and problem-solving.

Benefits:

- Promotes active learning and collaboration
- Provides more time for application and analysis
- Encourages self-directed learning

Example:
Students listen to podcasts or watch tutorials on lesson planning, then collaboratively design lesson plans during class.

3. Gamification

Gamification involves using **game elements** like points, badges, leaderboards, or challenges to motivate learners. It turns learning into an interactive and competitive experience.

Benefits:

- Increases engagement and motivation

- Encourages mastery through repeated practice
- Fosters healthy competition and goal-oriented learning

Example:
A classroom management course can include digital simulations where learners earn points for effective decision-making in virtual scenarios.

4. Collaborative Learning

Technology facilitates **collaboration** through online discussion forums, shared documents, virtual group projects, and video conferencing.

Benefits:

- Develops communication and teamwork skills
- Encourages peer-to-peer learning
- Provides platforms for global collaboration

Example:
Student-teachers work in Google Docs or Padlet to co-create lesson plans and provide feedback to each other.

5. Problem-Based Learning (PBL)

Problem-Based Learning uses real-world problems as a context for learners to develop knowledge and skills. Technology supports PBL through simulations, online research, and collaborative tools.

Benefits:

- Enhances critical thinking and problem-solving

- Connects theory to practice
- Encourages self-directed learning

Example:
Students simulate classroom management challenges using virtual classrooms and design solutions collaboratively.

6. Multimedia Integration

Integrating **videos, animations, podcasts, and interactive modules** enriches the learning experience. Multimedia caters to visual, auditory, and kinesthetic learners.

Benefits:

- Increases engagement and understanding
- Supports complex concept visualization
- Encourages active learning

Example:
Teaching science concepts using interactive simulations and educational videos.

7. Learning Analytics and Adaptive Learning

Technology enables tracking learners' progress and personalizing instruction based on their performance. Adaptive learning systems recommend content tailored to individual needs.

Benefits:

- Personalized learning pathways
- Immediate feedback for learners

- Data-driven insights for instructors

Example:
Adaptive quizzes in an LMS identify knowledge gaps and suggest additional exercises for improvement.

4.3 Visual Aids, Simulations, and Charts

Introduction

Visual aids, simulations, and charts are essential tools in educational technology that enhance understanding, retention, and engagement. They help transform abstract or complex concepts into concrete, easily understandable forms. For B.Ed. and M.Ed. students, mastering the use of these tools is vital for designing lessons that are interactive, learner-centered, and cognitively effective.

1. Visual Aids

Visual aids include images, diagrams, photographs, videos, and slides that support verbal instruction. They provide **dual coding**—information is processed both visually and verbally, improving comprehension and memory retention.

Types of Visual Aids:

- **Charts and Graphs:** Represent data and relationships clearly.
- **Infographics:** Summarize information visually for quick understanding.
- **Slides and Posters:** Enhance lectures and presentations.
- **Images and Animations:** Make abstract ideas tangible.

Benefits:

- Improves comprehension of complex concepts
- Captures learners' attention and increases engagement
- Supports different learning styles (visual, auditory, and kinesthetic)

Example:
Using a flowchart to explain the process of photosynthesis helps learners visualize the sequence of events clearly.

2. Simulations

Simulations are interactive, virtual models that mimic real-world processes or phenomena. They provide learners with **hands-on experience** in a risk-free environment.

Types of Simulations:

- **Virtual Labs:** Conduct experiments digitally when physical labs are unavailable.
- **Classroom Management Simulations:** Practice managing student behavior or lesson delivery.
- **Environmental or Scientific Simulations:** Observe natural or scientific processes virtually.

Benefits:

- Encourages experiential learning and problem-solving
- Reduces the risk of mistakes in real-world scenarios
- Provides immediate feedback and allows repeated practice

Example:
Student-teachers use a virtual classroom simulator to practice handling difficult classroom situations before entering a real classroom.

3. Charts and Graphs

Charts and graphs represent data visually, allowing learners to **analyze patterns, trends, and relationships** quickly. They simplify complex information, making it easier to interpret and remember.

Common Types:

- **Bar and Column Charts:** Compare quantities or frequencies.
- **Pie Charts:** Show proportions or percentages.
- **Line Graphs:** Represent trends over time.
- **Flowcharts:** Visualize processes and decision-making paths.

Benefits:

- Simplifies data interpretation and enhances analytical skills
- Supports critical thinking and discussion
- Provides a clear reference for teaching and assessment

Example:
Using a pie chart to show the distribution of students' learning preferences in a classroom helps plan differentiated instruction.

Integration of Visual Aids, Simulations, and Charts

Effective instruction often combines these tools for maximum impact:

- A **simulation** can be paired with **charts** to analyze outcomes.
- **Visual aids** like infographics can summarize simulation results.
- Teachers can create interactive lessons using slides with embedded simulations and data charts.

Benefits:

- Enhances engagement, comprehension, and retention
- Supports active and experiential learning
- Encourages learners to analyze, evaluate, and apply knowledge

Visual aids, simulations, and charts are powerful tools in educational technology. They transform abstract concepts into meaningful learning experiences, promote active engagement, and support cognitive processes like analysis, synthesis, and evaluation. For B.Ed. and M.Ed. students, effectively integrating these tools into teaching strategies ensures lessons are **interactive, learner-centered, and outcomes-driven**, preparing student-teachers to create dynamic and impactful learning environments.

4.4 Integrating Technology in Classroom Teaching

Introduction

Integrating technology in classroom teaching transforms traditional learning into an **interactive, learner-centered, and dynamic experience**. For B.Ed. and M.Ed. students, understanding how to blend technology with pedagogy is essential to enhance engagement, personalize learning, and improve learning outcomes. Effective integration ensures that technology serves as a **tool to support**

teaching, rather than a replacement for effective instructional strategies.

1. Planning for Technology Integration

Successful integration begins with **planning**: aligning technology tools with learning objectives, content, and assessment strategies.

Key Steps:

- Identify learning goals suitable for technology-supported instruction.
- Select appropriate tools (LMS, multimedia, simulations, interactive apps).
- Design lesson plans that combine traditional methods with digital resources.

Example:
For a lesson on environmental science, teachers may use videos, interactive simulations, and online quizzes alongside classroom discussions.

Benefits:

- Ensures purposeful use of technology
- Maintains alignment between objectives, activities, and assessments

2. Enhancing Student Engagement

Technology increases student engagement through **interactive and participatory learning experiences**.

Strategies:

- Use multimedia presentations (videos, animations, audio) to illustrate concepts.
- Conduct virtual labs and simulations for hands-on experience.
- Incorporate gamified learning to motivate and challenge students.

Example:
A history lesson may include an interactive timeline app where students explore events, answer questions, and receive immediate feedback.

Benefits:

- Active participation improves attention and motivation
- Supports diverse learning styles and multiple intelligences

3. Facilitating Collaborative Learning

Technology enables students to collaborate beyond the physical classroom using **digital platforms**.

Tools:

- Google Docs, Padlet, and Microsoft Teams for collaborative projects
- Online discussion forums and video conferencing for debates and peer interactions

Example:
Student-teachers co-create lesson plans in Google Docs, providing peer feedback and suggestions in real time.

Benefits:

- Builds communication and teamwork skills
- Encourages peer-to-peer learning and shared responsibility

4. Personalizing Learning

Technology allows **adaptive and personalized learning experiences** tailored to individual learner needs.

Strategies:

- Use learning management systems to assign personalized tasks based on performance.
- Offer digital resources for self-paced learning.
- Track progress and adjust instructional support accordingly.

Example:
An LMS platform may provide remedial exercises for students struggling with a topic, while offering advanced content to those excelling.

Benefits:

- Addresses diverse learning abilities
- Promotes self-directed learning and autonomy

5. Assessing Learning with Technology

Technology supports **formative and summative assessment**, providing immediate feedback and data-driven insights.

Tools:

- Online quizzes, polls, and interactive games
- Digital rubrics for evaluating projects and presentations
- Analytics in LMS to track engagement and performance

Example:
Teachers use an online quiz to assess comprehension of a lesson, analyze the results, and adjust subsequent instruction accordingly.

Benefits:

- Provides timely feedback
- Enhances data-informed decision-making for teaching

6. Overcoming Challenges

While integrating technology, teachers may face challenges such as lack of resources, technical issues, or learner digital literacy gaps. Solutions include:

- Training for teachers and students
- Ensuring reliable internet and digital infrastructure
- Using low-cost or offline tools when necessary

Integrating technology in classroom teaching enables **interactive, collaborative, and personalized learning**. For B.Ed. and M.Ed. students, mastering this integration ensures they can create lessons that enhance engagement, cater to diverse learners, and improve educational outcomes. Effective integration involves **planning, tool**

selection, student engagement, collaboration, personalized learning, and assessment, all while addressing challenges proactively. By blending pedagogy with technology thoughtfully, educators can transform traditional classrooms into dynamic, technology-enhanced learning environments.

4.5 Assessment Tools and Feedback Mechanisms in Technology-Enhanced Learning

Introduction

Assessment and feedback are crucial components of effective teaching, ensuring that learning objectives are achieved and guiding both instructors and learners in improving performance. In technology-enhanced learning, digital tools streamline assessment processes, provide immediate feedback, and support data-driven instructional decisions. For B.Ed. and M.Ed. students, understanding these tools is essential for designing **efficient, learner-centered, and interactive evaluation strategies**.

1. Online Quizzes and Tests

Online quizzes and tests allow educators to evaluate learners' knowledge and understanding in a structured manner.

Features:

- Multiple-choice, short-answer, or essay formats
- Automatic grading and immediate feedback
- Customizable question banks for adaptive assessment

Example:
An LMS like Moodle can administer weekly quizzes for a course on

educational technology, instantly scoring and providing explanations for incorrect answers.

Benefits:

- Saves time and resources
- Provides instant feedback to learners
- Enables tracking of learner progress over time

2. E-Portfolios

E-portfolios are digital collections of learners' work, showcasing skills, knowledge, and achievements over time.

Features:

- Includes assignments, projects, reflections, and multimedia submissions
- Supports continuous assessment and self-reflection
- Can be shared with peers and instructors for feedback

Example:
Student-teachers maintain an e-portfolio documenting lesson plans, classroom videos, and reflections on teaching practices.

Benefits:

- Encourages self-directed learning and reflection
- Provides a holistic view of learner development
- Facilitates formative and summative assessment

3. Interactive Polls and Surveys

Interactive polls and surveys engage learners while collecting data on their understanding, opinions, or learning preferences.

Tools:

- Kahoot, Mentimeter, Poll Everywhere, Google Forms

Example:
During a virtual lesson, the instructor conducts a live poll to assess understanding of classroom management strategies.

Benefits:

- Provides real-time feedback
- Increases learner engagement
- Helps instructors adjust instruction based on learners' responses

4. Rubrics and Digital Grading Tools

Rubrics provide clear criteria for evaluating assignments, projects, or presentations, promoting transparency and fairness. Digital grading tools in LMS platforms streamline assessment and record-keeping.

Example:
A rubric is used to evaluate student-teachers' lesson plans on creativity, clarity, and use of technology, with scores and comments uploaded digitally.

Benefits:

- Standardizes evaluation and reduces bias

- Provides detailed feedback to learners
- Supports consistent assessment across multiple evaluators

5. Peer and Self-Assessment Tools

Technology enables learners to evaluate their own work and that of peers, fostering reflection and collaborative learning.

Tools:

- Online discussion forums, peer-review platforms, Google Docs comments

Example:
Student-teachers provide feedback on each other's multimedia lesson plans using a structured rubric in a shared document.

Benefits:

- Promotes critical thinking and reflective practice
- Encourages collaborative learning and accountability
- Enhances understanding of assessment criteria

6. Learning Analytics

Learning analytics involves using digital data from LMS and other educational tools to monitor learners' engagement, performance, and progression.

Example:
An LMS dashboard shows which modules learners have completed, time spent on activities, and quiz performance, allowing instructors to identify struggling students.

Benefits:

- Enables data-driven instructional decisions
- Supports personalized learning pathways
- Identifies trends and areas for improvement

Assessment tools and feedback mechanisms in technology-enhanced learning provide **timely, actionable, and learner-centered evaluation**. By leveraging online quizzes, e-portfolios, polls, rubrics, peer assessments, and learning analytics, B.Ed. and M.Ed. students can create **dynamic assessment strategies** that promote engagement, reflection, and continuous improvement. Effective integration of these tools ensures that assessment becomes not just a measure of learning, but a **powerful driver of teaching effectiveness and student growth**.

Chapter 5
Use of Technology in Teaching Practice

5.1 Online and Blended Learning Models

Introduction

Online and blended learning models have transformed the way education is delivered, providing flexibility, accessibility, and personalization. For B.Ed. and M.Ed. students, understanding these models is crucial to design effective teaching strategies that leverage technology while maintaining pedagogical integrity. These models cater to diverse learning styles, encourage active participation, and support self-directed learning.

1. Online Learning Models

Online learning refers to **fully digital instruction** where learners access content, activities, and assessments entirely through digital platforms, often without face-to-face interaction.

Key Features:

- Learning management systems (LMS) such as Moodle, Canvas, or Google Classroom
- Multimedia content including videos, podcasts, e-books, and interactive modules
- Asynchronous and synchronous modes of instruction

Types of Online Learning:

- **Synchronous Online Learning:** Real-time interactions via video conferencing, webinars, or live chats.
- **Asynchronous Online Learning:** Learners access materials, lectures, and assignments at their own pace without real-time interaction.

Example:
Student-teachers attend live online seminars on educational technology (synchronous) and complete discussion boards, quizzes, and recorded lectures on the LMS (asynchronous).

Benefits:

- Flexible and accessible, allowing learners to study from any location
- Supports self-paced learning and review of materials
- Facilitates access to a wide range of resources and global expertise

2. Blended Learning Models

Blended learning combines **face-to-face instruction with online learning**, integrating traditional classroom methods with digital resources and activities.

Key Features:

- Combines classroom discussions, group work, and hands-on activities with online lectures, quizzes, and multimedia content
- Allows flexibility in pace and mode of learning
- Encourages active and collaborative learning

Types of Blended Learning Models:

1. **Flipped Classroom Model:** Students study instructional content online before class, using classroom time for problem-solving and collaborative activities.
2. **Rotation Model:** Learners rotate between different modalities—online learning, classroom instruction, and independent study—according to a fixed schedule.
3. **Flex Model:** Core instruction is delivered online, and teachers provide support and enrichment in the classroom as needed.
4. **Enriched Virtual Model:** Mostly online learning, with occasional in-person sessions for hands-on activities or assessments.

Example:
A lesson on classroom management may include online tutorials, quizzes, and discussion forums, while classroom sessions focus on simulations, role plays, and group discussions.

Benefits:

- Combines the advantages of online flexibility and face-to-face engagement
- Encourages collaborative learning, critical thinking, and problem-solving
- Supports differentiated instruction for diverse learners

3. Best Practices for Implementing Online and Blended Learning

- **Clear Learning Objectives:** Ensure digital and in-person activities align with objectives.
- **Interactive Content:** Use multimedia, quizzes, and discussion forums to engage learners.
- **Regular Feedback:** Provide timely feedback to guide learner progress.
- **Learner Support:** Offer technical support and guidance for digital tools.
- **Assessment Integration:** Incorporate both formative and summative assessments within online platforms.

5.2 Virtual Laboratories and Simulated Environments

Introduction

Virtual laboratories and simulated environments have become essential components of modern education, particularly in technology-enhanced learning. They provide **safe, cost-effective, and interactive platforms** for learners to explore concepts, practice skills, and experiment with real-world scenarios without the constraints of physical labs. For B.Ed. and M.Ed. students, understanding these tools is critical for designing practical, engaging, and learner-centered instruction.

1. Virtual Laboratories

Virtual laboratories are digital platforms that allow learners to conduct experiments and practice skills **in a simulated environment**. They replicate the functionality of real laboratories, enabling experimentation without physical constraints.

Key Features:

- Interactive simulations of experiments and lab procedures
- Real-time data collection and analysis
- Step-by-step guidance with built-in tutorials and instructions
- Safe environment with no risk of accidents or material wastage

Example:
A virtual science lab allows student-teachers to conduct chemistry experiments, measure reactions, and observe results digitally.

Benefits:

- Provides hands-on experience without the cost and safety concerns of physical labs
- Enhances understanding of complex concepts through visualization
- Supports repeated practice and experimentation
- Encourages self-directed and inquiry-based learning

2. Simulated Environments

Simulated environments replicate real-world scenarios to **develop practical skills, decision-making, and problem-solving abilities**. They are widely used in education, teacher training, and professional development.

Types of Simulations:

- **Classroom Management Simulations:** Learners practice managing student behavior, lesson flow, and classroom interactions.

- **Environmental or Scientific Simulations:** Students explore ecological systems, chemical reactions, or physics phenomena virtually.
- **Professional Scenario Simulations:** Trainees experience virtual teaching, counseling, or administrative situations to build competence.

Example:
Student-teachers use a classroom simulation platform to handle difficult classroom situations, apply teaching strategies, and receive instant feedback on their actions.

Benefits:

- Provides experiential learning without real-world risks
- Develops critical thinking, problem-solving, and decision-making skills
- Encourages engagement and active learning through interactive experiences

3. Advantages of Virtual Labs and Simulations in Teacher Education

- **Accessibility:** Students can access labs anytime, anywhere, facilitating flexible learning.
- **Cost-Effective:** Reduces expenses for equipment, materials, and physical space.
- **Safe Learning Environment:** Eliminates risks associated with chemical, electrical, or mechanical experiments.
- **Immediate Feedback:** Many platforms provide real-time feedback and performance analytics.

- **Scalable Learning:** Large numbers of learners can participate simultaneously without resource limitations.

4. Best Practices for Using Virtual Labs and Simulations

1. **Align with Learning Objectives:** Ensure simulations support specific skills and knowledge outcomes.
2. **Blend with Traditional Methods:** Use virtual labs alongside hands-on experiments when possible for holistic learning.
3. **Facilitate Reflection:** Encourage learners to analyze outcomes, discuss results, and connect theory with practice.
4. **Integrate Assessment:** Incorporate quizzes, performance tracking, and feedback within the simulation environment.
5. **Provide Technical Support:** Ensure learners have guidance to navigate software or online platforms effectively.

Virtual laboratories and simulated environments offer **innovative, interactive, and practical learning experiences**. They enhance understanding of complex concepts, develop critical skills, and provide safe, cost-effective alternatives to traditional labs. For B.Ed. and M.Ed. students, mastering these tools enables the design of **technology-enhanced teaching strategies** that promote active, experiential, and learner-centered education. By integrating virtual labs and simulations, educators can create engaging learning environments that prepare student-teachers for real-world classroom challenges.

5.3 Game-Based Learning and Interactive Methods

Introduction

Game-based learning (GBL) and interactive methods leverage technology to make education **engaging, motivating, and learner-centered**. These approaches transform traditional lessons into active, participatory experiences where learners explore, experiment, and solve problems through games, simulations, and interactive activities. For B.Ed. and M.Ed. students, mastering these methods is essential to design **dynamic classrooms that foster creativity, critical thinking, and collaboration**.

1. Game-Based Learning (GBL)

Game-based learning integrates **educational content with game mechanics**, such as challenges, rewards, and progress tracking, to enhance learning outcomes.

Key Features:

- Incorporates points, levels, badges, and leaderboards
- Encourages problem-solving and critical thinking
- Provides immediate feedback on performance
- Engages learners through interactive storytelling and challenges

Example:
A history lesson uses an online simulation game where learners role-play as historical figures, make strategic decisions, and observe consequences, earning points for accuracy and creativity.

Benefits:

- Increases motivation and engagement
- Enhances retention through experiential learning

- Encourages risk-taking and experimentation in a safe environment
- Supports differentiated learning by allowing students to progress at their own pace

2. Interactive Learning Methods

Interactive methods involve **active participation of learners** through discussions, simulations, quizzes, and collaborative digital tools. These methods foster engagement, deepen understanding, and develop higher-order thinking skills.

Examples of Interactive Methods:

1. **Quizzes and Polls:** Tools like Kahoot, Mentimeter, or Quizizz engage learners and provide instant feedback.
2. **Discussion Forums:** Platforms such as Google Classroom or Padlet facilitate collaborative learning and peer feedback.
3. **Simulations and Role-Plays:** Learners practice real-world scenarios digitally or in-class to develop problem-solving skills.
4. **Interactive Videos and Multimedia:** Videos with embedded questions or decision points promote active learning.

Benefits:

- Encourages participation and collaboration
- Provides immediate feedback and reflection opportunities
- Supports varied learning styles and multiple intelligences
- Develops practical, analytical, and decision-making skills

3. Combining Game-Based and Interactive Methods

Integrating GBL with interactive methods maximizes engagement and learning outcomes:

- Students participate in game-based quizzes to reinforce content knowledge.
- Simulations combined with scoring systems encourage competition and mastery.
- Collaborative problem-solving games promote teamwork while applying theoretical concepts.

Example:
A mathematics lesson uses an interactive puzzle game where groups solve problems collaboratively, earn badges for correct solutions, and discuss strategies to improve understanding.

4. Best Practices for Implementation

1. **Align with Learning Objectives:** Ensure games and interactive activities support curriculum goals.
2. **Balance Fun and Learning:** Activities should engage learners without overshadowing educational content.
3. **Provide Guidance:** Facilitate reflection, discussion, and debriefing after activities.
4. **Use Technology Appropriately:** Select tools and platforms suitable for learners' age, skill level, and subject area.
5. **Monitor Progress:** Track learners' performance and provide feedback to enhance learning outcomes.

5.4 Case Studies from Schools, Colleges, and Universities

Introduction

Case studies provide **real-world examples of technology integration in education**, illustrating how schools, colleges, and universities use digital tools to enhance teaching and learning. For B.Ed. and M.Ed. students, examining these case studies helps bridge theory with practice, offering insights into **successful strategies, challenges, and outcomes**.

1. Case Studies from Schools

Schools often adopt technology to **improve engagement, personalize learning, and support teachers in classroom management**.

Example 1: Smart Classrooms in Urban Schools

- **Context:** A network of urban schools implemented smart classrooms equipped with interactive whiteboards, projectors, and tablets.
- **Strategy:** Teachers used multimedia lessons, virtual experiments, and online quizzes to supplement traditional teaching.
- **Outcome:** Student engagement increased significantly, and conceptual understanding improved due to interactive and visual learning.
- **Lessons Learned:** Adequate teacher training and technical support are crucial for effective implementation.

Example 2: Blended Learning in Rural Schools

- **Context:** A rural school introduced blended learning using low-cost tablets and offline educational content.
- **Strategy:** Students studied digital lessons at home and participated in collaborative classroom activities.

- **Outcome:** Attendance improved, and students demonstrated better problem-solving and digital literacy skills.
- **Lessons Learned:** Offline content and simple technology can be highly effective where internet connectivity is limited.

2. Case Studies from Colleges

Colleges often use technology to **support higher-order thinking, research skills, and professional preparation**.

Example 1: Virtual Labs in Science Colleges

- **Context:** A science college integrated virtual chemistry and physics labs into the curriculum.
- **Strategy:** Students performed experiments online, recorded observations, and submitted reports through LMS.
- **Outcome:** Students gained practical experience safely, and learning outcomes improved despite limited physical lab resources.
- **Lessons Learned:** Virtual labs complement, but do not entirely replace, physical labs; a hybrid approach is ideal.

Example 2: Flipped Classroom in Teacher Education

- **Context:** A B.Ed. college implemented a flipped classroom model for pedagogy courses.
- **Strategy:** Students accessed video lectures and readings before class and engaged in lesson planning, simulations, and peer discussions during sessions.
- **Outcome:** Active participation, critical thinking, and lesson design skills improved.
- **Lessons Learned:** Pre-class preparation by students is essential for successful implementation.

3. Case Studies from Universities

Universities leverage technology for **research, large-scale learning, and global collaboration**.

Example 1: MOOCs and Online Learning Platforms

- **Context:** A university offered Massive Open Online Courses (MOOCs) in education and technology.
- **Strategy:** Students from different regions accessed lectures, discussion forums, quizzes, and peer assignments online.
- **Outcome:** Learners acquired skills beyond geographic constraints, and collaborative learning thrived.
- **Lessons Learned:** Clear guidance and structured assignments enhance MOOC effectiveness.

Example 2: Learning Analytics in Higher Education

- **Context:** A university used LMS analytics to monitor student engagement and performance.
- **Strategy:** Faculty tracked module completion, quiz results, and participation to identify struggling students.
- **Outcome:** Timely interventions improved retention and learning outcomes.
- **Lessons Learned:** Data-driven insights are invaluable for personalized instruction.

5.5 Teacher Training and Capacity Building in Technology-Enhanced Learning

Introduction

Effective integration of technology in education depends largely on **teachers' knowledge, skills, and confidence** in using digital tools. Teacher training and capacity building are therefore critical to ensure that technology enhances teaching and learning rather than simply serving as an accessory. For B.Ed. and M.Ed. students, understanding strategies for training and professional development equips them to become competent educators in technology-rich classrooms.

1. Importance of Teacher Training in Technology Integration

- **Enhances Digital Literacy:** Teachers learn to navigate software, LMS platforms, multimedia tools, and online assessment systems.
- **Improves Pedagogical Practices:** Training helps integrate technology with teaching strategies like blended learning, flipped classrooms, and gamification.
- **Promotes Confidence and Motivation:** Teachers are more likely to experiment with new methods when adequately trained.
- **Ensures Effective Classroom Management:** Technology-rich classrooms require teachers to manage digital resources, monitor online engagement, and maintain discipline.

Example:
A B.Ed. program includes workshops on using virtual labs and educational apps, enabling student-teachers to design interactive lessons effectively.

2. Models of Teacher Training

1. **Workshops and Short-Term Courses**
   - Hands-on sessions focusing on specific tools like LMS, multimedia software, or online assessment platforms.
   - Encourage practical application rather than only theoretical knowledge.
2. **In-Service Training Programs**
   - Continuous professional development for in-service teachers to update their skills with emerging technologies.
   - Often includes mentoring, peer learning, and collaborative projects.
3. **Online Professional Development (OPD)**
   - Flexible, self-paced online courses, webinars, and MOOCs allow teachers to learn at their convenience.
   - Combines theory, demonstration, and interactive practice.
4. **Peer Learning and Communities of Practice**
   - Teachers learn from each other through collaborative platforms, discussion forums, and shared lesson plans.
   - Encourages knowledge sharing, problem-solving, and innovation in instructional strategies.

3. Key Components of Capacity Building

1. **Technical Skills**
   - Operating hardware (computers, tablets, projectors) and software (LMS, apps, multimedia tools).
2. **Pedagogical Integration**
   - Aligning technology with learning objectives, content, and assessment strategies.

3. **Assessment and Feedback**
    - Using digital tools for formative and summative evaluation, learning analytics, and providing timely feedback.
4. **Digital Citizenship and Ethics**
    - Promoting safe, responsible, and ethical use of technology in classrooms.

4. Challenges in Teacher Training

- Limited access to updated infrastructure and resources
- Resistance to change or lack of motivation among some teachers
- Time constraints for attending training programs
- Varying levels of digital literacy among educators

Solutions:

- Provide ongoing support and mentoring
- Offer flexible, context-based, and hands-on training
- Promote collaborative learning among teachers to share experiences and best practices

Chapter 6

Digital Assessment and Evaluation

6.1 Online Tests, Quizzes, and Assignments

Introduction

Assessment is a crucial component of the teaching-learning process, and technology has significantly transformed the way evaluations are conducted. Online tests, quizzes, and assignments offer **flexibility, immediacy, and data-driven insights**, enabling educators to measure learning outcomes effectively. For B.Ed. and M.Ed. students, understanding these tools is essential to design **efficient, interactive, and learner-centered assessment strategies**.

1. Online Tests

Online tests are structured assessments conducted digitally to evaluate knowledge, comprehension, and application skills.

Key Features:

- Can include multiple-choice, short-answer, or essay-type questions
- Automated grading for objective questions
- Integration with Learning Management Systems (LMS) for seamless tracking
- Supports both formative and summative evaluation

Example:
A student-teacher submits an online test on child development

concepts via Moodle, receiving instant feedback and a detailed score report.

Benefits:

- Saves time in grading and record-keeping
- Provides immediate feedback to learners
- Facilitates large-scale assessments without physical constraints

2. Online Quizzes

Quizzes are short, often interactive assessments designed to reinforce learning and check understanding.

Key Features:

- Can be gamified with points, timers, and leaderboards to increase engagement
- Flexible scheduling: quizzes can be timed or untimed
- Adaptive quizzes adjust difficulty based on learner responses
- Instant feedback highlights correct answers and explanations

Example:
In a pedagogy course, a Kahoot quiz helps student-teachers review educational psychology theories, reinforcing concepts in an engaging manner.

Benefits:

- Encourages active learning and participation
- Enhances retention through repeated retrieval practice

- Provides formative insights for instructors to adjust teaching strategies

3. Online Assignments

Assignments submitted digitally allow learners to **demonstrate understanding, creativity, and application** of concepts.

Key Features:

- Can include essays, projects, multimedia submissions, and collaborative group work
- Facilitates peer assessment and feedback
- Easy tracking and archiving through LMS platforms

Example:
Student-teachers create a digital lesson plan using Google Docs, incorporating multimedia resources, and submit it via the college LMS for evaluation.

Benefits:

- Supports diverse modes of expression and creativity
- Enables collaboration among students through shared platforms
- Provides detailed feedback, fostering reflection and improvement

4. Best Practices for Online Assessments

1. **Align Assessments with Learning Objectives:** Ensure online tests, quizzes, and assignments measure intended outcomes.

2. **Use a Variety of Formats:** Combine objective questions, essays, projects, and multimedia tasks for holistic assessment.
3. **Provide Clear Instructions:** Avoid confusion by detailing requirements, deadlines, and submission guidelines.
4. **Ensure Academic Integrity:** Use plagiarism checkers, randomized questions, and timed quizzes.
5. **Feedback and Reflection:** Provide constructive feedback and encourage learners to reflect on their performance.

5. Challenges and Solutions

- **Technical Issues:** Ensure stable internet and device accessibility.
- **Digital Literacy Gaps:** Offer orientation sessions for learners unfamiliar with online tools.
- **Engagement:** Use interactive quizzes and multimedia assignments to maintain interest.
- **Assessment Validity:** Design well-structured questions aligned with learning objectives.

6.2 Automated Grading Systems

Introduction

Automated grading systems are digital tools that evaluate student performance **quickly, accurately, and consistently**. These systems are widely used in technology-enhanced education to save time, provide instant feedback, and generate data-driven insights. For B.Ed. and M.Ed. students, understanding automated grading systems is essential for designing **efficient assessment strategies** that support both teachers and learners.

1. What Are Automated Grading Systems?

Automated grading systems use software algorithms to evaluate student responses on assessments such as quizzes, assignments, or exams. They are particularly effective for **objective and structured assessments** but can also support some forms of subjective evaluation using AI-based tools.

Key Features:

- Instant scoring for multiple-choice, true/false, and fill-in-the-blank questions
- AI-assisted evaluation for essays and open-ended responses
- Integration with Learning Management Systems (LMS) for tracking and reporting
- Analytics for monitoring learner progress and identifying areas of improvement

Example:
A Moodle LMS automatically grades weekly quizzes in an educational technology course and generates performance reports for both students and instructors.

2. Types of Automated Grading Systems

1. **Objective Assessment Grading:**
    - Multiple-choice, matching, and true/false questions are automatically scored.
    - Provides immediate feedback and explanations for correct and incorrect answers.
2. **AI-Based Essay Grading:**

   - Uses natural language processing (NLP) algorithms to evaluate essays on content, grammar, coherence, and style.
   - Provides scores along with feedback on improvement areas.
3. **Rubric-Based Grading:**
   - Automated systems can apply rubrics to projects, presentations, and digital assignments.
   - Ensures consistent and transparent evaluation according to defined criteria.

3. Benefits of Automated Grading Systems

- **Time-Saving:** Reduces the time instructors spend on grading repetitive tasks.
- **Consistency:** Eliminates human bias and ensures uniformity in evaluation.
- **Immediate Feedback:** Students receive instant results, supporting timely learning adjustments.
- **Data-Driven Insights:** Generates reports on learner performance, helping educators identify strengths, weaknesses, and trends.
- **Scalability:** Handles large numbers of students efficiently, suitable for MOOCs and large classrooms.

Example:
In a B.Ed. program, automated grading allows instructors to quickly assess multiple student lesson plan submissions and provide structured feedback through an LMS.

4. Best Practices for Implementing Automated Grading

1. **Align with Learning Objectives:** Ensure the system evaluates outcomes effectively.
2. **Use Mixed Assessment:** Combine automated grading with teacher evaluation for subjective tasks.
3. **Maintain Transparency:** Explain scoring criteria and provide detailed feedback to learners.
4. **Regular System Updates:** Keep software updated to handle new assessment formats and AI improvements.
5. **Monitor Performance:** Review automated scores periodically to ensure accuracy and fairness.

5. Challenges and Solutions

- **Limitations in Subjective Evaluation:** AI may misinterpret complex essays; supplement with teacher review.
- **Technical Issues:** Provide stable infrastructure and technical support.
- **Resistance to Adoption:** Train teachers and student-teachers in using these systems effectively.
- **Cost Constraints:** Explore open-source or institution-provided platforms to reduce expenses.

6.3 Data-Driven Performance Analysis

Introduction

Data-driven performance analysis refers to the use of **educational data collected from digital platforms and tools** to assess, monitor, and improve student learning outcomes. In technology-enhanced education, it enables teachers to make informed decisions, personalize learning, and identify trends that support academic success. For B.Ed. and M.Ed. students, understanding data-driven performance analysis is critical for designing **evidence-based teaching and assessment strategies**.

1. What is Data-Driven Performance Analysis?

Data-driven performance analysis involves collecting, analyzing, and interpreting data from various educational technologies, such as Learning Management Systems (LMS), online quizzes, e-portfolios, and automated grading systems.

Key Features:

- Tracks learner engagement, progress, and completion rates
- Monitors performance in assignments, quizzes, and tests
- Identifies knowledge gaps and learning trends
- Supports timely interventions and personalized learning pathways

Example:
A B.Ed. college uses LMS analytics to track which modules student-teachers have completed, their quiz scores, and participation in online discussions, helping instructors tailor support for each learner.

2. Sources of Data

1. **LMS Activity Logs:** Tracks logins, time spent on modules, assignment submissions, and participation in discussions.
2. **Online Assessments:** Provides scores, time taken, and question-level performance.
3. **E-Portfolios:** Monitors progress, reflections, and skill development over time.

4. **Interactive Tools:** Collects data from simulations, gamified quizzes, and collaborative projects.

Benefits:

- Offers a comprehensive view of learning patterns
- Facilitates continuous improvement in teaching and learning
- Supports objective and evidence-based decision-making

3. Uses of Data-Driven Performance Analysis

1. **Identifying Learning Gaps:** Teachers can detect concepts that learners struggle with and plan remedial instruction.
2. **Personalized Learning:** Data enables the creation of tailored learning paths based on individual performance.
3. **Monitoring Engagement:** Analysis of participation metrics ensures students are actively involved in learning activities.
4. **Improving Teaching Strategies:** Insights from data inform instructional adjustments, resource allocation, and content pacing.
5. **Assessment and Feedback:** Performance analytics allows targeted feedback, helping learners reflect and improve.

Example:
In a pedagogical methods course, LMS analytics reveal that students consistently underperform in classroom management simulations, prompting additional workshops and mentoring.

4. Best Practices for Implementing Data-Driven Analysis

1. **Define Objectives:** Identify what aspects of learning and teaching need to be measured.

2. **Collect Reliable Data:** Use trusted platforms and consistent metrics to ensure accuracy.
3. **Analyze Regularly:** Monitor trends weekly or monthly to respond promptly.
4. **Act on Insights:** Adjust instruction, provide interventions, and support students based on data findings.
5. **Maintain Privacy and Ethics:** Protect student data and adhere to ethical guidelines in analysis and reporting.

5. Challenges and Solutions

- **Data Overload:** Focus on key metrics aligned with learning objectives.
- **Technical Limitations:** Ensure stable infrastructure and skilled personnel to manage analytics.
- **Interpretation Issues:** Train educators in data literacy to derive meaningful insights.
- **Resistance to Change:** Foster a culture of data-informed teaching and continuous improvement.

6.4 Designing Effective Assessments

Introduction

Designing effective assessments is a cornerstone of teaching and learning, ensuring that educational objectives are measured accurately and meaningfully. In technology-enhanced education, assessments can be **dynamic, interactive, and data-driven**, allowing for immediate feedback and continuous improvement. For B.Ed. and M.Ed. students, mastering assessment design is essential to create **learner-centered, fair, and impactful evaluation strategies**.

1. Principles of Effective Assessment

1. **Alignment with Learning Objectives:** Assessments should directly measure what students are expected to learn.
2. **Validity and Reliability:** Questions must accurately assess the intended knowledge or skills and produce consistent results.
3. **Diversity of Methods:** Use a combination of quizzes, projects, simulations, e-portfolios, and presentations to evaluate different competencies.
4. **Formative and Summative Balance:** Include ongoing assessments for feedback (formative) and final evaluations for grading (summative).
5. **Clarity and Transparency:** Instructions, grading criteria, and expectations should be clearly communicated to learners.

Example:
In an educational technology course, a formative quiz tests understanding of multimedia components, while a summative project evaluates the creation of an interactive lesson plan.

2. Steps in Designing Effective Assessments

1. **Define Learning Outcomes:** Identify cognitive, affective, and psychomotor objectives.
2. **Select Assessment Methods:** Choose appropriate tools—online quizzes, practical assignments, simulations, or peer evaluations.
3. **Develop Assessment Items:** Create clear, concise, and unbiased questions or tasks aligned with objectives.

4. **Set Rubrics and Criteria:** Establish scoring guidelines for consistency and transparency.
5. **Pilot and Revise:** Test assessments on a small group to identify potential issues and make improvements.
6. **Integrate Feedback Mechanisms:** Provide learners with detailed, timely feedback to guide improvement.

Example:
A teacher designs a rubric for evaluating multimedia lesson plans, considering creativity, content accuracy, instructional strategy, and technical integration.

3. Technology-Enhanced Assessment Tools

- **Quizzes and Tests:** Platforms like Moodle, Kahoot, and Google Forms provide instant feedback.
- **E-Portfolios:** Digital portfolios document ongoing work, reflections, and skill development.
- **Simulations and Virtual Labs:** Assess applied skills in controlled digital environments.
- **Automated Grading Systems:** Provide efficiency and consistency for objective assessments.
- **Learning Analytics:** Use data to identify trends, learning gaps, and performance patterns.

Benefits:

- Facilitates timely, data-driven decision-making
- Supports diverse learning styles and multiple competencies
- Enhances engagement through interactive and gamified assessments

4. Best Practices for Assessment Design

1. **Integrate Variety:** Combine multiple formats to assess different skills and knowledge.
2. **Use Formative Assessment Regularly:** Offer ongoing feedback to improve learning.
3. **Encourage Self-Assessment:** Involve learners in evaluating their own progress.
4. **Maintain Accessibility:** Ensure all learners can engage with assessments regardless of technical or physical limitations.
5. **Continuously Review:** Refine assessments based on learner performance, feedback, and evolving educational goals.

6.5 Feedback for Continuous Improvement

Introduction

Feedback is a critical component of the teaching-learning process, providing learners with insights into their performance and guiding improvements. In technology-enhanced education, feedback can be **timely, personalized, and data-driven**, enhancing learning outcomes and supporting continuous improvement. For B.Ed. and M.Ed. students, understanding effective feedback strategies is essential to **foster learner engagement, reflection, and skill development**.

1. Importance of Feedback

- **Promotes Learning:** Helps learners identify strengths, weaknesses, and areas for improvement.
- **Encourages Reflection:** Stimulates self-assessment and critical thinking about learning strategies.
- **Guides Instruction:** Enables teachers to adjust content, teaching methods, and pace based on learner needs.

- **Supports Motivation:** Constructive feedback boosts confidence and encourages persistence.

Example:
After an online lesson on classroom management, a teacher provides personalized comments on student-teachers' lesson plans, highlighting effective strategies and suggesting improvements.

2. Types of Feedback in Technology-Enhanced Learning

1. **Immediate Feedback:**
   - Delivered instantly through online quizzes, automated grading, or interactive modules.
   - Reinforces learning and corrects misconceptions quickly.
2. **Formative Feedback:**
   - Continuous guidance during the learning process via assignments, e-portfolios, or discussion forums.
   - Helps learners refine skills before summative assessment.
3. **Peer Feedback:**
   - Learners provide constructive comments to each other using discussion boards or collaborative tools.
   - Encourages reflection, collaboration, and critical evaluation skills.
4. **Teacher Feedback:**
   - Personalized feedback from instructors highlighting performance, providing guidance, and suggesting improvement strategies.

Example:
In a virtual lab, after completing a simulation, learners receive

instant automated feedback on their results, followed by teacher comments addressing deeper conceptual understanding.

3. Best Practices for Providing Feedback

1. **Be Specific and Actionable:** Focus on particular aspects of performance and suggest clear improvements.
2. **Timely Delivery:** Provide feedback soon after tasks or assessments to maintain relevance.
3. **Balance Positive and Constructive Feedback:** Reinforce strengths while addressing areas for improvement.
4. **Encourage Reflection:** Prompt learners to analyze their own performance and identify strategies for improvement.
5. **Use Technology Effectively:** Leverage LMS analytics, automated feedback tools, and digital rubrics for personalized guidance.

Example:
A student-teacher receives a rubric-based evaluation of a lesson plan with scores for clarity, engagement, and assessment integration, along with specific recommendations for improvement.

4. Feedback for Continuous Improvement

- **Data-Informed Decisions:** Use analytics to identify trends, gaps, and areas needing reinforcement.
- **Iterative Learning:** Encourage learners to revise assignments or projects based on feedback.
- **Collaborative Improvement:** Facilitate peer discussions and mentor guidance to reinforce learning.
- **Goal Setting:** Support learners in setting specific, measurable goals for improvement.

Example:
Following feedback on teaching simulations, learners revise their instructional strategies and re-submit lesson plans, demonstrating enhanced understanding and skill application.

Chapter 7
Learning Analytics and Educational Data Mining

7.1 Importance of Data in Education

Introduction

Data has become a cornerstone of modern education, guiding decision-making, improving teaching effectiveness, and enhancing student learning outcomes. In technology-enhanced education, the collection, analysis, and interpretation of data allow educators to adopt **evidence-based practices**, personalize instruction, and monitor academic progress. For B.Ed. and M.Ed. students, understanding the importance of data is critical to becoming **data-literate educators** capable of informed decision-making in classrooms.

1. Defining Data in Education

Data in education refers to **quantitative and qualitative information** collected from various sources such as student assessments, learning management systems, attendance records, classroom interactions, and surveys. This data can include:

- Test scores and grades
- Participation metrics in online learning platforms
- Student engagement in assignments, discussions, and simulations
- Behavioral and socio-emotional indicators

Example:
A college tracks student participation in virtual labs and online quizzes to identify patterns in learning and engagement.

2. Importance of Data in Educational Decision-Making

1. **Improves Teaching Effectiveness:**
   - Data enables teachers to identify areas where students struggle and adjust instructional strategies accordingly.
   - Provides insights into which teaching methods are most effective.
2. **Supports Personalized Learning:**
   - Enables tailoring of lessons, resources, and interventions to meet individual learner needs.
   - Helps accommodate diverse learning styles and paces.
3. **Enhances Assessment Practices:**
   - Informs the design of formative and summative assessments.
   - Allows objective evaluation of student performance and progress.
4. **Promotes Accountability:**
   - Provides evidence for institutional decision-making, accreditation processes, and policy formulation.
   - Ensures transparency and accountability in educational practices.
5. **Identifies Trends and Predicts Outcomes:**
   - Analysis of historical data helps predict potential learning gaps, dropouts, and performance trends.
   - Facilitates proactive interventions to improve outcomes.

Example:
A teacher uses LMS analytics to determine that students who engage in discussion forums score higher in assessments, prompting increased integration of collaborative activities.

3. Sources of Educational Data

- **Student Performance Data:** Grades, test scores, assignments, and e-portfolios
- **Engagement Data:** Attendance, login frequency, participation in online activities
- **Behavioral and Social Data:** Feedback from peers and teachers, classroom observations
- **Institutional Data:** Curriculum completion rates, teacher evaluations, resource utilization

Benefits:

- Provides a holistic view of learner development
- Supports continuous monitoring and improvement
- Enables research and policy-making in education

4. Best Practices for Using Data in Education

1. **Ensure Accuracy and Reliability:** Collect and validate data from trusted sources.
2. **Analyze Data Regularly:** Use dashboards, reports, and analytics tools to extract actionable insights.
3. **Make Data-Driven Decisions:** Use evidence from data to guide teaching strategies, resource allocation, and intervention programs.

4. **Maintain Ethical Standards:** Protect student privacy, ensure confidentiality, and use data responsibly.
5. **Promote Data Literacy:** Train educators and student-teachers to understand, interpret, and apply data effectively.

7.2 Tracking Student Progress

Introduction

Tracking student progress is a fundamental aspect of education, allowing teachers to **monitor learning outcomes, identify challenges, and provide timely interventions**. In technology-enhanced classrooms, digital tools enable **continuous, accurate, and data-driven monitoring** of learner performance. For B.Ed. and M.Ed. students, understanding strategies for tracking progress is essential to foster **personalized learning, evidence-based teaching, and improved student outcomes**.

1. Importance of Tracking Student Progress

1. **Identifies Learning Gaps:** Continuous monitoring highlights areas where students struggle, allowing for remedial instruction.
2. **Supports Personalized Learning:** Helps tailor lessons and resources to individual student needs.
3. **Enhances Motivation:** Students receive feedback on their progress, fostering engagement and goal-setting.
4. **Informs Teaching Practices:** Teachers can adjust instructional strategies, pace, and content based on performance data.

5. **Facilitates Communication:** Progress reports keep parents, administrators, and students informed about learning outcomes.

Example:
A B.Ed. student-teacher monitors quiz scores and class participation through Google Classroom to identify which students need additional support in pedagogical methods.

2. Tools for Tracking Student Progress

1. **Learning Management Systems (LMS):**
   - Platforms like Moodle, Canvas, and Google Classroom provide detailed analytics on assignment submissions, quiz scores, and participation.
   - Allows teachers to track progress over time and generate reports.
2. **E-Portfolios:**
   - Digital portfolios document students' work, reflections, and skill development across different activities.
   - Teachers can review progress, provide feedback, and assess competency growth.
3. **Online Assessment Tools:**
   - Quizzes, tests, and assignments graded automatically provide instant feedback and performance records.
   - Adaptive assessments adjust difficulty based on student performance.
4. **Attendance and Engagement Tracking:**
   - Digital attendance systems, participation in online discussions, and interaction logs help monitor engagement and commitment to learning.

Example:
A student-teacher observes that learners who regularly participate in discussion forums perform better in assessments, prompting strategies to increase engagement.

3. Methods of Progress Tracking

1. **Formative Assessment:** Regular quizzes, assignments, and classroom activities that provide ongoing insight into learning.
2. **Summative Assessment:** End-of-unit or term exams that evaluate cumulative knowledge and skills.
3. **Peer and Self-Assessment:** Encourages reflection and collaborative evaluation, allowing students to track their own progress.
4. **Data Analytics:** Use LMS dashboards, performance charts, and reports to visualize trends and gaps.

Benefits:

- Continuous insights into student learning
- Early detection of difficulties and timely interventions
- Supports goal-setting and self-regulated learning

4. Best Practices for Effective Progress Tracking

1. **Set Clear Learning Objectives:** Define measurable outcomes to track accurately.
2. **Use Multiple Data Sources:** Combine quizzes, assignments, participation, and e-portfolios for a holistic view.
3. **Provide Regular Feedback:** Inform learners about strengths and areas needing improvement.

4. **Ensure Transparency:** Share progress reports with students and stakeholders.
5. **Adapt Instruction Based on Data:** Use insights to modify teaching strategies and support mechanisms.

7.3 Learning Patterns and Interventions

Introduction

Understanding learning patterns is crucial for designing **effective teaching strategies and interventions**. Technology-enhanced education allows educators to collect and analyze data on student behaviors, engagement, and performance, helping identify trends and learning needs. For B.Ed. and M.Ed. students, recognizing these patterns and implementing targeted interventions is key to **promoting personalized learning, improving outcomes, and supporting all learners effectively**.

1. Understanding Learning Patterns

Learning patterns refer to **recurring behaviors, approaches, and performance trends** exhibited by students during the learning process. These can include:

- **Engagement Patterns:** Frequency and quality of participation in class, online discussions, and assignments.
- **Performance Patterns:** Strengths and weaknesses across subjects, topics, or skills.
- **Study Habits:** Time management, resource usage, and preferred learning modalities (visual, auditory, kinesthetic).
- **Progression Trends:** Rate of improvement or decline over time.

Example:
Analytics from an LMS indicate that students who frequently revisit course materials perform better in assessments, highlighting the importance of revision habits.

2. Importance of Identifying Learning Patterns

1. **Early Identification of Struggling Students:** Detects learners who may need additional support before issues become severe.
2. **Informing Instructional Design:** Helps educators plan lessons, activities, and resources based on actual student behaviors.
3. **Supporting Differentiated Instruction:** Enables the customization of learning experiences to suit diverse learning needs.
4. **Enhancing Engagement:** Recognizing patterns allows teachers to adapt methods to maintain student interest.

Example:
A B.Ed. student-teacher notices that students perform poorly in problem-solving tasks but excel in theory-based assessments, indicating the need for more practical exercises.

3. Interventions Based on Learning Patterns

1. **Targeted Remedial Support:**
   - Offer extra sessions, tutorials, or online resources for students struggling in specific areas.
2. **Adaptive Learning Strategies:**
   - Use technology tools that adjust difficulty levels based on individual performance.

3. **Collaborative Learning Opportunities:**
    - Form study groups or peer mentoring for learners showing similar patterns.
4. **Feedback and Reflection:**
    - Provide personalized feedback highlighting strengths, weaknesses, and strategies for improvement.
5. **Motivational Interventions:**
    - Recognize achievements, encourage goal-setting, and use gamification to maintain engagement.

Example:
In a virtual science lab, students who repeatedly make errors in simulations receive additional guided exercises and tutorials to reinforce concepts.

4. Tools for Tracking and Intervention

- **Learning Management Systems (LMS):** Track completion rates, quiz scores, and participation.
- **Analytics Dashboards:** Visualize trends, identify gaps, and compare performance across groups.
- **Digital Rubrics and E-Portfolios:** Monitor skills development and progression over time.
- **Communication Platforms:** Provide timely support through chats, forums, and video conferencing.

Benefits:

- Enables timely and effective interventions
- Supports evidence-based instructional decisions
- Encourages self-regulation and learner responsibility

7.4 Using Dashboards and Reports

Introduction

Dashboards and reports are powerful tools in technology-enhanced education that provide **real-time insights into student learning, engagement, and performance**. They allow educators to monitor trends, evaluate instructional effectiveness, and make data-driven decisions. For B.Ed. and M.Ed. students, understanding how to interpret and use dashboards and reports is essential for **evidence-based teaching and effective classroom management**.

1. Understanding Dashboards and Reports

- **Dashboards:** Visual interfaces that display key metrics and indicators about students' learning progress. Dashboards can include graphs, charts, heatmaps, and summary statistics.
- **Reports:** Detailed documents that provide structured information on student performance, participation, and engagement over time. Reports can be generated daily, weekly, or at the end of a term.

Example:
An LMS dashboard shows the percentage of students who have completed weekly assignments, quiz scores, and forum participation. A detailed report highlights individual student strengths and areas needing improvement.

2. Importance of Dashboards and Reports

1. **Quick Overview of Performance:** Allows teachers to monitor class progress at a glance.
2. **Data-Driven Instruction:** Provides insights to adjust teaching strategies, resources, and pacing.

3. **Identifying Trends and Patterns:** Highlights consistent struggles or areas where learners excel.
4. **Facilitates Accountability:** Supports transparent evaluation for students, parents, and administrators.
5. **Supports Continuous Improvement:** Teachers can track the effectiveness of interventions and modify them as needed.

Example:
A B.Ed. student-teacher notices from the dashboard that students struggle with interactive simulations. This prompts the teacher to introduce guided practice sessions to enhance understanding.

3. Key Features of Effective Dashboards and Reports

- **Real-Time Updates:** Provide up-to-date information about learner engagement and performance.
- **Customizable Views:** Teachers can filter data by student, subject, topic, or activity type.
- **Visual Analytics:** Graphs, charts, and heatmaps make complex data easy to interpret.
- **Comparative Analysis:** Track performance trends over time and compare groups or cohorts.
- **Actionable Insights:** Highlight areas requiring intervention and suggest targeted strategies.

4. Using Dashboards and Reports for Teaching and Learning

1. **Monitoring Student Progress:**
    - Track assignment submissions, quiz performance, and engagement levels.

- Identify students needing extra support or enrichment activities.

2. **Evaluating Teaching Effectiveness:**
    - Analyze class-wide performance patterns to assess instructional strategies.
    - Determine which topics require reteaching or additional resources.
3. **Planning Interventions:**
    - Use reports to implement remedial programs, peer mentoring, or adaptive learning modules.
4. **Communicating with Stakeholders:**
    - Share insights with students, parents, and administrators to foster collaboration and accountability.

Example:
A weekly report shows that a group of students consistently underperforms in formative assessments. The teacher organizes small group sessions and tracks improvement using subsequent dashboards.

5. Best Practices

1. **Focus on Relevant Metrics:** Avoid information overload; concentrate on indicators that matter most.
2. **Regular Monitoring:** Check dashboards and reports frequently to respond promptly.
3. **Interpret Data Correctly:** Understand the context behind numbers to make informed decisions.
4. **Integrate Feedback:** Combine dashboard insights with teacher observations and student feedback.

5. **Ensure Accessibility:** Make dashboards user-friendly and accessible to all educators involved.

7.5 Ethical Considerations in Data Use

Introduction

The use of data in education offers immense opportunities for improving teaching, learning, and decision-making. However, it also raises important **ethical concerns** related to privacy, security, equity, and responsible usage. For B.Ed. and M.Ed. students, understanding these ethical considerations is crucial to ensure that data is used in a way that **protects learners, maintains trust, and promotes fairness**.

1. Importance of Ethics in Educational Data Use

- **Protecting Privacy:** Student information is sensitive and must be safeguarded from unauthorized access.
- **Maintaining Trust:** Ethical data practices foster trust among learners, parents, and educators.
- **Ensuring Fairness:** Data must not be misused to discriminate against or stigmatize students.
- **Promoting Responsible Use:** Data should guide learning improvement, not punitive actions.

Example:
A teacher collects online assessment data to improve instruction but ensures that scores are only accessible to relevant educators, maintaining confidentiality.

2. Key Ethical Considerations

1. **Data Privacy and Security:**
    - Protect personal information, academic records, and behavioral data.
    - Use secure platforms with encryption and controlled access.
2. **Informed Consent:**
    - Ensure students and parents are aware of what data is collected, how it will be used, and who can access it.
3. **Equity and Fairness:**
    - Avoid bias in data interpretation that may disadvantage certain students.
    - Ensure interventions based on data are supportive, not punitive.
4. **Transparency:**
    - Share data policies and practices with all stakeholders.
    - Explain how analytics inform teaching, assessment, and feedback.
5. **Accountability:**
    - Educators and institutions must be accountable for ethical data collection, storage, and usage.
    - Regular audits and reviews can help maintain ethical standards.

3. Challenges in Ethical Data Use

1. **Data Breaches:** Cybersecurity threats can expose sensitive student information.
2. **Misinterpretation of Data:** Incorrect conclusions can lead to unfair treatment or misinformed decisions.
3. **Digital Divide:** Unequal access to technology may result in incomplete or biased data.

4. **Over-Surveillance:** Excessive tracking may infringe on student autonomy and trust.

Example:
A school using an AI tool to monitor online student activity must balance performance tracking with respect for privacy, ensuring that students are not constantly monitored inappropriately.

4. Best Practices for Ethical Data Use

1. **Adopt Privacy Policies:** Clearly define data collection, storage, and usage procedures.
2. **Use Data Minimally:** Collect only the data necessary to support learning and teaching.
3. **Ensure Accessibility:** Make data and insights understandable to educators, learners, and parents.
4. **Train Educators:** Equip teachers with skills to use data responsibly and interpret it accurately.
5. **Review and Update Practices:** Continuously evaluate ethical guidelines in response to new technologies and educational contexts.

Chapter 8
Inclusive Education with Technology

8.1 Assistive Technologies for Differently-Abled Students

Introduction

Assistive technologies are tools and devices designed to support students with disabilities or learning difficulties, enabling them to access educational content, participate actively, and achieve academic success. In technology-enhanced education, these tools play a crucial role in ensuring **inclusive learning environments** where all students, regardless of their abilities, can thrive. For B.Ed. and M.Ed. students, understanding assistive technologies is essential for **creating equitable and supportive classrooms**.

1. What are Assistive Technologies?

Assistive technologies refer to devices, software, and equipment that help students with physical, sensory, cognitive, or learning disabilities to perform tasks that might otherwise be challenging. These technologies aim to enhance **accessibility, participation, and independence**.

Example:
Screen readers help visually impaired students access written content by converting text into audio, while speech recognition tools assist students with motor disabilities in composing essays.

2. Types of Assistive Technologies

1. **Screen Readers and Text-to-Speech Software:**

- Convert written content into audio.
- Help visually impaired or dyslexic students comprehend text.

2. **Speech-to-Text Tools:**
    - Allow students with writing or motor difficulties to dictate responses.
    - Increase efficiency in completing assignments or exams.
3. **Hearing Aids and Captioning Services:**
    - Support students with hearing impairments through audio amplification or subtitles.
4. **Alternative Input Devices:**
    - Include adaptive keyboards, eye-tracking systems, and switch devices for students with mobility issues.
5. **Cognitive Support Tools:**
    - Software that breaks down instructions, offers reminders, and provides interactive learning activities for students with learning disabilities like ADHD or autism.
6. **Accessible Learning Platforms:**
    - LMS and e-learning tools designed with customizable fonts, color contrast options, and navigation aids to support diverse learners.

3. Importance of Assistive Technologies

1. **Promotes Inclusive Education:** Enables differently-abled students to participate fully alongside their peers.
2. **Improves Academic Access:** Provides tools that help students engage with curriculum content effectively.
3. **Encourages Independence:** Supports self-directed learning by reducing reliance on external assistance.

4. **Enhances Confidence and Motivation:** When students overcome barriers, they feel empowered and more willing to participate in learning activities.
5. **Facilitates Personalized Learning:** Allows teachers to tailor instruction based on individual needs.

Example:
A student with hearing impairment uses captioning tools during virtual lectures, ensuring they can follow along and participate without missing key points.

4. Implementation in Classrooms

1. **Assess Needs Individually:** Understand each student's disability and learning requirements before selecting technologies.
2. **Integrate Seamlessly:** Use assistive tools alongside regular instructional methods to avoid segregation.
3. **Provide Training:** Educate students and teachers on how to use assistive tools effectively.
4. **Collaborate with Specialists:** Work with therapists, counselors, and special educators to design comprehensive support plans.
5. **Ensure Accessibility:** Choose platforms and materials that adhere to accessibility guidelines.

5. Challenges and Solutions

- **Cost Barriers:** Seek government grants, community support, or low-cost alternatives.
- **Resistance to Adoption:** Raise awareness among teachers and students about the benefits of assistive tools.

- **Technical Difficulties:** Provide ongoing technical support and training sessions.
- **Privacy Concerns:** Ensure data protection and confidentiality in assistive software usage.

8.2 Accessibility Guidelines and Tools

Introduction

Accessibility in education ensures that learning materials, environments, and teaching methods are designed to accommodate all students, including those with disabilities or special learning needs. Accessibility guidelines and tools help educators create inclusive classrooms where every learner can access, engage with, and benefit from educational content. For B.Ed. and M.Ed. students, understanding accessibility principles is vital to promote **equity, participation, and effective learning**.

1. What is Accessibility in Education?

Accessibility refers to the design and delivery of educational resources, platforms, and environments in ways that make learning possible for all students, regardless of their physical, sensory, cognitive, or socio-economic barriers. It involves removing obstacles, providing accommodations, and using tools that support diverse learning needs.

Example:
Providing text alternatives for images in digital content allows visually impaired learners to understand the material through screen readers.

2. Accessibility Guidelines

1. **Universal Design for Learning (UDL):**
   - Offers multiple ways for students to access content, engage with materials, and demonstrate learning.
   - Encourages flexibility to accommodate individual learning styles.
2. **Web Content Accessibility Guidelines (WCAG):**
   - A set of internationally recognized standards for creating accessible digital content.
   - Includes principles like providing text alternatives, ensuring contrast, and making content navigable by keyboard.
3. **Section 508 (U.S. Accessibility Standards):**
   - Focuses on making electronic and information technology accessible to people with disabilities.
   - Encourages compatibility with assistive technologies.
4. **Accessible Pedagogy:**
   - Incorporates flexible teaching strategies, alternative formats, and supportive assessment methods to address diverse learning needs.

3. Tools That Support Accessibility

1. **Screen Readers:**
   - Examples: JAWS, NVDA
   - Converts digital text into speech for visually impaired learners.
2. **Text-to-Speech Software:**
   - Examples: NaturalReader, Kurzweil
   - Assists learners with reading difficulties by vocalizing written content.

3. **Speech-to-Text Tools:**
    - Examples: Google Docs Voice Typing, Dragon NaturallySpeaking
    - Helps students with motor impairments or writing challenges.
4. **Captioning and Subtitling Tools:**
    - Examples: YouTube automatic captions, Microsoft Stream
    - Supports learners with hearing impairments by providing written transcripts.
5. **Alternative Input Devices:**
    - Includes adaptive keyboards, eye-tracking systems, and touch screens for learners with mobility limitations.
6. **Screen Magnifiers and Color Adjustment Tools:**
    - Examples: ZoomText, Windows Magnifier
    - Assists learners with low vision by enlarging text or adjusting screen contrast.
7. **Accessible Learning Platforms:**
    - Many LMS platforms, such as Moodle and Google Classroom, include built-in accessibility features like adjustable fonts, keyboard navigation, and audio support.

4. Best Practices for Accessibility Implementation

1. **Conduct Accessibility Audits:**
    - Evaluate learning materials, websites, and classroom layouts to ensure compliance with guidelines.
2. **Provide Multiple Formats:**
    - Offer content in text, audio, video, and interactive formats to cater to different learning preferences.

3. **Involve Students in Planning:**
    - Seek feedback from learners about what works best for their needs.
4. **Integrate Assistive Tools Seamlessly:**
    - Use technology in ways that enhance learning without making accommodations feel separate or stigmatized.
5. **Train Educators and Staff:**
    - Ensure teachers are aware of accessibility guidelines, tools, and best practices.

8.3 Personalized Learning Approaches

Introduction

Personalized learning refers to educational strategies that are tailored to meet the individual needs, abilities, interests, and learning styles of each student. With advancements in educational technology and accessibility tools, personalized learning has become a key approach in creating inclusive classrooms. For B.Ed. and M.Ed. students, understanding personalized learning approaches is essential for designing lessons that **encourage student autonomy, engagement, and academic success** while supporting differently-abled learners.

1. What is Personalized Learning?

Personalized learning is a student-centered approach where instruction, content, learning pace, and assessment methods are adapted based on each learner's strengths and challenges. It aims to create **flexible learning pathways** that allow students to learn in ways that suit their needs while achieving learning objectives.

Example:
A student with reading difficulties may receive learning materials in audio format, while another student may prefer interactive simulations to understand complex concepts. Both learners follow customized pathways toward the same learning goal.

2. Key Elements of Personalized Learning

1. **Learner Profiles:**
   - Information about a student's learning style, strengths, disabilities, interests, and pace is gathered to guide instructional decisions.
2. **Adaptive Learning Tools:**
   - Software and platforms that adjust difficulty levels and content delivery based on learner performance, ensuring students are neither overwhelmed nor under-challenged.
3. **Flexible Learning Paths:**
   - Students can choose from a variety of learning activities and resources to master topics in ways that are most effective for them.
4. **Continuous Assessment:**
   - Ongoing assessments provide real-time data to guide teaching strategies, ensuring that interventions are timely and targeted.
5. **Student Autonomy:**
   - Students are encouraged to set learning goals, track their own progress, and take responsibility for their learning journey.

3. Personalized Learning Approaches for Differently-Abled Students

1. **Customized Content Delivery:**
   - Students with visual impairments may access content through screen readers, while others may use large-print materials.
2. **Assistive Technologies Integration:**
   - Tools like speech-to-text software, captioning, or alternative keyboards support students in interacting with content more easily.
3. **Individualized Support Plans:**
   - Teachers collaborate with special educators to create learning plans that align with each student's abilities and challenges.
4. **Peer Collaboration Opportunities:**
   - Personalized learning can also include group projects where students with complementary skills collaborate, enhancing mutual support and learning.

4. Benefits of Personalized Learning

1. **Enhanced Engagement:**
   - Students feel more motivated when learning experiences align with their interests and abilities.
2. **Improved Academic Outcomes:**
   - Targeted interventions and adaptive content support better understanding and retention.
3. **Inclusive Learning Environments:**
   - Differently-abled students receive the accommodations they need to participate fully in classroom activities.
4. **Fostering Independence and Confidence:**
   - By taking ownership of their learning, students build self-confidence and lifelong learning skills.

5. Best Practices for Implementing Personalized Learning

1. **Collect Comprehensive Learner Data:**
   - Use surveys, assessments, and observations to understand student needs and preferences.
2. **Incorporate Technology Thoughtfully:**
   - Select tools that enhance learning without overwhelming students.
3. **Encourage Goal Setting:**
   - Support students in setting realistic, measurable learning objectives.
4. **Collaborate with Support Services:**
   - Work with counselors, therapists, and special educators to provide holistic support.
5. **Review and Revise:**
   - Continuously monitor progress and adjust learning paths based on student feedback and assessment data.

8.4 Addressing Diverse Learning Needs

Introduction

Classrooms today are diverse, with students coming from different cultural, linguistic, social, and ability backgrounds. Addressing these diverse learning needs is essential for ensuring that every student has an equal opportunity to learn and succeed. Technology plays a significant role in helping educators design learning experiences that accommodate differences in learning styles, abilities, and pace. For B.Ed. and M.Ed. students, understanding how to address diverse learning needs is crucial for **promoting inclusion, equity, and academic growth**.

1. Understanding Diverse Learning Needs

Diverse learning needs can arise from multiple factors, including:

- **Physical or sensory disabilities** – such as visual or hearing impairments.
- **Learning disabilities** – including dyslexia, attention deficit disorder (ADD), or autism.
- **Language barriers** – learners from different linguistic backgrounds.
- **Socio-economic factors** – limited access to resources, technology, or stable learning environments.
- **Cultural differences** – variations in values, beliefs, and learning styles.

Understanding these factors helps educators design lessons that are **flexible, adaptive, and supportive**.

Example:
A student from a rural area may have limited internet access, requiring offline learning materials or downloadable resources. Another student with hearing impairment may benefit from captioned videos and transcripts.

2. Strategies to Address Diverse Learning Needs

1. **Differentiated Instruction:**
    - Vary content, process, and product based on students' abilities and preferences.
    - Provide multiple ways for students to engage with material and demonstrate learning.
2. **Universal Design for Learning (UDL):**

- Create learning experiences that accommodate a wide range of learners without the need for separate adaptations.

3. **Use of Assistive Technologies:**
   - Implement tools like screen readers, magnifiers, and speech-to-text programs to support learners with disabilities.
4. **Flexible Assessment Methods:**
   - Offer alternative forms of evaluation such as oral presentations, project work, or interactive activities instead of only written exams.
5. **Multilingual Resources:**
   - Provide learning materials in different languages or use translation tools to support students with limited language proficiency.
6. **Culturally Relevant Teaching:**
   - Incorporate examples, case studies, and learning materials that reflect students' diverse backgrounds and experiences.

3. Role of Technology in Supporting Diverse Needs

1. **Adaptive Learning Platforms:**
   - Adjust learning content and activities based on the student's performance and pace.
2. **Learning Management Systems (LMS):**
   - Offer personalized dashboards, progress tracking, and access to varied content formats.
3. **Interactive Tools:**
   - Engage learners through gamified activities, simulations, and multimedia resources.
4. **Collaboration Platforms:**

- Foster peer-to-peer support, discussion forums, and group projects that encourage shared learning.

Example:
An online platform allows students to choose between video lectures, text summaries, or interactive exercises, catering to different learning preferences.

4. Challenges and Considerations

1. **Equity of Access:**
   - Not all learners have access to devices or stable internet connections. Teachers must provide offline options or community support.
2. **Training Needs:**
   - Educators need ongoing professional development to implement technology-based solutions effectively.
3. **Avoiding Stigmatization:**
   - Accommodations should be integrated seamlessly into learning experiences, ensuring that students do not feel singled out.
4. **Monitoring and Feedback:**
   - Regular assessments and communication with students help in identifying evolving needs and making necessary adjustments.

8.5 Case Studies in Inclusive Education

Introduction

Case studies provide real-life examples of how inclusive education practices are implemented in diverse classroom settings. They illustrate the challenges, strategies, and outcomes of using technology and pedagogical approaches to support differently-abled and diverse learners. For B.Ed. and M.Ed. students, studying these cases helps in **understanding practical applications, learning from experiences, and adopting best practices** for inclusive teaching.

Case Study 1: Integrating Assistive Technology for Visually Impaired Students

Context:
A secondary school implemented screen reader software and audio textbooks to support visually impaired students. The school identified that students faced difficulties accessing printed learning materials and participating fully in classroom discussions.

Strategy:

- Teachers collaborated with specialists to integrate tools like JAWS screen reader and audio files of lessons.
- Classrooms were equipped with accessible learning platforms that allowed adjustable font sizes and high-contrast settings.
- Students received training sessions on how to use assistive devices effectively.

Outcome:
Students showed improved academic performance and greater participation in class activities. They reported feeling more confident and independent in managing their studies. Teachers noted a more inclusive learning environment where all students could engage meaningfully.

Case Study 2: Blended Learning for Students with Learning Disabilities

Context:
A teacher in an inclusive primary school worked with students diagnosed with dyslexia and attention deficit disorder (ADD). These students struggled with reading comprehension and staying focused during lessons.

Strategy:

- The school adopted a blended learning model combining face-to-face teaching and interactive online modules.
- Text-to-speech tools, interactive quizzes, and video explanations were used to reinforce learning.
- Students could access learning materials at their own pace and receive instant feedback through adaptive learning software.

Outcome:
Students showed increased engagement and improved reading and comprehension skills. The flexible learning paths allowed them to work at their own pace without feeling pressured. The teacher observed that students were more willing to participate and ask for help when needed.

Case Study 3: Multilingual Learning for Language Barriers

Context:
In a metropolitan college, many students spoke different regional

languages and struggled to understand lessons conducted in the official instructional language.

Strategy:

- The institution integrated multilingual subtitles, translation tools, and audio support into its digital learning platforms.
- Teachers created bilingual worksheets and encouraged peer-assisted learning where students with stronger language skills helped others.
- Regular workshops were conducted to train faculty in culturally responsive teaching methods.

Outcome:
Students became more comfortable participating in class discussions and group projects. Language barriers were reduced, and learners felt more connected to the curriculum. The college reported improved attendance and academic outcomes among previously hesitant students.

Case Study 4: Promoting Social Inclusion through Collaborative Projects

Context:
A higher education institution wanted to address social exclusion and foster empathy among students with and without disabilities.

Strategy:

- Collaborative projects were designed where students from diverse backgrounds worked together in mixed-ability groups.

- Assistive tools like captioning, screen readers, and simplified content were incorporated into project planning.
- Teachers facilitated reflection sessions encouraging students to share experiences and perspectives.

Outcome:

Students developed stronger communication skills and empathy. The collaborative approach reduced stigma and helped build friendships across diverse groups. Academic achievements also improved due to shared learning and mutual support.

Chapter 9

Ethical and Legal Aspects of Technology in Education

9.1 Data Privacy and Consent

Introduction

With the growing use of technology in education, data privacy and consent have become critical concerns. Educational institutions collect, store, and analyze large amounts of data from students, teachers, and parents to improve learning experiences, track progress, and enhance educational outcomes. However, handling this data responsibly requires strict attention to privacy laws, ethical standards, and informed consent. For B.Ed. and M.Ed. students, understanding data privacy and consent is essential to ensure that **learning environments are safe, trustworthy, and respectful of individual rights**.

1. What is Data Privacy in Education?

Data privacy refers to the protection of personal and sensitive information collected from students and other stakeholders. This includes academic records, health information, behavioral data, location details, and interaction history on digital platforms. Ensuring data privacy means safeguarding this information from unauthorized access, misuse, or breaches.

Example:

A learning management system collects student login details, grades, and participation metrics. Privacy policies ensure that this data is accessible only to authorized educators and administrators.

2. Why Consent is Important

Consent is a fundamental principle that ensures individuals are aware of what data is being collected, how it will be used, and who will have access to it. Consent empowers students and parents by providing them with control over their personal information.

Key elements of informed consent include:

- **Clear communication:** Data collection processes and purposes should be explained in simple terms.
- **Voluntary agreement:** Participation should not be forced or conditioned upon agreeing to data sharing.
- **Right to withdraw:** Individuals must have the option to revoke consent without facing penalties or exclusion from learning activities.

Example:
Before implementing an online assessment tool, the school shares a consent form detailing what data will be collected, how it will be stored, and how feedback will be used to support learning. Students and parents sign the form after understanding its content.

3. Legal and Ethical Frameworks

1. **Data Protection Laws:**
    - Many countries have data protection regulations that govern how personal data should be handled in educational settings. These laws often require secure

data storage, encryption, and accountability mechanisms.

2. **Educational Standards and Policies:**
   - Institutions are encouraged to develop privacy policies aligned with ethical guidelines, including respecting student dignity, minimizing data collection, and using data only for educational purposes.
3. **Ethical Responsibilities:**
   - Educators must ensure that student data is used fairly, without discrimination or bias.
   - Institutions should regularly audit data use and address concerns raised by stakeholders.

4. Best Practices for Data Privacy and Consent

1. **Transparent Communication:**
   - Clearly outline data collection processes in student handbooks and online platforms.
2. **Secure Storage and Access Controls:**
   - Use encryption, passwords, and role-based access to protect sensitive information.
3. **Regular Training:**
   - Educate teachers, administrators, and students about privacy policies and safe data handling.
4. **Minimal Data Collection:**
   - Collect only necessary information to reduce exposure to data breaches.
5. **Consent Forms:**
   - Provide easy-to-understand consent forms and explain rights to students and parents.

9.2 Plagiarism, Copyright, and Fair Use

Introduction

In today's digital learning environments, content is widely accessible, and students and teachers frequently use online resources, multimedia tools, and educational platforms. While technology offers vast opportunities for learning, it also raises ethical and legal concerns related to plagiarism, copyright, and fair use. For B.Ed. and M.Ed. students, understanding these concepts is essential to maintain academic integrity, respect intellectual property, and use educational materials responsibly.

1. What is Plagiarism?

Plagiarism is the act of using someone else's work—whether text, images, videos, or ideas—without proper acknowledgment or citation. It is considered unethical because it misrepresents another's intellectual property as one's own and undermines academic honesty.

Example:
A student copies large sections from a website into their assignment without citing the source or adding original analysis.

2. Consequences of Plagiarism

1. **Academic Penalties:**
    - Students may receive reduced grades, warnings, or disciplinary actions.
2. **Loss of Credibility:**

  - Repeated plagiarism can harm a student's or educator's reputation.
3. **Legal Issues:**
  - Using copyrighted materials without permission may lead to legal consequences, including fines or lawsuits.
4. **Impact on Learning:**
  - Plagiarism discourages critical thinking and self-expression, preventing students from developing their own voice and creativity.

3. Understanding Copyright

Copyright is a legal framework that protects creators' original works, including books, articles, videos, artwork, and software. It grants the creator exclusive rights to reproduce, distribute, and display their work, usually for a fixed period.

Key Aspects of Copyright:

- Protects original works from unauthorized use.
- Requires permission or licensing for reproduction or distribution.
- Encourages innovation and creative efforts by ensuring recognition and control over one's work.

Example:
A teacher cannot distribute a textbook in its entirety without obtaining permission from the publisher or author.

4. Fair Use in Education

Fair use is a legal doctrine that allows limited use of copyrighted materials without permission under specific conditions, particularly for educational, research, or commentary purposes. Fair use is not a blanket permission but depends on factors such as:

1. **Purpose of Use:** Non-commercial, educational purposes are more likely to qualify.
2. **Nature of the Work:** Using factual or published works is easier to justify than unpublished creative works.
3. **Amount Used:** Using only a small portion of the content may be allowed.
4. **Effect on the Market:** If the use doesn't affect the original creator's ability to profit, it's more likely to be fair.

Example:
A teacher may use a short excerpt from a book during class discussion, provided it is attributed and does not affect the original market.

5. Best Practices to Avoid Plagiarism and Respect Copyright

1. **Proper Citation:**
   - Always give credit to the original creator by citing books, articles, websites, and images correctly.
2. **Use Open Educational Resources (OER):**
   - Choose freely available, licensed materials that allow adaptation and reuse for educational purposes.
3. **Paraphrasing:**
   - Rewrite content in your own words and include proper references to avoid direct copying.
4. **Check for Plagiarism:**

  - Use plagiarism detection tools to ensure originality in assignments and research.
5. **Educate Students:**
  - Teach learners about ethical research practices, proper citation methods, and responsible content use.

9.3 Ethical Challenges in Digital Education

Introduction

Digital education has transformed how students learn and teachers instruct, offering flexibility, access to vast resources, and personalized learning experiences. However, alongside these benefits, it has introduced new ethical challenges that educators must navigate. Issues like data misuse, bias in artificial intelligence, inequity in access, and concerns about privacy have raised important questions about fairness, responsibility, and accountability in digital learning environments. For B.Ed. and M.Ed. students, understanding these ethical challenges is essential to ensure that technology is used responsibly and equitably in educational settings.

1. Data Misuse and Privacy Concerns

Digital platforms collect extensive data, including personal details, learning behaviors, and performance metrics. Without strict safeguards, this data may be exposed to misuse, hacking, or commercial exploitation. Students may unknowingly share sensitive information, and institutions may not always be transparent about how data is used.

Example:
An online learning app tracks students' progress and shares it with third-party advertisers without clear consent.

Ethical Concern: Educators must ensure informed consent, transparent data policies, and secure storage systems to protect learners' privacy.

2. Equity and Accessibility Issues

Not all students have equal access to devices, high-speed internet, or supportive learning environments. Digital education can unintentionally widen the gap between privileged and underprivileged students, affecting learning outcomes.

Example:
A student from a rural area struggles to participate in online classes due to limited internet connectivity, while others access resources freely.

Ethical Concern: Institutions must work to provide inclusive solutions, such as offline materials, community support programs, or subsidized technology access.

3. Algorithmic Bias and Artificial Intelligence

Artificial intelligence (AI) tools are increasingly used for adaptive learning, automated grading, and personalized recommendations. However, these algorithms may reflect biases present in their training data, leading to unfair treatment or reinforcing stereotypes.

Example:
An AI-driven assessment tool penalizes students from certain

backgrounds due to patterns in its dataset, affecting their academic evaluation.

Ethical Concern: Educators and developers must audit algorithms regularly, ensure diverse datasets, and incorporate human oversight in decision-making.

4. Academic Integrity and Online Learning

Digital platforms make it easier for students to access information quickly, but this convenience can also lead to plagiarism, cheating, and academic dishonesty. Tools that assist in answering questions may tempt learners to bypass critical thinking and independent effort.

Example:
Students copy entire solutions from online sources without engaging in problem-solving.

Ethical Concern: Educators must balance providing resources with fostering authentic learning experiences, promoting ethical conduct, and developing assignments that encourage original thinking.

5. Psychological and Social Well-being

Extended screen time, online distractions, and isolation can affect students' mental health, leading to anxiety, burnout, or reduced motivation. The lack of personal interaction may also impact social learning and emotional development.

Example:
Students attending virtual classes for long hours without breaks may experience stress and fatigue.

Ethical Concern: Teachers should design balanced schedules, encourage collaborative activities, and provide support networks to safeguard students' well-being.

9.4 Protecting Students and Educators

Introduction

As digital education becomes more prevalent, protecting both students and educators from ethical, legal, and psychological risks is critical. Technology-based learning environments offer convenience and expanded access but also pose challenges related to privacy, security, cyberbullying, misinformation, and mental health. For B.Ed. and M.Ed. students, understanding strategies to safeguard learners and teachers ensures that technology is used in ways that promote safety, trust, and well-being while maintaining educational integrity.

1. Ensuring Data Security and Privacy

Protecting sensitive data is one of the foremost concerns in digital education. Educational platforms often collect information such as personal details, academic records, and interaction histories. Educators must ensure that proper security measures are in place.

Strategies:

- Use secure platforms with encryption and access controls.
- Limit data collection to what is necessary for learning objectives.
- Provide clear privacy policies and obtain informed consent before collecting data.

- Educate students on safe online behavior, password management, and how to report suspicious activities.

2. Preventing Cyberbullying and Online Harassment

The anonymity and distance in online learning environments can lead to instances of bullying, harassment, or exclusion. Both students and educators can face such threats, impacting their mental health and sense of security.

Strategies:

- Establish clear behavioral expectations and codes of conduct for online interactions.
- Monitor discussions and forums for inappropriate content.
- Provide reporting mechanisms and ensure that complaints are addressed confidentially and swiftly.
- Encourage empathy, respectful communication, and peer support among learners.

3. Promoting Mental Health and Emotional Well-Being

Prolonged screen time, isolation from peers, and academic pressure in virtual classrooms can affect learners' and teachers' emotional well-being. Addressing these issues is as important as academic achievement.

Strategies:

- Encourage breaks between sessions and promote healthy study routines.
- Offer counseling services or helplines for students facing anxiety, stress, or depression.

- Organize group activities, collaborative projects, and interactive sessions that foster social interaction.
- Train teachers to recognize signs of burnout or emotional distress and refer students to appropriate support resources.

4. Upholding Academic Integrity

In the digital space, it is easier for students to access unauthorized resources or share answers during assessments. Protecting academic integrity is crucial for fair and meaningful learning.

Strategies:

- Design assessments that test critical thinking rather than rote memorization.
- Use plagiarism detection tools and ensure that students are educated about ethical academic practices.
- Foster a culture of honesty by rewarding effort and original thought rather than merely correct answers.

5. Supporting Educators in Ethical Technology Use

Educators also face challenges, including stress from adapting to new technologies, lack of training, and fear of data misuse or harassment. Protecting teachers is equally important to ensure that they feel empowered and supported.

Strategies:

- Provide professional development workshops on digital tools and ethical teaching practices.
- Offer peer networks or mentoring systems where educators can share experiences and solutions.

- Encourage teachers to set boundaries regarding availability and communication times.
- Ensure that institutional policies clearly outline support mechanisms for educators facing online harassment or ethical dilemmas.

9.5 Policy Frameworks and Guidelines

Introduction

The integration of technology in education requires well-structured policies and guidelines that ensure ethical, secure, and effective use of digital tools. Without clear frameworks, both students and educators may face risks related to privacy breaches, misuse of data, inequity, and mental health concerns. For B.Ed. and M.Ed. students, understanding policy frameworks and guidelines helps them implement technology responsibly and create learning environments that are safe, inclusive, and aligned with legal and ethical standards.

1. Importance of Policy Frameworks in Digital Education

Policy frameworks serve as formal guidelines that direct how technology is used within educational settings. They provide clarity on rights, responsibilities, acceptable behavior, and procedures for handling challenges. Having such frameworks:

- Protects students' and educators' privacy and dignity.
- Establishes standards for data security, access, and ethical conduct.
- Encourages equitable access to technology.
- Ensures accountability and transparency in decision-making.

2. Key Elements of Policy Frameworks

1. **Data Protection and Privacy Policies:**
   - Clearly define what data will be collected, how it will be stored, who will access it, and how consent will be obtained.
   - Ensure that encryption, passwords, and secure servers are used to safeguard data.
2. **Guidelines on Acceptable Use of Technology:**
   - Specify what types of content can be shared, what platforms are approved, and how communication should be conducted.
   - Set clear expectations for academic integrity, prohibiting plagiarism and inappropriate behavior.
3. **Accessibility and Inclusion Policies:**
   - Outline procedures to ensure that all students, including those with disabilities or limited access, can participate fully.
   - Promote the use of assistive technologies, flexible learning paths, and culturally sensitive teaching materials.
4. **Mental Health and Well-being Support:**
   - Include provisions for counseling services, peer support, stress management programs, and wellness resources.
5. **Training and Capacity Building:**
   - Provide ongoing training for educators on ethical technology use, privacy safeguards, and inclusive teaching methods.
6. **Monitoring and Evaluation:**

- Establish mechanisms to regularly review and update policies based on feedback, technological advancements, and changing educational needs.

3. Examples of Policy Frameworks

1. **Institutional Guidelines:**
    - Many universities and schools have adopted policies aligned with national data protection laws and international ethical standards, such as GDPR (General Data Protection Regulation).
2. **Government Regulations:**
    - Governments issue directives for educational technology use, focusing on cybersecurity, data management, and equal access to technology.
3. **Professional Organizations' Codes of Conduct:**
    - Organizations like UNESCO and national education boards provide recommendations on responsible, ethical, and inclusive use of technology in classrooms.

4. Implementing Effective Guidelines

1. **Stakeholder Involvement:**
    - Engage students, teachers, parents, administrators, and technology experts while drafting and reviewing policies.
2. **Transparency:**
    - Clearly communicate policies through workshops, handbooks, and online portals to ensure that everyone understands their rights and responsibilities.
3. **Feedback Mechanisms:**

- Encourage students and educators to report issues, suggest improvements, and participate in discussions about ethical technology use.

4. **Continuous Improvement:**
    - Policies should be living documents that evolve with technological advancements, educational needs, and social changes.

Chapter 10
Teacher Professional Development through Technology

10.1 Online Workshops and Certifications

Introduction

Online workshops and certifications have become an essential part of modern education, especially with the increasing use of technology in teaching and learning. These programs offer flexible learning opportunities, skill enhancement, and professional growth for students and educators alike. For B.Ed. and M.Ed. students, engaging in online workshops and earning certifications helps in staying updated with the latest educational tools, methodologies, and best practices while also building a credible academic and professional profile.

1. What are Online Workshops and Certifications?

- **Online Workshops:** These are structured learning sessions conducted virtually, where participants can attend lectures, demonstrations, and interactive activities in real-time or through recorded content. Workshops focus on specific topics such as digital pedagogy, assessment techniques, or inclusive teaching strategies.
- **Certifications:** Certifications are formal acknowledgments awarded after successful completion of a course or workshop. They validate the participant's knowledge, skills, and expertise in a particular area and can enhance employability and professional development.

Example:

A workshop on "Integrating ICT in Classroom Teaching" may include sessions on using learning management systems, multimedia tools, and virtual classrooms, followed by an assessment and certificate of completion.

2. Importance of Online Workshops and Certifications

1. **Skill Development:**
   - Workshops offer hands-on training with tools and resources that educators can implement in their classrooms.
2. **Flexibility:**
   - Students and teachers can learn at their own pace and schedule, making it easier to balance academic, professional, and personal commitments.
3. **Professional Growth:**
   - Certifications add value to a resume, showcasing specialized skills and updated knowledge, which is especially helpful for career advancement.
4. **Networking Opportunities:**
   - Virtual sessions bring together learners from different regions and backgrounds, encouraging collaboration and exchange of ideas.
5. **Access to Expert Knowledge:**
   - Many workshops are led by experienced educators, researchers, or technology specialists, giving participants access to high-quality training.

3. Platforms Offering Online Workshops and Certifications

1. **MOOCs (Massive Open Online Courses):**
   - Platforms like Coursera, edX, and FutureLearn offer courses from reputed universities and institutions.
2. **Government Portals:**
   - Initiatives like SWAYAM (Study Webs of Active Learning for Young Aspiring Minds) provide free or subsidized courses for teachers and students in India.
3. **Professional Associations:**
   - Organizations like NCERT, NCTE, and state education boards conduct workshops on curriculum development, pedagogy, and research methodologies.
4. **Private EdTech Platforms:**
   - Websites like Udemy and LinkedIn Learning offer skill-based certifications in digital tools, classroom management, and communication techniques.

4. Guidelines for Selecting Workshops and Certifications

1. **Relevance:**
   - Choose programs aligned with academic goals, teaching methods, or areas requiring improvement.
2. **Accreditation:**
   - Ensure that the certificate is recognized by educational or professional bodies to enhance credibility.
3. **Content Quality:**
   - Look for workshops that offer practical demonstrations, real-life case studies, and interactive sessions rather than just theoretical lectures.
4. **Feedback and Support:**

- Check if there is guidance from instructors, discussion forums, or mentoring options during the course.

10.2 Communities of Practice and Peer Learning

Introduction

With the growth of technology in education, learning is no longer confined to classrooms or textbooks. Communities of practice and peer learning have emerged as effective methods for enhancing knowledge, skills, and professional development. These approaches encourage collaboration, sharing of resources, and collective problem-solving among learners and educators. For B.Ed. and M.Ed. students, engaging in communities of practice and peer learning helps build networks, exchange ideas, and gain diverse perspectives while fostering a culture of continuous learning.

1. What are Communities of Practice and Peer Learning?

- **Communities of Practice (CoP):** A community of practice is a group of individuals who share a common interest or profession and learn through interaction, experience sharing, and mutual support. Members engage in discussions, share resources, and work together to solve challenges and enhance their skills.
- **Peer Learning:** Peer learning is an educational practice where students learn from each other through collaborative activities such as group discussions, mentoring, project work, or problem-solving tasks. It promotes active

participation and reinforces understanding by explaining concepts to others.

Example:
A group of teachers from different schools forms a community where they exchange lesson plans, discuss classroom management strategies, and support one another in implementing technology-enhanced teaching methods.

2. Importance of Communities of Practice and Peer Learning

1. **Collaborative Learning:**
    - Working together helps learners solve problems faster and gain insights that may not be available through formal instruction alone.
2. **Knowledge Sharing:**
    - Members share experiences, research findings, teaching resources, and best practices that benefit the entire group.
3. **Building Confidence:**
    - Discussing challenges openly in a supportive environment helps learners develop confidence and reduce feelings of isolation.
4. **Encouraging Innovation:**
    - Peer discussions often lead to creative solutions, experimentation, and improvements in teaching strategies and learning tools.
5. **Professional Growth:**
    - Exposure to diverse perspectives helps learners broaden their understanding and apply new methods in classrooms or research.

3. How Technology Supports Communities of Practice and Peer Learning

1. **Online Forums and Discussion Groups:**
   - Platforms like Google Classroom, Microsoft Teams, and WhatsApp allow members to share ideas, ask questions, and collaborate virtually.
2. **Social Media Groups:**
   - Facebook groups, LinkedIn communities, and Telegram channels bring together educators from across the globe to exchange ideas and learning resources.
3. **Collaborative Tools:**
   - Shared documents, cloud storage, and project management tools enable real-time cooperation and feedback.
4. **Webinars and Video Calls:**
   - Live discussions, workshops, and group coaching sessions help build relationships and foster peer support.

4. Best Practices for Effective Communities of Practice and Peer Learning

1. **Set Clear Goals:**
   - Define the purpose of the community and the expected outcomes, such as improving classroom teaching or exploring educational research.
2. **Encourage Participation:**
   - Provide opportunities for all members to contribute, ask questions, and share experiences without fear of judgment.

3. **Use Structured Activities:**
   - Organize webinars, workshops, collaborative projects, and group discussions to encourage regular interaction and learning.
4. **Foster Inclusivity:**
   - Ensure that all members, regardless of experience or background, feel welcomed and valued.
5. **Evaluate and Reflect:**
   - Periodically assess the effectiveness of the community and encourage members to reflect on what they have learned.

10.3 Mentoring and Support Systems

Introduction

Mentoring and support systems play a vital role in guiding learners and educators through the complexities of academic life, professional development, and personal growth. With the increasing use of technology in education, these systems have expanded beyond traditional face-to-face interactions to include online platforms, virtual mentoring, and peer support networks. For B.Ed. and M.Ed. students, access to structured mentoring and support systems helps build confidence, provide guidance, and create pathways for academic and career advancement in a rapidly changing educational landscape.

1. What are Mentoring and Support Systems?

- **Mentoring:** Mentoring is a relationship where an experienced educator or professional (mentor) provides advice, guidance, and encouragement to a learner or less experienced individual (mentee). This relationship helps mentees develop skills, overcome challenges, and achieve personal or academic goals.

- **Support Systems:** Support systems refer to structured networks that provide assistance, resources, and emotional encouragement to learners and educators. These can include academic counseling, mental health services, peer groups, helplines, or professional associations.

Example:
A mentor may guide a student teacher on classroom management strategies, help them reflect on their teaching practices, and offer career advice based on their own experiences. Support systems, such as an online helpdesk, may offer resources for managing stress or preparing for examinations.

2. Importance of Mentoring and Support Systems

1. **Personal and Academic Growth:**
   - Mentors help students set realistic goals, plan their learning paths, and build self-confidence.
2. **Emotional and Psychological Support:**
   - Support systems create a safe space for students to share concerns, cope with stress, and access counseling services.
3. **Professional Networking:**
   - Mentoring relationships often lead to connections with industry experts, academic communities, and research networks.
4. **Enhanced Learning Experience:**

- Guided learning and feedback from mentors improve classroom practices, teaching strategies, and educational outcomes.

5. **Motivation and Retention:**
    - Students who feel supported are more likely to remain engaged, complete their studies, and pursue higher education or career opportunities.

3. Role of Technology in Mentoring and Support Systems

1. **Virtual Mentoring Platforms:**
    - Tools like Zoom, Microsoft Teams, or Google Meet allow mentors and mentees to interact regularly, share documents, and conduct video sessions.
2. **Online Counseling and Helplines:**
    - Educational institutions offer chat support, mental health counseling, and academic assistance accessible anytime through dedicated portals.
3. **Learning Communities:**
    - Online forums, discussion groups, and social networks provide peer-to-peer support, helping students learn collaboratively and resolve doubts.
4. **Mobile Applications:**
    - Apps offer scheduling tools, reminders, and progress tracking, making mentoring relationships more structured and efficient.

4. Best Practices for Effective Mentoring and Support Systems

1. **Clear Objectives:**

   - Mentoring relationships should have defined goals, timelines, and expected outcomes to ensure purposeful interaction.
2. **Training for Mentors:**
   - Mentors should be trained in communication, counseling, and conflict resolution to handle diverse mentee needs effectively.
3. **Confidentiality and Trust:**
   - Support systems must ensure that students feel safe sharing concerns without fear of judgment or breach of privacy.
4. **Regular Feedback:**
   - Both mentors and mentees should engage in regular reviews to reflect on progress, challenges, and areas for improvement.
5. **Inclusivity:**
   - Systems should be designed to support diverse learners, including those with disabilities, different cultural backgrounds, and varying academic abilities.

10.4 Using Technology for Professional Growth

Introduction

In today's fast-paced educational environment, technology offers a range of opportunities for teachers and students to pursue continuous professional growth. For B.Ed. and M.Ed. students, leveraging technology is essential not only for academic excellence but also for enhancing pedagogical skills, research capabilities, leadership qualities, and career prospects. With online platforms, digital tools, and global networks at their disposal, learners can access knowledge, connect with experts, and refine their teaching methods beyond traditional classroom boundaries.

1. Importance of Technology in Professional Growth

1. **Access to Global Knowledge:**
   - Technology enables access to research papers, e-books, webinars, and educational conferences worldwide, broadening learning horizons.
2. **Skill Enhancement:**
   - Through online courses, certifications, and workshops, teachers and students can develop new skills such as instructional design, data analysis, educational software usage, and digital communication.
3. **Networking Opportunities:**
   - Online forums, social media groups, and professional networks connect learners with peers, experts, and educational communities, encouraging collaboration and exchange of ideas.
4. **Research Development:**
   - Digital libraries, citation tools, and collaborative platforms make it easier to conduct, share, and publish research, contributing to academic growth.
5. **Career Advancement:**
   - Certificates, training programs, and mentorship opportunities build credibility and improve job prospects by showcasing expertise and commitment to lifelong learning.

2. Tools and Platforms for Professional Growth

1. **Learning Management Systems (LMS):**
   - Platforms like Moodle, Google Classroom, and Canvas offer structured content delivery, progress tracking, and interaction opportunities.
2. **Online Courses and MOOCs:**
   - Websites like Coursera, edX, and SWAYAM provide free or affordable courses on a wide range of topics relevant to education.
3. **Professional Social Networks:**
   - LinkedIn and ResearchGate allow learners to build profiles, share research, and engage with professionals in education and related fields.
4. **Educational Apps:**
   - Apps for note-taking, time management, and collaborative work support efficient learning and project organization.
5. **Virtual Conferences and Webinars:**
   - Attending virtual events keeps learners updated with trends, research developments, and best practices from around the world.

3. Strategies to Use Technology for Professional Growth

1. **Set Clear Learning Goals:**
   - Identify areas for improvement and choose courses or tools that directly address those needs.
2. **Engage in Continuous Learning:**
   - Regularly participate in webinars, workshops, and discussion groups to remain informed about advancements in educational methods and technology.
3. **Build a Professional Online Presence:**

   - Maintain an updated profile, share academic achievements, and connect with mentors and peers to create collaborative opportunities.
4. **Apply Learning Practically:**
   - Implement newly acquired skills in classroom teaching, research projects, or community initiatives to enhance practical knowledge.
5. **Seek Feedback and Reflect:**
   - Encourage peer reviews, mentor guidance, and self-assessment to identify strengths and areas requiring further development.

4. Challenges and Solutions

1. **Digital Literacy Gaps:**
   - **Solution:** Participate in basic technology training sessions and peer learning groups.
2. **Information Overload:**
   - **Solution:** Curate resources carefully, focus on priority learning goals, and schedule study routines.
3. **Lack of Motivation or Support:**
   - **Solution:** Join communities of practice and seek mentors who provide encouragement and accountability.

10.5 Challenges and Best Practices

Introduction

While technology offers significant benefits for professional growth, it also presents challenges that educators and students must address. Understanding these challenges and adopting best practices is crucial for making the most of digital tools while minimizing risks. For B.Ed. and M.Ed. students, learning how to navigate technological barriers, maintain ethical standards, and stay motivated ensures that technology remains a supportive force in education rather than a source of stress or confusion.

1. Common Challenges in Using Technology for Professional Growth

1. **Digital Divide and Accessibility Issues:**
   - Not all learners have access to devices, stable internet, or assistive technologies. This can create disparities in learning opportunities and limit participation.
2. **Lack of Technical Skills:**
   - Some teachers or students may struggle to use educational tools effectively due to limited training or experience.
3. **Time Management and Motivation:**
   - Balancing technology-based learning with other responsibilities can be overwhelming, resulting in procrastination or burnout.
4. **Information Overload:**
   - The vast amount of online content can be confusing, making it difficult for learners to focus on relevant materials or trust reliable sources.
5. **Privacy and Security Concerns:**
   - Online platforms may expose users to risks such as data breaches, cyberbullying, or misuse of personal information.
6. **Maintaining Academic Integrity:**

- Easy access to information increases the temptation to copy content, leading to plagiarism or reduced learning engagement.

2. Best Practices to Overcome These Challenges

1. **Promote Equal Access:**
    - Institutions should provide support like device loans, offline content, and internet subsidies for students in underserved areas.
    - Teachers should ensure materials are accessible through various formats and platforms.
2. **Offer Training and Orientation:**
    - Conduct workshops on how to use educational software, manage digital content, and stay safe online.
    - Encourage peer mentoring where tech-savvy students assist others in navigating platforms.
3. **Encourage Time Management:**
    - Help students create structured learning schedules and set achievable goals.
    - Integrate breaks, reflection sessions, and group discussions to prevent mental fatigue.
4. **Curate Learning Resources:**
    - Educators should guide learners to trustworthy websites, recommended reading lists, and validated research tools.
    - Encourage learners to focus on purpose-driven content aligned with their academic or career objectives.
5. **Ensure Data Privacy and Ethical Use:**

- Use platforms with strong security protocols and clearly explain privacy policies.
- Teach students how to create secure passwords, avoid phishing scams, and report suspicious activities.

6. **Foster Academic Integrity:**
   - Design assessments that require critical thinking, analysis, and original work rather than rote memorization.
   - Promote discussions about ethical learning and the value of honest effort.

3. Building a Supportive Learning Environment

1. **Encourage Collaboration:**
   - Group projects, peer feedback, and shared problem-solving help learners build trust and feel supported.
2. **Provide Continuous Feedback:**
   - Regular interaction with mentors and teachers helps learners stay motivated and correct mistakes early.
3. **Celebrate Achievements:**
   - Recognizing milestones and accomplishments reinforces commitment and builds a positive learning culture.

Chapter 11
Collaborative Tools and Social Learning

11.1 Online Discussion Platforms

Introduction

Online discussion platforms have become an essential part of modern education, providing spaces where learners and educators can exchange ideas, ask questions, and engage in collaborative learning beyond the classroom. For B.Ed. and M.Ed. students, these platforms offer opportunities to discuss teaching strategies, explore academic topics, and solve problems collectively, helping them develop communication skills, critical thinking, and a sense of community in a technology-driven environment.

1. What are Online Discussion Platforms?

Online discussion platforms are virtual spaces where participants interact through text, video, or audio messages. These platforms facilitate conversations on academic subjects, research projects, or professional development topics. Unlike face-to-face interactions, online forums allow learners to engage asynchronously, offering flexibility and enabling participation from diverse geographical locations.

Example:
A discussion forum for student teachers may include threads on lesson planning, classroom management techniques, and challenges faced during teaching practice, where participants post queries and share insights.

2. Importance of Online Discussion Platforms

1. **Enhanced Engagement:**
   - Students participate actively in discussions, fostering deeper understanding and encouraging curiosity.
2. **Collaborative Problem-Solving:**
   - Learners can share solutions, best practices, and personal experiences to address common challenges in education.
3. **Development of Communication Skills:**
   - Articulating thoughts clearly, listening to others, and responding respectfully improves academic and interpersonal communication.
4. **Flexible Learning Environment:**
   - Discussions can occur at any time, allowing students to learn at their own pace while balancing other responsibilities.
5. **Access to Diverse Perspectives:**
   - Interaction with learners from different backgrounds helps students explore new ideas, methods, and cultural approaches to education.

3. Types of Online Discussion Platforms

1. **Learning Management Systems (LMS):**
   - Platforms like Moodle and Google Classroom include discussion boards where students and teachers can post and reply to queries.
2. **Social Media Groups:**
   - Facebook groups, WhatsApp communities, and Telegram channels allow informal, interactive discussions among educators.

3. **Educational Forums:**
   - Platforms such as Edmodo and Quora provide spaces dedicated to learning topics where users can ask questions and exchange information.
4. **Video Conferencing Tools:**
   - Zoom, Microsoft Teams, and Google Meet facilitate live discussions, workshops, and brainstorming sessions.

4. Best Practices for Using Discussion Platforms

1. **Set Clear Rules and Objectives:**
   - Establish guidelines regarding respectful communication, participation frequency, and the focus of discussions.
2. **Encourage Thoughtful Contributions:**
   - Promote questions, insights, and reflections that are well-researched and contribute meaningfully to the topic.
3. **Moderation and Guidance:**
   - Teachers or facilitators should actively moderate discussions to ensure relevance and prevent misinformation or disruptive behavior.
4. **Integrate with Learning Goals:**
   - Discussions should align with course content, assignments, and assessments to reinforce learning objectives.
5. **Provide Feedback:**
   - Encourage peer reviews and timely responses to maintain engagement and validate contributions.

5. Challenges and Solutions

1. **Low Participation:**
    - o Solution: Encourage group tasks and assign discussion points as part of course requirements.
2. **Misinformation:**
    - o Solution: Moderators should fact-check content and guide learners toward reliable sources.
3. **Overwhelming Volume of Messages:**
    - o Solution: Organize discussions into categories or threads and highlight key posts to streamline learning.

11.2 Group Projects and Virtual Teams

Introduction

Group projects and virtual teams are important components of collaborative learning in modern education. With advancements in technology, B.Ed. and M.Ed. students can work together beyond physical classrooms, connecting with peers from different locations and backgrounds. These collaborative efforts not only enhance knowledge sharing but also build essential skills such as communication, leadership, problem-solving, and teamwork—qualities that are critical for future educators.

1. What are Group Projects and Virtual Teams?

- **Group Projects:** Group projects are tasks assigned to a team of learners who collaborate to research, plan, and present solutions or findings on a given topic. They promote interaction, brainstorming, and joint responsibility.
- **Virtual Teams:** Virtual teams consist of learners who work together online using digital tools like video calls, shared

documents, and messaging platforms. This allows students to coordinate tasks, share resources, and contribute despite geographical distances.

Example:
A group project may involve designing an innovative classroom activity that integrates technology, where team members research ideas, create lesson plans, and present their proposals via a video conferencing platform.

2. Benefits of Group Projects and Virtual Teams

1. **Enhanced Learning:**
    - Working with peers exposes learners to diverse viewpoints, experiences, and teaching methods that deepen understanding.
2. **Skill Development:**
    - Students learn how to manage time, communicate effectively, and resolve conflicts—skills that are invaluable for teaching careers.
3. **Accountability and Responsibility:**
    - Group work encourages participants to share responsibilities, meet deadlines, and support each other's learning journey.
4. **Innovation and Creativity:**
    - Collaborative discussions often lead to creative solutions, encouraging experimentation with new tools and teaching techniques.
5. **Networking:**
    - Virtual teams help learners build professional relationships that can support research, internships, and future employment opportunities.

3. Tools Used for Group Projects and Virtual Teams

1. **Video Conferencing Tools:**
   - Platforms like Zoom, Google Meet, and Microsoft Teams facilitate face-to-face interactions for planning and presentations.
2. **Collaborative Documents:**
   - Google Docs, Microsoft OneDrive, and Dropbox allow real-time editing and sharing of content such as reports, presentations, and lesson plans.
3. **Communication Platforms:**
   - WhatsApp groups, Slack channels, and discussion forums keep teams connected for quick updates and idea sharing.
4. **Project Management Tools:**
   - Trello, Asana, and Monday.com help in task allocation, tracking progress, and setting deadlines.

4. Best Practices for Effective Group Projects and Virtual Teams

1. **Define Roles and Responsibilities:**
   - Assign specific tasks to each member based on strengths and interests to ensure equal participation.
2. **Set Clear Objectives:**
   - Clearly outline project goals, expected outcomes, and timelines to guide the team's efforts.
3. **Encourage Open Communication:**
   - Foster an environment where all members feel comfortable sharing ideas, asking questions, and giving constructive feedback.
4. **Use Structured Meetings:**

- Regularly scheduled virtual meetings help in tracking progress, addressing challenges, and maintaining focus.

5. **Promote Mutual Respect:**
    - Encourage team members to respect each other's opinions, time, and expertise to build trust and cooperation.

5. Challenges and Solutions

1. **Coordination Issues:**
    - Solution: Use shared calendars and task management tools to organize meetings and track assignments.
2. **Technical Difficulties:**
    - Solution: Provide training on using collaborative tools and have backup communication channels.
3. **Uneven Participation:**
    - Solution: Set accountability measures, assign rotating leadership roles, and monitor contribution levels.

11.3 Peer Feedback and Interaction

Introduction

Peer feedback and interaction are vital components of collaborative learning in education. They enable B.Ed. and M.Ed. students to learn from one another's experiences, reflect on their practices, and develop a sense of responsibility and mutual respect. Technology has made peer interaction more accessible, allowing learners to share ideas, critique work, and provide support beyond traditional classroom settings. Through structured peer feedback, students enhance critical thinking, problem-solving, and communication skills, which are essential for professional teaching and lifelong learning.

1. What is Peer Feedback and Interaction?

- **Peer Feedback:** Peer feedback is a process where students review each other's work, provide constructive criticism, and offer suggestions for improvement. It is a form of collaborative learning that encourages reflection, self-assessment, and skill enhancement.
- **Peer Interaction:** Peer interaction involves discussions, brainstorming, sharing experiences, and collaborative learning activities where students exchange knowledge and support each other's academic or professional growth.

Example:
A group of student teachers may review each other's lesson plans and provide feedback on clarity, instructional strategies, and assessment methods. These discussions help identify strengths and areas for improvement, fostering deeper learning.

2. Importance of Peer Feedback and Interaction

1. **Promotes Critical Thinking:**
    - Reviewing others' work encourages learners to analyze content deeply, ask questions, and offer thoughtful suggestions.
2. **Encourages Self-Reflection:**
    - Giving and receiving feedback helps students reflect on their teaching practices and identify areas for improvement.
3. **Enhances Communication Skills:**

- Students learn how to articulate their thoughts respectfully and listen actively, improving interpersonal and professional communication.

4. **Builds Confidence and Motivation:**
   - Positive feedback boosts confidence, while constructive suggestions motivate learners to strive for excellence.
5. **Fosters Collaboration and Team Spirit:**
   - Working together builds trust, empathy, and a sense of community, which are essential qualities in teaching and learning environments.

3. Tools for Peer Feedback and Interaction

1. **Online Discussion Forums:**
   - Platforms like Moodle, Edmodo, and Google Classroom allow students to post assignments and exchange feedback asynchronously.
2. **Collaborative Documents:**
   - Google Docs or Microsoft OneDrive support real-time commenting and editing, enabling immediate peer interaction.
3. **Video Conferencing Tools:**
   - Zoom and Microsoft Teams allow live discussions where students can share feedback verbally and engage in group learning activities.
4. **Social Media Groups:**
   - WhatsApp, Telegram, and Facebook groups foster informal interaction and provide space for sharing ideas, tips, and educational resources.

4. Best Practices for Peer Feedback and Interaction

1. **Establish Clear Guidelines:**
   - Set rules for providing respectful, specific, and constructive feedback to ensure interactions are helpful and supportive.
2. **Encourage Balanced Feedback:**
   - Students should highlight both strengths and areas for improvement, ensuring feedback is encouraging and actionable.
3. **Promote Regular Interaction:**
   - Schedule peer review sessions and discussion groups to maintain consistent engagement and foster continuous learning.
4. **Integrate Reflection:**
   - Encourage students to reflect on the feedback received and incorporate it into their learning practices.
5. **Provide Facilitator Support:**
   - Teachers or mentors should guide discussions, clarify doubts, and ensure feedback aligns with learning objectives.

5. Challenges and Solutions

1. **Fear of Criticism:**
   - Solution: Create a supportive environment where feedback is framed positively and aimed at growth.
2. **Lack of Engagement:**
   - Solution: Assign tasks that require peer interaction and integrate feedback into assessments.
3. **Unstructured Feedback:**
   - Solution: Use rubrics and templates to guide students in providing structured and meaningful comments.

11.4 Social Learning Strategies

Introduction

Social learning strategies are methods that encourage learners to acquire knowledge, skills, and behaviors through interaction, observation, and shared experiences. In the context of B.Ed. and M.Ed. students, social learning not only supports academic growth but also helps build essential teaching competencies such as empathy, communication, and collaborative problem-solving. Technology enhances these strategies by providing platforms where learners can connect, observe best practices, and engage in meaningful dialogue regardless of geographical location.

1. What are Social Learning Strategies?

Social learning strategies involve structured and informal methods where learners learn from their peers, mentors, or experts through observation, discussion, and collaboration. These strategies are rooted in the belief that learning is a social process and that knowledge is best gained when learners interact with others in meaningful ways.

Example:
A group of student teachers may engage in peer observations, where one student teaches a lesson while others watch and provide feedback. They may also participate in discussion forums where they share classroom challenges and collectively brainstorm solutions.

2. Importance of Social Learning Strategies

1. **Encourages Active Participation:**
   - Learners are more engaged when they interact with others and contribute their thoughts rather than passively receiving information.
2. **Promotes Observation and Imitation:**
   - By watching how others approach teaching or solve problems, learners can incorporate new strategies into their own practice.
3. **Builds Communication and Collaboration Skills:**
   - Group activities, discussions, and shared projects improve interpersonal skills and foster cooperative learning environments.
4. **Enhances Motivation and Confidence:**
   - Positive interactions and shared successes boost learners' self-esteem and encourage them to take on new challenges.
5. **Supports Reflective Practice:**
   - Discussing experiences and receiving feedback helps learners critically assess their teaching methods and refine them.

3. Types of Social Learning Strategies

1. **Collaborative Projects:**
   - Teams work together to complete tasks, share resources, and solve problems, promoting interdependence and cooperation.
2. **Peer Observations:**
   - Students observe each other's teaching practices to learn effective strategies and receive constructive feedback.
3. **Discussion Forums and Study Groups:**

   - These platforms encourage learners to ask questions, share insights, and debate topics, fostering critical thinking.
4. **Role-Playing and Simulations:**
   - Learners simulate classroom scenarios or teaching challenges, allowing them to practice problem-solving and decision-making.
5. **Mentorship and Coaching:**
   - Experienced educators guide learners by offering advice, modeling best practices, and encouraging self-directed learning.

4. Implementing Social Learning Strategies

1. **Create Safe and Inclusive Spaces:**
   - Encourage learners to express ideas without fear of judgment, ensuring that everyone feels valued and supported.
2. **Use Technology Effectively:**
   - Integrate tools like video conferencing, collaborative documents, and social media groups to facilitate interaction and resource sharing.
3. **Align Activities with Learning Goals:**
   - Ensure that social learning exercises are directly related to course objectives and real-life teaching scenarios.
4. **Encourage Reflective Discussions:**
   - After activities, prompt learners to discuss what they learned, what challenges they faced, and how they can apply new strategies.
5. **Recognize Contributions:**

  - Celebrate group achievements and individual efforts to maintain motivation and promote continuous participation.

5. Challenges and Solutions

1. **Unequal Participation:**
   - **Solution:** Assign roles and responsibilities to ensure that every group member is actively involved.
2. **Communication Barriers:**
   - **Solution:** Provide training on effective communication tools and strategies for overcoming language or technological difficulties.
3. **Managing Conflicts:**
   - **Solution:** Teach conflict-resolution techniques and encourage respectful dialogue to maintain a positive learning environment.

11.5 Creating Engaging Collaborative Environments

Introduction

Creating engaging collaborative environments is essential for effective learning, especially for B.Ed. and M.Ed. students who are preparing to become educators themselves. Collaboration fosters teamwork, communication, creativity, and critical thinking—skills that are crucial in a classroom setting. With the support of technology, collaborative learning can be made more interactive, inclusive, and enjoyable. This section explores how to build environments where students feel encouraged to participate, share ideas, and learn from one another.

1. What Makes a Collaborative Environment Engaging?

An engaging collaborative environment is one where learners feel safe, motivated, and connected. It encourages open communication, values every contribution, and promotes shared responsibility. The learning atmosphere should foster trust, curiosity, and respect, allowing students to freely exchange knowledge and explore new ideas.

Example:
In a teacher training program, students might work together to create a lesson plan incorporating educational technology tools. When guided thoughtfully, they learn from each other's strengths and weaknesses while feeling supported in their learning process.

2. Key Elements of an Engaging Collaborative Environment

1. **Clear Purpose and Goals:**
   - When students understand the purpose of their collaboration and the outcomes they are expected to achieve, they stay focused and invested in the learning process.
2. **Inclusive Participation:**
   - Every student should feel that their voice matters. Encouraging contributions from all members helps to create a sense of ownership and belonging.
3. **Safe and Supportive Atmosphere:**
   - Psychological safety is crucial for fostering open discussions. Students should feel comfortable sharing opinions without fear of judgment or criticism.
4. **Interactive and Flexible Activities:**

- Incorporating interactive tasks like role plays, case studies, and brainstorming sessions keeps students engaged and allows for diverse learning styles.

5. **Recognition and Encouragement:**
    - Celebrating individual and group achievements motivates learners to continue collaborating and exploring new ideas.

3. Strategies to Create an Engaging Collaborative Environment

1. **Set Expectations Early:**
    - Define roles, timelines, and responsibilities at the beginning of the project to ensure everyone is aligned and accountable.
2. **Use Technology Tools Effectively:**
    - Leverage tools like shared documents, video conferencing platforms, and messaging apps to enhance interaction and simplify communication.
3. **Encourage Dialogue and Feedback:**
    - Regular check-ins and feedback sessions allow learners to share insights, reflect on their experiences, and adjust their approach collaboratively.
4. **Facilitate Peer Learning:**
    - Pair students with diverse strengths to promote knowledge sharing and mutual learning.
5. **Provide Real-World Contexts:**
    - Relating tasks to practical classroom scenarios helps students see the relevance of collaboration and increases their engagement.

4. Challenges and Solutions

1. **Lack of Motivation:**
   - **Solution:** Incorporate gamification elements, such as points or badges, to make learning more fun and rewarding.
2. **Dominance by Certain Individuals:**
   - **Solution:** Assign rotating leadership roles to ensure everyone gets a chance to contribute.
3. **Communication Gaps:**
   - **Solution:** Offer workshops on active listening and conflict resolution to enhance team dynamics.

Chapter 12
Mobile Learning and Micro learning

12.1 Learning Anytime, Anywhere

Introduction

"Learning anytime, anywhere" is a flexible approach that allows learners to access educational content and interact with peers or instructors without being confined to a traditional classroom setting. With the advancement of technology, this approach has become increasingly significant for B.Ed. and M.Ed. students, who often balance studies with internships, teaching practice, and personal responsibilities. Learning outside conventional boundaries empowers students to take control of their education, access resources on demand, and tailor their learning experiences to suit individual needs.

1. What is "Learning Anytime, Anywhere"?

Learning anytime, anywhere refers to the use of digital tools and platforms that enable learners to study, collaborate, and engage with educational material from any location and at any time. It emphasizes learner autonomy and accessibility, ensuring that education is not restricted by time zones, schedules, or geographic limitations.

Example:
A student teacher preparing for classroom observations might access lesson planning resources, video tutorials, or group discussions on

their smartphone while traveling or during a free period, allowing learning to continue seamlessly.

2. Importance of Learning Anytime, Anywhere

1. **Flexibility:**
   - Students can learn at their own pace and fit educational activities around other commitments such as internships, part-time jobs, or family responsibilities.
2. **Accessibility:**
   - Learning materials are available online, making it possible for students in remote areas or with limited access to educational institutions to participate fully.
3. **Self-Directed Learning:**
   - Learners can choose topics based on their interests or weaknesses, promoting personalized learning experiences.
4. **Real-Time Collaboration:**
   - Students can connect with peers and instructors from different locations, encouraging broader perspectives and collaborative problem-solving.
5. **Continuous Learning:**
   - Educational activities are no longer confined to scheduled classes, enabling learners to engage in study, practice, and reflection whenever it suits them.

3. Tools that Support Learning Anytime, Anywhere

1. **Learning Management Systems (LMS):**
   - Platforms like Moodle, Canvas, and Google Classroom provide course materials, assignments,

and discussion boards that students can access at any time.

2. **Mobile Learning Apps:**
    - Apps such as Khan Academy, Coursera, and Byju's offer video lessons, quizzes, and practice exercises optimized for smartphones and tablets.
3. **Cloud Storage and Shared Documents:**
    - Tools like Google Drive and Dropbox allow learners to upload, edit, and share resources from any device with internet access.
4. **Online Discussion Forums:**
    - Platforms like Edmodo and WhatsApp groups foster peer interaction, providing space for questions, feedback, and collaborative learning.
5. **Video Conferencing:**
    - Tools such as Zoom and Microsoft Teams facilitate live interactions for classes, mentoring sessions, or group discussions, regardless of location.

4. Best Practices for Effective Anytime, Anywhere Learning

1. **Create a Learning Schedule:**
    - While flexibility is a strength, setting a structured schedule helps maintain discipline and prevents procrastination.
2. **Set Learning Goals:**
    - Clear, achievable objectives guide students in selecting resources and tracking progress effectively.
3. **Use Diverse Resources:**

- Incorporating videos, podcasts, quizzes, and articles caters to different learning styles and keeps the content engaging.

4. **Encourage Interaction:**
    - Regular communication with peers and instructors through forums or live sessions enhances motivation and accountability.
5. **Practice Self-Reflection:**
    - Periodically reviewing what has been learned and identifying areas for improvement helps learners stay focused and continuously grow.

5. Challenges and Solutions

1. **Lack of Motivation:**
    - **Solution:** Set small, achievable goals and celebrate progress to maintain enthusiasm.
2. **Technical Barriers:**
    - **Solution:** Ensure students are trained to use available tools and provide offline alternatives where necessary.
3. **Feeling Isolated:**
    - **Solution:** Create peer networks and mentorship programs to foster a sense of community and belonging.

12.2 Designing Microlearning Content

Introduction

Microlearning is an educational strategy that delivers content in short, focused segments, making it easier for learners to grasp and retain information. For B.Ed. and M.Ed. students, microlearning provides a practical way to study complex topics without feeling overwhelmed. It supports learning anytime, anywhere by offering small modules that can be completed in minutes rather than hours. Designing effective microlearning content requires careful planning to ensure that each learning piece is meaningful, engaging, and aligned with learning objectives.

1. What is Microlearning Content?

Microlearning content consists of brief, self-contained learning modules that focus on specific skills or topics. These modules are typically 5–10 minutes long and may include videos, infographics, quizzes, podcasts, or interactive tasks. The goal is to provide learners with easily digestible pieces of information that they can access on-demand.

Example:
A microlearning module on "Classroom Management Techniques" may include a short video explaining strategies, followed by an infographic summarizing key points and a quick quiz to test understanding.

2. Importance of Designing Microlearning Content

1. **Improves Retention:**
    - Smaller learning segments help learners process information better, leading to improved recall and understanding.
2. **Encourages Regular Learning:**
    - Short modules can be easily integrated into daily routines, encouraging consistent study habits.

3. **Supports Personalized Learning:**
   - Learners can choose modules based on their needs, allowing them to focus on areas where they require improvement.
4. **Offers Flexibility:**
   - Microlearning fits into busy schedules, enabling learners to access content anytime without the pressure of long study sessions.
5. **Promotes Engagement:**
   - Interactive tasks and multimedia formats keep learners interested and motivated.

3. Steps to Design Effective Microlearning Content

1. **Identify Specific Learning Objectives:**
   - Focus on one learning goal per module to ensure clarity and purpose.
2. **Select Relevant and Concise Content:**
   - Avoid unnecessary details. Include only the essential information required to understand the topic.
3. **Use Interactive and Multimedia Elements:**
   - Videos, animations, quizzes, and infographics make learning more engaging and help explain complex concepts.
4. **Incorporate Real-World Examples:**
   - Use practical scenarios, case studies, or classroom experiences to make the content relatable.
5. **Ensure Accessibility:**
   - Provide subtitles, downloadable materials, and alternative formats to support learners with different needs.
6. **Design for Mobile Devices:**

   - Optimize content for smartphones and tablets since learners are likely to access modules on the go.

4. Best Practices in Designing Microlearning Content

1. **Keep It Short and Focused:**
   - Limit each module to one topic and keep videos or lessons under 10 minutes.
2. **Use Visual Aids:**
   - Graphics, charts, and diagrams enhance understanding and make content easier to remember.
3. **Incorporate Assessment:**
   - Use quizzes or polls at the end of each module to reinforce learning and encourage self-assessment.
4. **Encourage Reflection:**
   - Include prompts or journaling activities that help learners think about how they can apply the content in real situations.
5. **Provide Immediate Feedback:**
   - Offering feedback helps learners correct mistakes and understand concepts more clearly.

5. Challenges and Solutions

1. **Risk of Superficial Learning:**
   - **Solution:** Link multiple microlearning modules to cover broader topics in depth without overwhelming learners.
2. **Lack of Motivation:**
   - **Solution:** Use gamification elements like badges, points, or rewards to encourage progress.
3. **Technology Access Issues:**

- **Solution:** Provide offline options or downloadable content for learners with limited internet access.

12.3 Apps and Educational Tools for Mobile Platforms

Introduction

With the increasing use of smartphones and tablets, mobile learning has become an integral part of modern education. B.Ed. and M.Ed. students benefit from apps and educational tools that provide on-the-go access to learning materials, interactive exercises, and collaborative spaces. Mobile platforms make learning more flexible, personalized, and engaging, helping future educators integrate technology into their teaching practices. This section explores popular apps and tools, their features, and best practices for using them effectively.

1. Why Use Apps and Educational Tools on Mobile Platforms?

1. **Convenience and Flexibility:**
    - Students can access learning materials anytime, anywhere, whether during travel, breaks, or at home.
2. **Interactive Learning:**
    - Many apps offer quizzes, games, and simulations that encourage active participation and deeper understanding.
3. **Personalization:**
    - Mobile apps often adapt to learners' progress, offering tailored content and practice based on individual strengths and weaknesses.
4. **Collaboration:**

   - Tools allow learners to interact with peers, share documents, and participate in group activities.
5. **Real-Time Feedback:**
   - Instant feedback helps learners correct mistakes and reinforce learning immediately.

2. Popular Educational Apps and Tools

1. **Google Classroom:**
   - A widely used platform where teachers can create, share, and grade assignments. It integrates seamlessly with other Google tools like Docs, Sheets, and Drive.
2. **Khan Academy:**
   - Offers free video lessons, practice exercises, and quizzes across various subjects, helping students reinforce foundational concepts.
3. **Edmodo:**
   - A social learning platform where students and teachers can interact, share resources, and collaborate on projects.
4. **Quizlet:**
   - Allows learners to create and study digital flashcards, quizzes, and games to memorize terms, definitions, and concepts effectively.
5. **Microsoft OneNote:**
   - A versatile note-taking tool that supports multimedia inputs, annotations, and collaboration, making it ideal for class notes and project work.

6. **Nearpod:**
    - Provides interactive lessons, polls, and quizzes that teachers can share with students in real time, enhancing classroom engagement.
7. **Padlet:**
    - A virtual bulletin board where learners can post ideas, documents, images, and links, fostering creativity and collaboration.
8. **Trello or Asana:**
    - Project management tools that help teams organize tasks, set deadlines, and track progress efficiently.

3. Features to Look for in Educational Apps

1. **User-Friendly Interface:**
    - Simple navigation ensures learners of all tech levels can use the app effectively.
2. **Offline Access:**
    - Downloadable resources allow students to learn even without internet access.
3. **Security and Privacy:**
    - Apps should protect personal data and adhere to educational privacy standards.
4. **Customization Options:**
    - Flexible settings that let learners adjust difficulty levels, content types, and learning pace.
5. **Integration Capabilities:**
    - Tools that connect with other apps or learning management systems enhance overall usability.

4. Best Practices for Using Mobile Educational Tools

1. **Set Clear Goals:**
    - Define what learners should achieve with each app to ensure purposeful use.
2. **Blend with Traditional Learning:**
    - Combine app-based learning with classroom discussions, assignments, and assessments for a balanced approach.
3. **Encourage Exploration:**
    - Allow students to explore apps independently, helping them discover features that suit their learning styles.
4. **Monitor Progress:**
    - Use apps' analytics features to track performance and provide targeted support when needed.
5. **Provide Training:**
    - Offer tutorials or workshops to help learners and teachers maximize the potential of mobile tools.

12.4 Engagement Techniques for Mobile Learners

Introduction

Mobile learning offers flexibility and convenience, but it also presents challenges in keeping learners actively engaged. For B.Ed. and M.Ed. students, who are training to become effective educators, understanding engagement techniques is critical to ensuring that learning remains interactive, motivating, and productive. Engagement strategies help learners stay focused, practice new skills, and collaborate with peers, even when learning remotely or at their own pace.

1. Why Engagement is Important in Mobile Learning

1. **Prevents Distractions:**
   - Mobile devices can be a source of distractions, so engaging learners helps them stay on task.
2. **Improves Retention:**
   - Interactive and enjoyable learning experiences enhance memory and understanding.
3. **Encourages Self-Directed Learning:**
   - When learners are actively involved, they take responsibility for their own progress and explore content more deeply.
4. **Builds a Learning Community:**
   - Engagement fosters communication and collaboration among peers, creating a supportive learning environment.

2. Effective Engagement Techniques for Mobile Learners

1. **Use Interactive Content:**
   - Incorporate videos, animations, quizzes, and polls that prompt learners to actively participate rather than passively consume information.
2. **Set Clear Learning Goals:**
   - Help learners understand the purpose of each module, breaking it into smaller, achievable tasks that build confidence and motivation.
3. **Incorporate Gamification:**
   - Introduce badges, points, or rewards for completing tasks, quizzes, or discussions. Gamification makes learning fun and fosters a sense of achievement.
4. **Encourage Peer Collaboration:**

- Use group chats, forums, and collaborative tools where learners can share ideas, discuss topics, and provide feedback to each other.

5. **Provide Instant Feedback:**
   - Apps that offer real-time feedback on quizzes or assignments help learners correct mistakes and reinforce concepts immediately.
6. **Design for Microlearning:**
   - Short, focused modules with interactive elements keep learners engaged without overwhelming them.
7. **Use Notifications and Reminders:**
   - Scheduled alerts help learners stay on track and remind them of pending assignments or new content, preventing procrastination.
8. **Encourage Reflection:**
   - Include prompts or journaling tasks that encourage learners to think about what they have learned and how they can apply it.

3. Best Practices to Sustain Engagement

1. **Blend Learning Methods:**
   - Combine video lessons, readings, interactive quizzes, and discussions to keep the learning experience diverse and stimulating.
2. **Personalize Learning Paths:**
   - Allow learners to choose topics or modules that interest them, helping them feel more connected to their learning journey.
3. **Foster Social Connections:**
   - Organize virtual meetups or group projects to help learners feel part of a community.

4. **Encourage Self-Assessment:**
    - Provide tools that allow learners to track their progress and set personal learning goals.
5. **Maintain Consistency:**
    - Regular updates and structured schedules help learners form healthy study habits and stay engaged over time.

4. Challenges and Solutions

1. **Low Motivation:**
    - **Solution:** Use storytelling, real-life examples, and relatable scenarios to make learning more appealing.
2. **Technical Issues:**
    - **Solution:** Ensure learners are trained in using mobile apps and provide support resources for troubleshooting.
3. **Isolation:**
    - **Solution:** Promote peer interaction through discussion boards and group activities to create a sense of belonging.

12.5 Accessibility and Offline Learning Solutions

Introduction

With the growing use of mobile devices in education, ensuring that learning is accessible to all has become increasingly important. Many learners face challenges due to disabilities, language barriers, or limited internet access. Accessibility features and offline learning solutions help overcome these obstacles, making education inclusive and available to a wider audience. These strategies support continuous learning, ensure equal opportunities, and promote self-paced study without being restricted by location or resources.

1. Importance of Accessibility and Offline Solutions

1. **Equal Learning Opportunities:**
   - Accessibility tools and offline resources help learners from diverse backgrounds engage with educational content without discrimination.
2. **Support for Remote Areas:**
   - Offline access allows learners in areas with unstable or no internet connectivity to continue their studies without interruption.
3. **Inclusive Education:**
   - Assistive technologies enable learners with disabilities to participate fully and independently in learning activities.
4. **Flexibility and Self-Paced Learning:**
   - Learners can access resources at their convenience, allowing them to study at their own pace without reliance on live instruction.

2. Accessibility Features

1. **Text-to-Speech and Speech-to-Text:**
   - These features assist learners with visual or writing difficulties by converting text to audio and vice versa.
2. **Subtitles and Captions:**
   - Adding captions to video content improves understanding for learners with hearing impairments and those studying in a second language.
3. **Screen Readers and Magnifiers:**

- Tools that enlarge content and describe elements on the screen support learners with low vision.

4. **Customizable Interfaces:**
    - Options such as font size, contrast adjustments, and color themes allow learners to personalize content according to their needs.
5. **Multilingual Support:**
    - Providing content in multiple languages helps learners from different linguistic backgrounds access information more easily.

3. Offline Learning Solutions

1. **Downloadable Content:**
    - Lessons, quizzes, and reading materials can be downloaded for later use without internet connectivity.
2. **Offline Apps:**
    - Certain apps allow learners to access resources offline and sync progress when the internet is available.
3. **External Storage Devices:**
    - USB drives or memory cards loaded with educational materials provide access where online platforms are not feasible.
4. **Printed Materials:**
    - Worksheets and guides serve as reliable alternatives for learners without access to digital devices.
5. **Community Learning Centers:**
    - Shared access to devices and resources in schools, libraries, or community hubs helps bridge the digital divide.

4. Best Practices

1. **Review for Accessibility:**
   - Regular audits ensure that materials meet diverse learning requirements.
2. **Provide Multiple Formats:**
   - Offering content in text, audio, and video formats accommodates different learning preferences.
3. **Train Users:**
   - Providing guidance on how to use assistive technologies and offline resources enhances effectiveness.
4. **Encourage Peer Assistance:**
   - Collaborative support networks ensure that learners help each other overcome access barriers.
5. **Monitor Progress:**
   - Tracking usage and performance helps identify learners needing additional support.

5. Challenges and Solutions

1. **Device Limitations:**
   - **Solution:** Share devices through local centers and supply downloadable content.
2. **Digital Literacy Gaps:**
   - **Solution:** Organize workshops to teach learners how to use apps and accessibility tools.
3. **Connectivity Issues:**
   - **Solution:** Design offline-first learning modules that require minimal internet interaction.

Chapter 13

Challenges in Educational Technology

13.1 Digital Divide and Inequality

Introduction

The digital divide refers to the gap between individuals or communities that have access to modern information and communication technologies (ICT) and those that do not. This divide creates inequalities in education, employment, healthcare, and other areas of life. As technology becomes increasingly integrated into learning environments, understanding the causes and effects of the digital divide is essential to ensuring that education remains fair, accessible, and inclusive for all learners.

1. What is the Digital Divide?

The digital divide is not just about having or not having internet access. It includes disparities in access to devices like smartphones, tablets, and computers, as well as access to digital skills and relevant content. It also reflects socio-economic differences, geographic location, gender, age, and disability.

For example, learners in urban areas may have fast internet and multiple devices, while those in rural or underdeveloped regions struggle with poor connectivity and limited access to technology. Similarly, some learners may lack the training required to use online tools effectively, making it difficult to benefit from digital education resources.

2. Causes of the Digital Divide

1. **Economic Barriers:**
   - Families with lower income may not be able to afford devices or internet services.
2. **Geographical Barriers:**
   - Remote or rural areas often lack infrastructure for stable internet connections.
3. **Educational Barriers:**
   - Lack of digital literacy or skills prevents some learners from making effective use of technology.
4. **Social and Gender Inequality:**
   - Women, minorities, or people with disabilities may face additional barriers in accessing technology.
5. **Language Barriers:**
   - Educational content may not be available in local languages, limiting access to knowledge.

3. Effects of the Digital Divide on Learning

1. **Unequal Educational Opportunities:**
   - Students without technology access fall behind their peers, missing out on interactive lessons, real-time feedback, and supplementary learning resources.
2. **Lower Academic Performance:**
   - Without consistent access to study materials, learners may struggle to keep up with coursework and assessments.
3. **Increased Dropout Rates:**
   - Frustration and a lack of support can lead to disengagement and higher dropout rates among disadvantaged students.

4. **Widening Social Gaps:**
    - Educational inequalities reinforce broader social and economic disparities, perpetuating cycles of poverty.

4. Bridging the Digital Divide

1. **Government and Policy Support:**
    - Subsidized internet services, affordable devices, and rural connectivity programs can improve access for underserved populations.
2. **Community-Based Initiatives:**
    - Local learning hubs, libraries, and shared device programs ensure that learners can access resources even in low-connectivity areas.
3. **Inclusive Content Development:**
    - Educational materials in multiple languages and formats ensure accessibility for diverse learners.
4. **Digital Literacy Training:**
    - Providing tutorials, workshops, and user-friendly guides empowers learners to navigate technology effectively.
5. **Partnerships with NGOs and Corporates:**
    - Collaborations can fund infrastructure, provide devices, and offer support programs for learners in need.

5. Challenges in Addressing the Divide

1. **Sustainability:**
    - Programs may face difficulties in maintaining funding and infrastructure over time.
2. **Cultural Resistance:**

- Some communities may hesitate to adopt new technologies due to mistrust or lack of awareness.

3. **Rapid Technological Changes:**
   - Keeping learners updated with the latest tools and platforms requires ongoing support.

13.2 Infrastructure and Connectivity Issues

Introduction

Infrastructure and connectivity are critical components that determine the effectiveness of digital learning. Even with advanced educational tools and content, learners cannot benefit from them without reliable internet access, electricity, and the necessary devices. Infrastructure and connectivity issues create significant barriers, particularly in rural, remote, and underdeveloped regions, contributing to educational inequality. Addressing these challenges is essential to ensure that technology-based learning reaches all learners, regardless of their location or socio-economic background.

1. Key Infrastructure Challenges

1. **Lack of Internet Access:**
   - Many areas, especially in rural and hilly regions, lack broadband services or stable mobile networks. Slow or intermittent connections disrupt online learning and limit access to educational platforms.
2. **Insufficient Electricity Supply:**
   - Regular power cuts or the absence of electricity prevent learners from charging devices or using them consistently.
3. **Limited Device Availability:**

   - Many learners rely on shared or outdated devices, which restricts their ability to participate in online learning activities.
4. **Inadequate School Facilities:**
   - Schools in underprivileged areas may lack computer labs, Wi-Fi infrastructure, or digital teaching tools, putting students at a disadvantage.
5. **Geographical Barriers:**
   - Difficult terrains, natural disasters, and long distances from urban centers hinder the establishment and maintenance of internet infrastructure.

2. Connectivity Issues Affecting Learning

1. **Bandwidth Limitations:**
   - Poor network speed makes it difficult to stream videos, attend virtual classes, or download learning materials.
2. **High Costs:**
   - Internet subscriptions, data packs, and devices may be expensive for economically weaker families.
3. **Device Compatibility:**
   - Some educational tools and apps require newer devices or higher processing power, excluding learners with basic smartphones.
4. **Technical Support Shortages:**
   - Learners in remote areas may not have access to help desks or technicians to resolve issues when devices or networks fail.

3. Impact on Education

1. **Interruption of Learning:**
    - Frequent disruptions prevent continuity in learning, affecting students' academic performance and motivation.
2. **Increased Dropout Rates:**
    - Students may lose interest or feel left out, especially when they cannot access lessons or assignments on time.
3. **Unequal Access to Resources:**
    - Learners with poor infrastructure cannot access rich digital content, limiting their academic growth.
4. **Strain on Teachers:**
    - Educators in areas with weak infrastructure struggle to deliver lessons and track student progress, affecting teaching effectiveness.

4. Possible Solutions

1. **Government Investment:**
    - Expanding broadband coverage, creating satellite internet networks, and providing subsidies for devices can improve infrastructure in underserved areas.
2. **Public-Private Partnerships:**
    - Collaborations between governments, NGOs, and corporations can fund infrastructure projects and offer affordable internet plans.
3. **Solar-Powered Solutions:**
    - Solar chargers and energy-efficient devices can help areas with unreliable electricity supply.
4. **Offline-Compatible Tools:**

- Designing apps that work offline or with low bandwidth ensures that learners can access content even in challenging conditions.

5. **Community Learning Centers:**
   - Establishing hubs with shared devices and internet access can support groups of learners in remote areas.

5. Challenges in Implementation

1. **High Initial Costs:**
   - Building infrastructure in remote areas requires significant investment in technology and manpower.
2. **Maintenance Issues:**
   - Infrastructure may deteriorate over time without proper maintenance and trained personnel.
3. **Digital Literacy Gaps:**
   - Even when infrastructure is provided, learners and teachers may lack the skills needed to make full use of it.

13.3 Resistance from Teachers and Students

Introduction

The integration of technology in education offers many benefits, but it is not without challenges. One of the significant barriers is resistance from teachers and students. This resistance may arise due to fear of change, lack of confidence in using new tools, or concerns about the relevance and effectiveness of technology in learning. Understanding the reasons behind this resistance is crucial for designing strategies that encourage the adoption of technology and ensure that it becomes a supportive rather than intimidating part of the educational process.

1. Reasons for Resistance

1. **Fear of Technology:**
   - Teachers and students unfamiliar with digital tools may fear making mistakes or being judged for their lack of experience, leading them to avoid using technology.
2. **Lack of Training:**
   - Without proper guidance or professional development, teachers may feel overwhelmed by new platforms or devices. Similarly, students may struggle to navigate apps or online resources.
3. **Preference for Traditional Methods:**
   - Many educators and learners are comfortable with conventional teaching methods, such as face-to-face interaction and printed textbooks, and may see technology as unnecessary or disruptive.
4. **Concerns About Effectiveness:**
   - Some believe that technology cannot replace human interaction or that it may reduce attention spans and critical thinking skills.
5. **Access Issues:**
   - Even when infrastructure is available, teachers and students may resist using it if they experience frequent technical problems or lack support.
6. **Privacy and Security Concerns:**
   - Worries about data security, misuse of information, and online bullying can lead to reluctance in adopting digital tools.

2. Effects of Resistance

1. **Slower Adoption of Educational Technology:**
   - Schools and institutions may face delays in implementing technology-based initiatives, limiting their effectiveness.
2. **Lower Participation in Online Activities:**
   - Students who are hesitant to use digital platforms may miss assignments, discussions, or assessments, affecting their academic growth.
3. **Reduced Innovation:**
   - Teachers who resist technology may avoid exploring new instructional methods, preventing improvements in pedagogy.
4. **Inequality in Learning:**
   - Learners more comfortable with technology advance faster, while others fall behind, widening the gap in educational outcomes.

3. Strategies to Overcome Resistance

1. **Professional Development Programs:**
   - Regular workshops, tutorials, and hands-on training can help teachers build confidence in using technology and integrate it effectively into lessons.
2. **Student Orientation:**
   - Introductory sessions on how to use apps, devices, and online platforms can reduce anxiety and build trust in the learning process.
3. **Demonstrating Benefits:**

- Showcasing successful case studies and highlighting how technology improves learning outcomes can encourage hesitant users to embrace change.

4. **Blended Learning Approaches:**
   - Combining traditional methods with technology helps ease learners into digital platforms without overwhelming them.
5. **Providing Technical Support:**
   - A dedicated help desk or peer-support groups can assist users when problems arise, ensuring that technology feels approachable rather than intimidating.
6. **Creating Safe Learning Spaces:**
   - Establishing clear guidelines for online behavior and ensuring privacy can alleviate concerns and encourage participation.

4. Role of Leadership

1. **Encouraging a Growth Mindset:**
   - Leaders should promote the idea that mistakes are part of the learning process and that technology use can be mastered over time.
2. **Recognizing Efforts:**
   - Celebrating small successes and acknowledging teachers and students who experiment with technology boosts morale and motivation.
3. **Providing Incentives:**
   - Offering certifications, awards, or recognition can encourage users to explore and adopt new tools.

13.4 Cyber Security and Data Protection

Introduction

With the growing reliance on digital tools and platforms in education, cyber security and data protection have become critical concerns. Educational institutions collect, store, and process vast amounts of personal and academic data, including students' identities, assessment records, and communication logs. At the same time, online platforms and mobile apps facilitate teaching, learning, and administration but also expose users to risks such as hacking, data theft, fraud, and privacy violations. Ensuring robust cyber security and data protection mechanisms is essential to maintain trust, safeguard sensitive information, and support the safe use of technology in education.

1. What is Cyber Security and Data Protection?

Cyber Security refers to the practices, tools, and processes designed to protect digital systems, networks, and data from unauthorized access, attacks, and damage. It includes securing devices, software applications, communication channels, and storage systems.

Data Protection is the set of legal, technical, and organizational measures that ensure personal and sensitive data is collected, stored, and used in ways that respect privacy and prevent misuse. It also involves ensuring data integrity, confidentiality, and availability.

Both are interlinked. Without proper cyber security measures, data protection cannot be guaranteed, and without ensuring data privacy, digital systems remain vulnerable to exploitation.

2. Why Cyber Security and Data Protection Matter in Education

1. **Protection of Sensitive Information:**
   - Schools and universities store personal data such as names, addresses, academic records, and health information, making them prime targets for cyber threats.
2. **Preventing Identity Theft:**
   - Hackers can misuse stolen data to impersonate students or staff, causing reputational damage and financial losses.
3. **Ensuring Continuity of Learning:**
   - Cyber attacks such as ransomware or denial-of-service attacks can disrupt online classes, assignments, and exams.
4. **Maintaining Trust:**
   - Students, parents, and staff need assurance that their data is safe. Without trust, users may resist adopting online learning platforms.
5. **Compliance with Laws and Regulations:**
   - Many countries have legal frameworks that mandate how educational institutions handle personal data. Non-compliance can lead to penalties or legal action.

3. Common Cyber Threats in Educational Environments

1. **Phishing Attacks:**
   - Fake emails or messages that trick users into revealing passwords or installing malware.
2. **Malware and Ransomware:**
   - Software that infects devices, corrupts files, or locks data until a ransom is paid.
3. **Data Breaches:**

- Unauthorized access to systems resulting in stolen or exposed data.

4. **Insecure Wi-Fi Networks:**
   - Open or poorly protected networks make it easy for attackers to intercept data.
5. **Weak Passwords:**
   - Easily guessable passwords can compromise accounts and sensitive information.
6. **Insider Threats:**
   - Data misuse by authorized users, whether intentional or accidental.

4. Key Principles of Data Protection

1. **Confidentiality:**
   - Ensuring that data is accessible only to authorized individuals.
2. **Integrity:**
   - Maintaining the accuracy and completeness of data throughout its lifecycle.
3. **Availability:**
   - Ensuring that data and systems are accessible when needed.
4. **Accountability:**
   - Assigning responsibility for protecting data and ensuring compliance with security protocols.
5. **Transparency:**
   - Informing users about how their data is collected, stored, and used.

5. Best Practices for Cyber Security and Data Protection

A. Technical Measures

1. **Strong Password Policies:**
   - Enforce complex passwords and regular updates to prevent unauthorized access.
2. **Encryption:**
   - Encrypt sensitive data during transmission and storage to prevent interception or misuse.
3. **Secure Networks:**
   - Use firewalls, VPNs, and secure Wi-Fi protocols to safeguard data exchanges.
4. **Regular Software Updates:**
   - Keep operating systems and applications patched to prevent vulnerabilities.
5. **Multi-Factor Authentication (MFA):**
   - Require additional verification steps, such as one-time codes, to ensure only authorized users access accounts.
6. **Data Backup Systems:**
   - Maintain regular backups to recover data in case of attacks or hardware failures.

B. Organizational Measures

1. **Access Control:**
   - Limit data access based on roles and responsibilities to minimize exposure.
2. **Training and Awareness:**
   - Educate teachers, students, and staff about phishing, password management, and safe browsing habits.
3. **Incident Response Plans:**

- Develop protocols to respond quickly to cyber incidents, including reporting, containment, and recovery steps.

4. **Monitoring and Auditing:**
   - Continuously monitor systems for unusual activities and conduct audits to ensure compliance with security policies.
5. **Third-Party Risk Management:**
   - Assess and manage the security protocols of software vendors, cloud services, and other partners.

6. Legal and Ethical Considerations

1. **Compliance with Data Protection Laws:**
   - Educational institutions must adhere to regulations such as GDPR (General Data Protection Regulation), FERPA (Family Educational Rights and Privacy Act), or national guidelines depending on the country.
2. **Obtaining Consent:**
   - Users must be informed about data collection and asked for explicit consent where required.
3. **Handling Sensitive Information:**
   - Data such as health records or financial information must be processed with heightened security measures.
4. **Ethical Responsibility:**
   - Institutions must ensure fairness, avoid discrimination, and protect user privacy even beyond legal requirements.

7. Emerging Trends in Cyber Security and Data Protection

1. **AI-Based Threat Detection:**
    - Artificial intelligence tools are increasingly used to identify unusual activities and potential threats in real time.
2. **Cloud Security Solutions:**
    - As educational institutions shift to cloud-based systems, advanced cloud security frameworks are being adopted to protect data storage and communication.
3. **Blockchain for Data Integrity:**
    - Blockchain technologies are being explored to ensure data immutability and reduce the risk of tampering.
4. **Digital Identity Management:**
    - Secure identity verification systems are being implemented to prevent fraud and unauthorized access.

8. Challenges in Implementing Cyber Security

1. **Budget Constraints:**
    - Many institutions lack the funds to invest in advanced security tools or hire dedicated personnel.
2. **Rapid Technological Change:**
    - Constantly evolving threats require continuous updates, training, and adaptation.
3. **Balancing Accessibility and Security:**
    - Overly restrictive policies may hinder learning, while loose security may expose systems to risk.
4. **User Behavior:**

- o Human error, such as weak passwords or careless browsing, remains a significant vulnerability.

Cyber security and data protection are vital for the safe and effective use of technology in education. As digital tools become integral to learning and teaching, safeguarding sensitive information and ensuring secure communication channels must be treated as priorities. Implementing strong technical measures, developing organizational policies, and educating users are essential steps toward creating a secure learning environment. Compliance with legal frameworks and ethical standards further reinforces trust and responsibility. By adopting best practices and staying informed about emerging threats, educational institutions can protect data, empower learners, and create a resilient digital ecosystem that supports innovation without compromising privacy or safety.

13.5 Psychological and Ethical Concerns

Introduction

The use of technology in education has transformed how students learn and how teachers instruct. However, alongside its many benefits, the increased reliance on digital platforms has raised significant psychological and ethical concerns. Issues such as stress, anxiety, screen fatigue, and privacy invasion are becoming more common. Ethical dilemmas around data misuse, plagiarism, and surveillance also challenge the integrity of educational environments. Addressing these concerns is essential to ensure that technology serves as a supportive tool rather than a source of harm.

1. Psychological Concerns

A. Stress and Anxiety

1. **Performance Pressure:**
   - Online learning often includes frequent assessments, notifications, and performance tracking. This constant monitoring can create pressure, leading to stress and anxiety among students.
2. **Fear of Failure:**
   - Students may fear making mistakes when using new tools or interacting in virtual environments, resulting in reduced participation and self-confidence.

B. Screen Fatigue and Physical Strain

1. **Extended Screen Time:**
   - Prolonged use of devices for learning, especially without breaks, can lead to headaches, eye strain, and sleep disturbances.
2. **Isolation and Loneliness:**
   - Lack of face-to-face interaction in digital environments may cause feelings of isolation, which can negatively impact mental health.

C. Attention and Concentration Issues

1. **Multitasking:**
   - Online platforms often allow students to switch between tasks easily, reducing sustained attention and deep learning.
2. **Distraction from Notifications:**
   - Frequent alerts and messages from various apps can interrupt learning sessions, making concentration difficult.

2. Ethical Concerns

A. Data Privacy and Surveillance

1. **Excessive Monitoring:**
    - Some learning platforms track student activities, attendance, and even behavior patterns, raising concerns about surveillance and loss of autonomy.
2. **Unauthorized Data Use:**
    - Sensitive data, such as academic records or personal information, may be shared without consent or used for commercial purposes.

B. Plagiarism and Academic Dishonesty

1. **Ease of Copying:**
    - Digital platforms make it easier for students to copy assignments or access unauthorized materials, compromising academic integrity.
2. **Lack of Ethical Awareness:**
    - Many students are unaware of what constitutes plagiarism or misuse of information, leading to unintentional academic violations.

C. Inequality and Exclusion

1. **Access Gaps:**
    - Students without devices or stable internet access may be excluded from educational opportunities, raising ethical concerns about fairness.
2. **Bias in Algorithms:**

- Educational software may inadvertently reinforce biases by using data-driven algorithms that do not account for cultural or socio-economic differences.

3. Addressing Psychological Concerns

A. Creating Balanced Learning Environments

1. **Encouraging Breaks:**
   - Structuring learning schedules with periodic breaks can reduce fatigue and enhance focus.
2. **Promoting Mental Health Awareness:**
   - Schools and institutions can offer counseling services and stress management programs to support students' well-being.

B. Fostering Social Connection

1. **Interactive Platforms:**
   - Using discussion forums, group projects, and video sessions can replicate in-person interactions and reduce feelings of isolation.
2. **Encouraging Peer Support:**
   - Structured group work encourages collaboration and builds a sense of community.

4. Addressing Ethical Concerns

A. Transparent Data Policies

1. **Informed Consent:**

- Institutions must clearly communicate how data is collected, stored, and used, ensuring students and parents understand their rights.

2. **Secure Systems:**
   - Strong encryption and data protection protocols must be in place to prevent unauthorized access.

B. Promoting Academic Integrity

1. **Awareness Campaigns:**
   - Educating students about plagiarism, proper citation, and responsible internet use helps instill ethical practices.
2. **Use of Plagiarism Detection Tools:**
   - Tools that check for similarities can guide students in learning how to reference sources properly.

C. Ensuring Inclusivity

1. **Equitable Access:**
   - Providing devices, internet subsidies, or offline resources ensures that all students can participate fairly.
2. **Bias Audits:**
   - Regular review of algorithms and platforms helps ensure that learning tools serve diverse learners without prejudice.

5. The Role of Educators and Institutions

1. **Modeling Ethical Behavior:**

- Teachers should exemplify honesty, empathy, and responsible technology use, creating a culture of trust.

2. **Encouraging Open Dialogue:**
    - Providing safe spaces where students can share their concerns helps address psychological stress and ethical dilemmas.
3. **Integrating Ethics into the Curriculum:**
    - Including modules on digital citizenship, online safety, and academic responsibility prepares students to navigate technology thoughtfully.

Chapter 14

Future Trends in Educational Technology

14.1 Artificial Intelligence in Learning

Introduction

Artificial Intelligence (AI) is rapidly transforming the landscape of education. From personalized learning pathways to automated assessments, AI technologies are making education more efficient, adaptive, and accessible. In learning environments, AI helps tailor content to individual needs, provide real-time feedback, and automate administrative tasks, enabling educators to focus on pedagogy rather than routine work. While AI offers remarkable opportunities, it also presents challenges such as privacy concerns, bias in algorithms, and dependence on technology. This section explores how AI is shaping modern learning, its benefits, challenges, ethical considerations, and future prospects.

1. Understanding Artificial Intelligence in Learning

Artificial Intelligence refers to the simulation of human intelligence in machines, enabling them to perform tasks such as reasoning, learning from data, recognizing patterns, and making decisions. In education, AI is applied through algorithms, machine learning models, natural language processing, and data analytics to create intelligent systems that can support, enhance, and transform teaching and learning processes.

AI's role in learning is not to replace teachers but to augment their work by offering tools that help analyze student performance, adapt instructional materials, and predict learning outcomes. AI systems can interpret vast amounts of data to identify learning gaps and offer targeted interventions.

2. Applications of AI in Learning

A. Personalized Learning

1. **Adaptive Learning Systems:**
   - AI-powered platforms can analyze student interactions and performance to customize learning content and pace. For example, if a student struggles with a math concept, the system can recommend additional exercises and tutorials.
2. **Learning Path Recommendations:**
   - AI can create personalized study plans based on learner profiles, interests, and performance history, making education more relevant and engaging.

B. Intelligent Tutoring Systems (ITS)

1. **Real-Time Feedback:**
   - ITS provides immediate responses to students' inputs, helping them understand concepts without waiting for teacher intervention.
2. **Interactive Problem-Solving:**
   - AI-based tutors guide learners through complex problems step-by-step, offering hints and explanations that mimic human tutoring.

C. Automated Assessments

1. **Grading and Evaluation:**
   - AI systems can assess assignments, quizzes, and tests quickly, reducing teachers' workload and providing consistent evaluation standards.
2. **Plagiarism Detection:**
   - AI tools scan submitted content to ensure originality and teach students proper citation practices.

D. Language Learning

1. **Speech Recognition:**
   - AI-powered language platforms help learners practice pronunciation and conversational skills by analyzing speech patterns.
2. **Translation Tools:**
   - Language barriers are overcome with AI tools that provide instant translations, enabling students to access global learning resources.

E. Learning Analytics

1. **Predictive Analytics:**
   - AI analyzes data trends to predict student performance and identify learners at risk of falling behind, allowing for timely interventions.
2. **Behavioral Insights:**
   - Patterns of engagement, participation, and resource use are analyzed to improve instructional methods.

F. Virtual Classrooms and Chatbots

1. **24/7 Support:**
   - AI-powered chatbots answer frequently asked questions, provide reminders, and guide learners through coursework at any time.
2. **Enhanced Interaction:**
   - Virtual classrooms with AI tools support collaboration, simulate lab environments, and offer multimedia content to enrich learning experiences.

3. Benefits of AI in Learning

A. Efficiency and Time-Saving

- Automated grading and data analysis allow teachers to focus more on instructional strategies and student engagement rather than routine tasks.

B. Accessibility

- AI helps learners access educational content in remote areas or those with disabilities by offering assistive technologies, language translation, and tailored learning paths.

C. Engagement and Motivation

- Interactive tools, gamified learning platforms, and adaptive exercises enhance student participation and sustain interest.

D. Scalability

- AI-powered platforms can support thousands of students simultaneously without compromising the quality of feedback or content delivery.

E. Data-Driven Decisions

- AI assists educators in making informed decisions by providing evidence-based insights into learning patterns and outcomes.

4. Challenges and Limitations

A. Privacy and Security Concerns

- The collection of personal data raises concerns about how information is stored, who can access it, and how it may be used.

B. Bias in AI Algorithms

- AI models trained on biased data can lead to unfair assessments or recommendations, affecting certain groups disproportionately.

C. Over-Dependence on Technology

- Excessive reliance on AI may reduce human interaction, critical thinking, and problem-solving skills among learners.

D. High Implementation Costs

- Developing and maintaining AI systems requires investments in infrastructure, software, and training, which may not be feasible for all institutions.

E. Digital Divide

- Unequal access to devices and internet connectivity can exacerbate learning disparities, preventing some students from benefiting from AI-driven solutions.

5. Ethical Considerations

A. Informed Consent

- Learners must be aware of how their data will be used and must give explicit permission before AI systems process their information.

B. Transparency

- AI systems should clearly explain how decisions are made, especially when grading or recommending learning resources.

C. Fairness and Inclusion

- AI tools should be designed to accommodate diverse learner profiles, ensuring that they support learners from different cultural, economic, and social backgrounds.

D. Human Oversight

- Educators should remain central to decision-making, ensuring that AI supports but does not replace human judgment and empathy.

6. The Future of AI in Learning

The potential of AI in education continues to expand with advancements in machine learning, natural language processing, and data analytics. Future developments include:

1. **Emotion Recognition:**
   - AI systems may be able to detect emotions such as frustration or confusion and adjust teaching strategies accordingly.
2. **Virtual Reality Integration:**
   - Combining AI with immersive technologies can create realistic simulations that enhance experiential learning.
3. **Global Collaboration Platforms:**
   - AI-driven platforms will connect learners across borders, enabling cross-cultural educational experiences.
4. **Self-Learning Systems:**
   - AI models that continuously learn and improve from interactions will personalize education even further, offering tailored solutions over time.

Artificial Intelligence is revolutionizing education by offering personalized, efficient, and accessible learning experiences. It empowers learners and educators alike by automating administrative tasks, offering real-time feedback, and tailoring content to individual needs. However, along with its many advantages, AI also brings challenges such as privacy risks, bias, and over-dependence on technology. Ethical considerations, informed consent, and human oversight are critical to ensuring that AI tools are used responsibly and inclusively.

As AI continues to evolve, it will increasingly shape the future of education. By balancing technological innovation with empathy, fairness, and ethical responsibility, educational institutions can harness AI's potential to create more meaningful, engaging, and equitable learning environments. Proper training, transparency, and support systems will be essential to ensuring that AI serves as a tool that enriches rather than replaces the human aspects of teaching and learning.

14.2 Virtual Reality (VR) and Augmented Reality (AR)

Introduction

Virtual Reality (VR) and Augmented Reality (AR) are advanced technologies that are transforming how learning takes place. By creating immersive, interactive, and engaging environments, these tools help learners experience concepts rather than just read about them. While VR fully immerses the user in a virtual environment, AR overlays digital information on the real world, enhancing understanding through interaction. Both have become powerful tools in education, making learning more experiential, accessible, and fun.

1. Virtual Reality (VR) in Learning

Virtual Reality uses headsets and motion-tracking devices to create a simulated environment where learners can explore topics in a 3D space. This technology allows students to:

1. **Experience Real-World Scenarios:**
   - VR simulations can recreate historical events, scientific experiments, or geographical locations, allowing students to interact with content and gain practical insights.
2. **Enhance Practical Learning:**
   - Medical students can practice surgeries in VR labs, while engineering students can explore mechanical structures without the risk of physical harm.
3. **Improve Focus and Engagement:**
   - The immersive experience reduces distractions, helping learners stay attentive and retain information better.
4. **Offer Safe Learning Environments:**
   - Complex, dangerous, or expensive experiments can be safely replicated in VR, providing opportunities for hands-on learning without real-world risks.

2. Augmented Reality (AR) in Learning

Unlike VR, Augmented Reality enhances the real environment by adding interactive digital elements such as images, videos, or 3D models. AR tools are widely accessible through smartphones or tablets and can be used to:

1. **Visualize Complex Concepts:**

- Students can scan textbooks or charts to access 3D models, animations, or diagrams that explain difficult topics in science, mathematics, or engineering.

2. **Support Field Learning:**
   - In biology or geography classes, AR apps can overlay information on plants, animals, or landscapes, making outdoor learning more informative and engaging.
3. **Encourage Interactive Learning:**
   - AR tools allow students to manipulate objects or explore scenarios, helping them learn by doing.
4. **Facilitate Collaborative Learning:**
   - Students can work together on AR projects, enhancing teamwork and communication skills.

3. Benefits of VR and AR in Education

1. **Enhanced Understanding:**
   - Interactive and visual learning helps students grasp abstract or complex concepts more easily.
2. **Inclusive Learning:**
   - VR and AR provide alternative ways to learn, catering to diverse learning styles and abilities.
3. **Motivation and Engagement:**
   - Gamified content and immersive experiences increase student interest and participation.
4. **Accessibility:**
   - VR and AR can bring real-world experiences into classrooms, especially for students in remote or resource-limited areas.

4. Challenges and Considerations

1. **Cost and Infrastructure:**
    - VR headsets and AR-enabled devices can be expensive and require stable internet access, limiting their use in some schools.
2. **Health and Safety:**
    - Prolonged use of VR headsets may cause motion sickness or eye strain in some learners.
3. **Content Development:**
    - Creating high-quality VR and AR educational content requires expertise, time, and investment.
4. **Training for Educators:**
    - Teachers need to be trained in using these tools effectively to integrate them into their curriculum.

14.3 Adaptive Learning Systems

Introduction

Adaptive Learning Systems are AI-powered platforms designed to personalize education by adjusting the learning experience to the unique needs of each student. These systems analyze data such as student responses, learning pace, and comprehension levels to create customized learning paths. The goal is to provide targeted support, optimize learning outcomes, and ensure that learners stay engaged and motivated throughout the educational process.

1. What are Adaptive Learning Systems?

Adaptive Learning Systems use algorithms, machine learning, and data analytics to continuously assess a learner's progress and adjust educational content accordingly. Unlike traditional classrooms where all students receive the same instruction, adaptive learning platforms respond dynamically to the learner's behavior, providing resources, quizzes, hints, and explanations that are suited to their needs.

Key features include:

1. **Personalized Content Delivery:**
   - Lessons are tailored based on the learner's strengths, weaknesses, and preferences.
2. **Real-Time Feedback:**
   - The system provides instant guidance, helping learners correct mistakes and reinforce concepts immediately.
3. **Performance Tracking:**
   - Learners' progress is continuously monitored, and learning plans are updated as new data is collected.
4. **Goal Setting and Motivation:**
   - The system can set achievable targets, reward progress, and encourage learners to stay engaged.

2. How Adaptive Learning Systems Work

1. **Data Collection:**
   - Systems gather data from quizzes, assignments, navigation patterns, time spent on tasks, and interaction with learning materials.
2. **Analysis and Pattern Recognition:**
   - Algorithms analyze how students learn, which areas they struggle with, and where they excel.
3. **Content Adjustment:**
   - Based on the analysis, the platform presents content that matches the learner's level, introduces

supplementary resources, or revises topics that need reinforcement.

4. **Continuous Improvement:**
   - As learners progress, the system adapts further, ensuring that new challenges are neither too easy nor too difficult.

3. Benefits of Adaptive Learning Systems

1. **Personalized Learning Experience:**
   - Students learn at their own pace, focusing on areas that need improvement without feeling left behind or overwhelmed.
2. **Improved Learning Outcomes:**
   - Targeted interventions and instant feedback help in better understanding and retention of knowledge.
3. **Increased Engagement:**
   - Interactive content, quizzes, and progress tracking keep students motivated and actively participating in their learning journey.
4. **Efficient Use of Time:**
   - Learners spend time on concepts they need to master, reducing unnecessary repetition and focusing on areas that require attention.
5. **Support for Diverse Learners:**
   - Students with different learning styles, disabilities, or language barriers benefit from customized learning experiences.

4. Applications in Education

1. **K-12 Education:**

- Adaptive systems help younger students build foundational skills in subjects such as mathematics and reading.

2. **Higher Education:**
   - Colleges and universities use adaptive platforms to support large classrooms by offering personalized learning resources to individual students.
3. **Online Courses and E-Learning:**
   - Platforms like MOOCs (Massive Open Online Courses) integrate adaptive learning to assist learners globally.
4. **Corporate Training:**
   - Adaptive systems are used for employee training programs to enhance skills and track professional development.

5. Challenges and Limitations

1. **Data Privacy:**
   - Collecting and analyzing personal learning data raises concerns about how information is stored and shared.
2. **Algorithmic Bias:**
   - If not properly designed, adaptive systems can favor certain learners while disadvantaging others.
3. **Over-Reliance on Technology:**
   - Learners may become dependent on the system, reducing their ability to solve problems independently.
4. **Implementation Costs:**

- Developing and maintaining adaptive platforms requires financial investment, technical expertise, and infrastructure support.

14.4 Global Collaboration and Remote Learning

Introduction

Artificial Intelligence (AI) is reshaping global collaboration and remote learning by enabling students and educators to connect, communicate, and learn across geographical boundaries. With AI-powered platforms, learners can participate in virtual classrooms, access educational resources from anywhere, and engage in collaborative projects with peers worldwide. This transformation not only increases access to education but also fosters cultural exchange, teamwork, and global competencies essential for the 21st-century learner.

1. AI in Remote Learning

Remote learning has become increasingly important, especially with the rise of online education platforms. AI enhances remote learning by:

1. **Personalizing Learning Experiences:**
   - AI algorithms analyze student performance, engagement levels, and learning patterns to deliver content tailored to individual needs, even in remote settings.
2. **Automating Administrative Tasks:**

- AI tools handle scheduling, grading, and assessment tracking, reducing the workload on educators and allowing them to focus on instruction.

3. **Providing Real-Time Feedback:**
   - Learners receive instant responses on assignments and quizzes, helping them correct mistakes and reinforce understanding without delay.
4. **Facilitating Language Support:**
   - AI-driven translation and language tools enable students from different linguistic backgrounds to participate in global online courses seamlessly.

2. AI for Global Collaboration

AI supports collaboration across countries and cultures in several ways:

1. **Virtual Classrooms and Discussion Platforms:**
   - AI moderates and facilitates discussions, ensuring that students from different time zones and backgrounds can engage effectively.
2. **Collaborative Project Management Tools:**
   - Platforms use AI to assign tasks, monitor progress, and suggest resources for group projects, enhancing teamwork among international students.
3. **Cross-Cultural Learning Experiences:**
   - AI can pair students from diverse regions based on learning objectives, encouraging cultural exchange and broadening perspectives.
4. **Enhanced Communication:**
   - AI-powered chatbots, video conferencing tools, and real-time collaboration software help overcome

communication barriers, ensuring smooth interactions among learners and instructors.

3. Benefits of AI in Global Collaboration and Remote Learning

1. **Increased Accessibility:**
   - Students from remote or underprivileged areas can access high-quality educational resources and global courses without physical travel.
2. **Flexibility and Convenience:**
   - AI-powered platforms allow learners to study at their own pace and schedule, accommodating different time zones and learning preferences.
3. **Enhanced Engagement:**
   - Gamified features, interactive simulations, and virtual labs keep students engaged in a remote environment.
4. **Data-Driven Insights:**
   - Educators can use AI analytics to track participation, performance, and collaboration effectiveness, enabling better support for learners.
5. **Skill Development:**
   - Students develop digital literacy, cross-cultural communication, and collaboration skills essential for global citizenship and employment in the modern workforce.

4. Challenges and Considerations

1. **Digital Divide:**

  - Unequal access to devices and internet connectivity can limit participation in remote learning and global projects.
2. **Privacy and Security:**
  - AI platforms collect significant amounts of data; securing this data and ensuring ethical use is crucial.
3. **Teacher Training:**
  - Educators must be trained to effectively integrate AI tools into global and remote learning contexts.
4. **Cultural Sensitivity:**
  - AI systems must account for diverse cultural norms and learning styles to ensure equitable and inclusive collaboration.

AI has the potential to revolutionize global collaboration and remote learning by bridging geographical gaps, personalizing education, and facilitating interactive, multicultural learning experiences. It enhances accessibility, engagement, and skill development, preparing learners for a globally connected world. However, challenges such as the digital divide, privacy concerns, and the need for educator training must be addressed to ensure equitable and effective implementation. By leveraging AI responsibly, educational institutions can create dynamic, inclusive, and globally collaborative learning environments that prepare students for the opportunities and challenges of the 21st century.

4.5 Innovations and Startups in EdTech

Introduction

The educational technology (EdTech) sector has witnessed tremendous growth in recent years, driven by innovative startups and advancements in Artificial Intelligence (AI), Virtual Reality (VR), Augmented Reality (AR), and adaptive learning systems. These innovations are reshaping how education is delivered, accessed, and experienced, making learning more personalized, interactive, and inclusive. Startups are at the forefront of this transformation, providing creative solutions to traditional educational challenges, such as accessibility, engagement, and scalability.

1. Role of EdTech Startups

EdTech startups leverage technology to develop platforms, applications, and tools that enhance teaching and learning processes. Their focus areas include:

1. **Personalized Learning Platforms:**
    - AI-driven systems analyze student performance and adapt lessons to individual needs. Startups like BYJU'S and DreamBox Learning use personalized learning algorithms to optimize learning outcomes.
2. **Interactive Content Creation:**
    - Companies are designing gamified content, simulations, and virtual labs to make learning engaging. Platforms such as Labster and Kahoot! create immersive, interactive experiences that encourage active participation.
3. **Online Assessment and Feedback Tools:**
    - Startups provide automated testing, real-time feedback, and data analytics to help educators track student performance and improve learning outcomes. Examples include Quizizz and Socrative.
4. **Collaboration and Communication Platforms:**

- Tools like Edmodo, Google Classroom, and Microsoft Teams enable students and teachers to interact seamlessly, fostering collaboration and peer learning.

2. Innovations Driving EdTech

A. AI-Powered Learning

- AI algorithms create adaptive learning paths, predict learning difficulties, and recommend personalized resources, making education more efficient and effective.

B. Immersive Learning with VR and AR

- Virtual Reality and Augmented Reality transform abstract concepts into experiential learning. Startups are developing VR/AR-based simulations for subjects like science, history, and engineering.

C. Mobile Learning Apps

- Mobile platforms allow students to access educational resources anytime and anywhere. Apps like Duolingo, Khan Academy, and BYJU'S Learning App provide interactive lessons on-the-go.

D. Gamification

- Startups integrate game-based elements, such as rewards, badges, and challenges, to increase motivation, engagement, and retention among learners.

E. Learning Analytics

- AI-driven analytics track learning patterns, identify gaps, and provide actionable insights for students and educators. Companies like Smart Sparrow and Knewton use data to enhance personalized learning.

3. Benefits of Innovations and Startups in EdTech

1. **Increased Accessibility:**
   - Students from remote or underserved areas can access high-quality education through online platforms.
2. **Enhanced Engagement:**
   - Interactive content, gamified learning, and immersive technologies make education more enjoyable and effective.
3. **Personalized Learning:**
   - AI and adaptive technologies enable customized learning experiences tailored to individual needs.
4. **Efficiency and Scalability:**
   - Automation of assessments, feedback, and administrative tasks allows educators to focus on teaching while reaching a larger number of learners.
5. **Skill Development:**
   - EdTech tools encourage critical thinking, problem-solving, collaboration, and digital literacy, preparing students for future careers.

4. Challenges and Considerations

1. **Digital Divide:**

- Access to devices and reliable internet remains a barrier for many students, limiting the reach of EdTech solutions.

2. **Quality of Content:**
   - Ensuring that educational content is accurate, relevant, and pedagogically sound is crucial for effective learning.
3. **Privacy and Security:**
   - Handling student data responsibly and protecting it from misuse is a major concern for EdTech startups.
4. **Teacher Training:**
   - Educators need training to effectively integrate new technologies into their classrooms.

Chapter 15
Educational Policies and Government Initiatives

15.1 Digital India Mission

Introduction

The **Digital India Mission** is a flagship initiative launched by the Government of India in 2015 to transform India into a digitally empowered society and knowledge economy. Its primary aim is to ensure that government services are made available to citizens electronically, promote digital literacy, and expand internet connectivity across the country. In the education sector, the mission plays a crucial role by enhancing access to digital resources, promoting e-learning platforms, and integrating technology into teaching and learning processes.

1. Objectives of Digital India Mission

1. **Digital Infrastructure as a Core Utility:**
    - Provide high-speed internet access to all citizens, particularly in rural and remote areas.
    - Ensure availability of online platforms for education, healthcare, and governance.
2. **Governance and Services on Demand:**
    - Make government services digitally accessible, including educational resources, certificates, and scholarship applications.
3. **Digital Empowerment of Citizens:**
    - Enhance digital literacy and skills among students, teachers, and citizens, enabling them to effectively use technology for education and personal growth.

4. **Promotion of e-Governance:**
   - Encourage the use of online platforms for school administration, learning management, and citizen engagement in educational planning.

2. Key Components Related to Education

1. **e-Education Platforms:**
   - Initiatives like **DIKSHA** (Digital Infrastructure for Knowledge Sharing) provide free online resources for students and teachers, including lesson plans, textbooks, and multimedia content.
   - The platform supports professional development for teachers through online courses and digital certification.
2. **Digital Classrooms:**
   - Schools and colleges are being equipped with ICT tools, smart boards, projectors, and internet connectivity to enhance teaching and learning experiences.
3. **Access to Learning Resources:**
   - Students in remote areas can access e-books, online lectures, and interactive content through government-supported digital platforms.
4. **Skill Development Programs:**
   - Digital India promotes skill-building initiatives for students and educators, including coding, digital literacy, and vocational skills.

3. Benefits of the Digital India Mission in Education

1. **Enhanced Accessibility:**

- Students from rural and underserved areas can access quality learning resources and online courses.

2. **Improved Teacher Training:**
    - Digital platforms provide continuous professional development, training modules, and best practices for educators.
3. **Efficiency and Transparency:**
    - Online services reduce paperwork, streamline administrative processes, and allow for better monitoring of school programs and student progress.
4. **Encouraging E-Learning Culture:**
    - By integrating ICT in classrooms and promoting digital content, the mission fosters a culture of e-learning, self-paced learning, and interactive education.
5. **Bridging the Digital Divide:**
    - Ensures that students from diverse socio-economic backgrounds gain equitable access to modern educational tools and resources.

4. Challenges in Implementation

1. **Infrastructure Limitations:**
    - Many rural areas still lack high-speed internet and electricity, limiting the effectiveness of digital education initiatives.
2. **Digital Literacy:**
    - Teachers and students may require additional training to utilize digital tools effectively.
3. **Maintenance and Sustainability:**

- Ensuring that digital classrooms, devices, and platforms remain functional and updated is a continuing challenge.

4. **Inclusivity:**
   - Efforts are needed to ensure differently-abled students and those from marginalized communities can equally benefit from digital initiatives.

15.2 National Education Policy (NEP)

Introduction

The **National Education Policy (NEP) 2020** is a landmark framework for transforming India's education system, replacing the earlier policies and aiming to make education holistic, flexible, multidisciplinary, and aligned with the needs of the 21st century. NEP 2020 envisions an education system that promotes critical thinking, creativity, and lifelong learning, while integrating technology into learning, teaching, and administration. The policy emphasizes inclusivity, equity, and access, ensuring that students from all socio-economic backgrounds receive quality education. It also lays special emphasis on higher education, vocational education, teacher training, and the use of Artificial Intelligence (AI) and digital tools in classrooms.

1. Objectives of NEP 2020

The core objectives of NEP 2020 include:

1. **Universalization of Education:**
   - Ensure equitable access to education from pre-primary to higher education for all children.

   - Focus on marginalized groups, including girls, differently-abled students, and students from disadvantaged regions.
2. **Holistic and Multidisciplinary Education:**
   - Promote curricula that integrate arts, sciences, humanities, vocational studies, and life skills.
   - Encourage critical thinking, creativity, and problem-solving over rote learning.
3. **Integration of Technology:**
   - Embed technology in teaching, learning, and administrative processes.
   - Support online learning platforms, digital classrooms, and AI-driven personalized learning.
4. **Flexibility in Learning:**
   - Enable students to choose subjects and learning paths based on their interests and career goals.
   - Encourage multiple entry and exit options in higher education.
5. **Teacher Training and Professional Development:**
   - Improve teacher quality through rigorous training, continuous professional development, and use of technology in pedagogy.
6. **Focus on Vocational Education and Skill Development:**
   - Integrate vocational training into school and higher education curricula from an early age.
   - Prepare students for employment and entrepreneurship opportunities.
7. **Research and Innovation:**
   - Strengthen research capabilities in universities and colleges.
   - Promote a culture of innovation and knowledge creation.

2. Key Features of NEP 2020

A. School Education

1. **Foundational Literacy and Numeracy:**
   - Emphasis on achieving literacy and numeracy by Grade 3.
   - Focus on interactive and activity-based learning at early stages.
2. **Curriculum and Pedagogy Reform:**
   - Shift from rote learning to competency-based learning.
   - Integration of experiential learning, arts, sports, and digital skills.
3. **5+3+3+4 Structure:**
   - Replacement of the 10+2 system with a 5+3+3+4 structure:
     - **Foundational Stage (5 years):** Play-based and discovery learning.
     - **Preparatory Stage (3 years):** Introduction to language, numeracy, and STEM concepts.
     - **Middle Stage (3 years):** Experiential and project-based learning.
     - **Secondary Stage (4 years):** Multidisciplinary education with flexibility in subject choices.
4. **Multilingualism and Mother Tongue Instruction:**
   - Promotion of teaching in the mother tongue or local language until at least Grade 5.
   - Encouragement of multilingual competency to enhance cultural understanding.
5. **Assessment Reforms:**

- Shift from high-stakes exams to formative, competency-based assessments.
- Emphasis on application, critical thinking, and creativity.

B. Higher Education

1. **Holistic and Multidisciplinary Universities:**
   - Institutions encouraged to offer broad-based education with flexibility in subject combinations.
   - Emphasis on liberal arts, sciences, vocational skills, and research.
2. **Multiple Entry-Exit Options:**
   - Students can leave programs with certificates, diplomas, or degrees based on completed years of study.
   - Encourages lifelong learning and reduces dropouts.
3. **Integration of Technology:**
   - Use of AI, learning management systems (LMS), and online courses to enhance teaching and learning.
   - Platforms like SWAYAM and DIKSHA promoted for accessible online education.
4. **Research and Innovation Hubs:**
   - Establishment of National Research Foundation to strengthen research ecosystems.
   - Encouragement of interdisciplinary research and global collaboration.
5. **Regulation and Accreditation:**
   - Separation of academic, administrative, and regulatory functions to improve governance.
   - Introduction of a single regulator for higher education institutions.

C. Teacher Education

1. **Four-Year Integrated Teacher Education Programs:**
   - Standardization of teacher training programs to improve quality and prepare educators for 21st-century classrooms.
2. **Continuous Professional Development:**
   - Mandatory in-service training and online programs to enhance teaching practices.
3. **Technology-Enabled Teaching:**
   - Use of AI tools, digital resources, and educational technology for lesson planning, assessments, and classroom management.

3. Technology Integration in NEP 2020

1. **Digital Infrastructure:**
   - Expansion of internet connectivity, smart classrooms, and ICT-enabled resources.
   - Digital repositories for curriculum, textbooks, and learning materials.
2. **AI and Personalized Learning:**
   - AI-driven adaptive learning platforms to address individual student needs.
   - Predictive analytics to monitor learning outcomes and provide interventions.
3. **Online and Blended Learning:**
   - Promotion of online courses, virtual labs, and blended learning models for flexible and continuous education.
4. **Capacity Building:**

    - Training teachers and administrators in using digital tools effectively.
5. **Equity and Accessibility:**
    - Technology to support differently-abled learners through assistive devices, screen readers, and audio-visual content.

4. Implementation Strategies

1. **Central and State Collaboration:**
    - NEP recommends strong coordination between central and state governments to ensure uniform quality and equitable access.
2. **Public-Private Partnerships (PPP):**
    - Engagement with EdTech companies, NGOs, and private institutions for technology deployment, teacher training, and content development.
3. **Monitoring and Evaluation:**
    - Use of data analytics to monitor progress, identify gaps, and improve educational outcomes.
    - Annual and periodic assessments for accountability and transparency.
4. **Investment in Infrastructure:**
    - Government funding for ICT-enabled classrooms, digital libraries, and online learning platforms.

5. Challenges in Implementing NEP 2020

1. **Digital Divide:**
    - Unequal access to devices and internet connectivity in rural and remote areas.
2. **Teacher Training Gaps:**

- Need for large-scale professional development to implement pedagogy reforms effectively.

3. **Financial and Resource Constraints:**
   - Significant investment required for infrastructure, content development, and technology adoption.
4. **Resistance to Change:**
   - Traditional mindset among educators and institutions may slow adoption of flexible, technology-enabled learning methods.
5. **Equity and Inclusion:**
   - Ensuring marginalized and differently-abled students benefit from policy reforms remains a challenge.

6. Impact and Potential of NEP 2020

1. **Holistic Development:**
   - Emphasis on life skills, creativity, and critical thinking prepares students for modern careers and societal challenges.
2. **Global Competitiveness:**
   - Aligning Indian education with international standards promotes research, innovation, and global collaboration.
3. **Increased Enrollment and Retention:**
   - Flexible learning paths, multiple exit options, and vocational integration reduce dropout rates.
4. **Technology-Driven Education:**
   - AI, digital classrooms, and online learning improve accessibility, efficiency, and learning outcomes.
5. **Empowered Educators:**

- Professional development and ICT integration enable teachers to deliver more effective, personalized, and engaging instruction.

The **National Education Policy (NEP) 2020** is a transformative framework aimed at modernizing India's education system, making it more inclusive, flexible, and technology-driven. By integrating digital tools, AI, adaptive learning, and skill-based curricula, NEP 2020 seeks to prepare students for the demands of the 21st century. While challenges such as the digital divide, infrastructure gaps, and teacher training persist, the policy provides a roadmap for a holistic, learner-centered, and multidisciplinary education system. With coordinated implementation, investment in digital infrastructure, and continuous monitoring, NEP 2020 has the potential to revolutionize education in India, fostering innovation, equity, and global competitiveness.

15.3 Government Programs for ICT Integration

Introduction

Information and Communication Technology (ICT) has become a cornerstone of modern education, enhancing teaching, learning, and administration. The Government of India has implemented several programs to integrate ICT into educational institutions at all levels. These initiatives aim to provide digital infrastructure, promote e-learning, train teachers, and ensure equitable access to technology for students across the country. ICT integration not only improves educational quality but also prepares learners for a technology-driven world.

1. National Mission on Education through ICT (NMEICT)

Overview:
Launched in 2009 by the Ministry of Education, NMEICT seeks to leverage ICT to enhance the reach and quality of education in India. Its primary goal is to provide access to high-quality educational resources to all learners, particularly in remote and underserved areas.

Key Components:

1. **E-Content Development:**
    - Creation of digital learning materials, including e-books, audio-visual modules, simulations, and interactive lessons.
    - Resources are made available through platforms like **SWAYAM**, **e-PG Pathshala**, and **NPTEL**.
2. **Virtual Classrooms and e-Learning:**
    - ICT-enabled classrooms connect students and teachers across institutions, facilitating distance learning.
    - Video lectures and virtual labs provide experiential learning opportunities.
3. **Connectivity and Digital Infrastructure:**
    - Provision of high-speed internet in universities, colleges, and schools.
    - Establishment of ICT labs and smart classrooms to facilitate technology-enabled education.
4. **Teacher Training and Capacity Building:**
    - Training programs for educators on using ICT tools effectively.

- Development of modules for online teaching and digital content creation.

Impact:

- Expanded access to higher education resources and MOOCs.
- Improved quality of education through interactive and multimedia content.
- Enabled remote learning, particularly in rural and difficult-to-reach areas.

2. Digital Infrastructure for Knowledge Sharing (DIKSHA)

Overview:
DIKSHA is a national platform for school education that provides digital content for students, teachers, and parents. It supports curriculum-aligned learning and teacher professional development.

Key Features:

1. **Curriculum-Based Learning Material:**
   - Free access to e-books, lesson plans, videos, and quizzes aligned with state and national curricula.
2. **Teacher Training Modules:**
   - Online courses and certification programs for teachers to improve digital pedagogical skills.
3. **Analytics and Assessment:**
   - Tools for tracking student progress and providing personalized feedback.
4. **Community Engagement:**

- Teachers and students can collaborate, share resources, and participate in discussion forums.

Impact:

- Promotes blended learning in classrooms.
- Enhances teacher capacity in integrating technology into pedagogy.
- Supports personalized learning for students across grades.

3. SWAYAM (Study Webs of Active-Learning for Young Aspiring Minds)

Overview:
SWAYAM is an initiative to provide free online courses across higher education subjects, from school to university levels. It integrates ICT into learning by offering Massive Open Online Courses (MOOCs).

Key Features:

- Courses developed by top Indian institutions and experts.
- Interactive video lectures, quizzes, assignments, and discussion forums.
- Certificates recognized by universities for academic credits.

Impact:

- Democratizes access to high-quality education.
- Encourages self-paced learning and lifelong learning opportunities.

4. National Digital Library of India (NDLI)

Overview:
NDLI is an initiative to provide a single-window access to digital educational resources, including books, theses, videos, and articles.

Key Features:

- Digital repository covering all academic disciplines.
- Resources available for free to students, researchers, and teachers.
- Integration with AI for content recommendation and personalized learning.

Impact:

- Facilitates easy access to quality resources for learners in remote areas.
- Supports research and higher education with comprehensive digital content.

5. Challenges in ICT Integration Programs

1. **Digital Divide:**
   - Limited access to devices and reliable internet in rural and marginalized regions.
2. **Teacher Preparedness:**
   - Many educators require training to use digital tools effectively.
3. **Infrastructure Limitations:**
   - Schools and colleges often lack sufficient ICT labs or smart classroom facilities.
4. **Content Quality and Relevance:**
   - Continuous updating and contextualization of digital resources are necessary to maintain effectiveness.

15.4 International Educational Technology Practices

Introduction

Educational technology (EdTech) has become a global phenomenon, transforming how teaching and learning occur worldwide. Countries across the globe have integrated technology into education in diverse ways, reflecting local needs, infrastructure, and policy frameworks. By studying international EdTech practices, India can adopt best practices, avoid pitfalls, and implement innovative approaches to enhance learning outcomes. This section highlights key international initiatives, technological integration strategies, and the impact of these practices on global education.

1. United States: Personalized and Blended Learning

Overview:
The U.S. education system emphasizes technology-driven personalized learning and blended learning models. Schools and universities use Learning Management Systems (LMS) to deliver content, track progress, and provide adaptive learning experiences.

Key Practices:

1. **Adaptive Learning Platforms:**
    - Tools like DreamBox Learning and Knewton use AI to customize content for individual students.
    - Students receive personalized exercises based on performance data.
2. **Blended Learning Models:**
    - Combination of online and face-to-face instruction.

    - Platforms like Google Classroom and Canvas facilitate collaboration, assessment, and content delivery.

Impact:

- Improved engagement and retention rates.
- Enhanced teacher ability to monitor individual student progress.

2. Finland: ICT Integration for Equity and Collaboration

Overview:
Finland is known for its innovative and equitable education system, where technology supports collaborative learning and equal access.

Key Practices:

1. **Student-Centered Learning:**
    - ICT tools enable project-based learning, collaboration, and creativity.
2. **Digital Literacy for All:**
    - Digital skills are integrated into the curriculum from an early age.
    - Teachers receive continuous professional development in EdTech.
3. **National Digital Learning Platforms:**
    - Platforms provide e-books, learning games, and virtual labs for all students, ensuring uniform access.

Impact:

- Promotes equity and inclusion in digital learning.

- Encourages critical thinking and problem-solving skills.

3. Singapore: Technology-Enhanced Curriculum and Assessment

Overview:
Singapore leverages technology to enhance curriculum delivery, student assessment, and teacher professional development.

Key Practices:

1. **Smart Classrooms:**
   - Integration of tablets, interactive whiteboards, and digital resources to make learning interactive.
2. **Data-Driven Decision Making:**
   - Use of analytics to monitor student progress and identify learning gaps.
3. **National EdTech Strategy:**
   - Policies encourage collaboration between schools, universities, and EdTech startups.

Impact:

- Facilitates evidence-based teaching and learning improvements.
- Prepares students for digital literacy and future-ready skills.

4. South Korea: Gamification and AI in Education

Overview:
South Korea has invested heavily in AI and gamified learning to engage students and improve academic outcomes.

Key Practices:

1. **AI Tutors and Virtual Assistants:**
   - AI tools help students practice subjects such as mathematics and language learning.
2. **Gamified Learning Platforms:**
   - Platforms include rewards, challenges, and interactive simulations to boost motivation.
3. **Digital Textbooks:**
   - Schools use tablets and e-books integrated with interactive content for a personalized learning experience.

Impact:

- Enhances engagement, motivation, and learning efficiency.
- Reduces achievement gaps through adaptive learning solutions.

5. Australia: Inclusive and Accessible EdTech

Overview:
Australia focuses on inclusivity and accessibility, ensuring that differently-abled students benefit from EdTech.

Key Practices:

1. **Assistive Technologies:**
   - Tools like screen readers, text-to-speech software, and adaptive keyboards support diverse learners.
2. **Professional Development for Educators:**
   - Teachers are trained to use technology effectively for inclusive education.

3. **Collaborative Online Platforms:**
   - Use of LMS and cloud-based collaboration tools promotes student interaction and peer learning.

Impact:

- Supports diverse learning needs and fosters equitable education.
- Encourages collaboration and critical thinking among students.

6. Key Lessons for India

1. **Personalized and Adaptive Learning:**
   - AI-driven adaptive platforms can address individual learning needs.
2. **Teacher Training and Professional Development:**
   - Continuous capacity building is essential for effective ICT integration.
3. **Equity and Inclusion:**
   - Ensure technology reaches all learners, including rural, marginalized, and differently-abled students.
4. **Policy and Governance:**
   - National EdTech strategies, public-private partnerships, and funding models are critical for successful implementation.
5. **Gamification and Engagement:**
   - Interactive content and gamified learning enhance motivation, retention, and performance.

15.5 Funding, Grants, and Institutional Support for EdTech in India

Introduction

The successful integration of educational technology (EdTech) in India relies heavily on adequate **funding, grants, and institutional support**. Government initiatives, public-private partnerships, and private investments play a crucial role in providing the financial and infrastructural backing required to implement ICT in education. Funding ensures the establishment of digital classrooms, development of e-learning content, teacher training programs, and research in EdTech, enabling equitable access and sustainable educational growth.

1. Government Funding and Initiatives

The Government of India has allocated substantial resources to promote EdTech integration in schools, colleges, and higher education institutions. Key funding avenues include:

1. **National Mission on Education through ICT (NMEICT):**
   - Funded by the Ministry of Education, this mission supports digital infrastructure, content development, online learning platforms (SWAYAM, e-PG Pathshala), and virtual labs.
   - Grants are provided to universities and colleges to set up ICT-enabled classrooms and develop digital repositories.
2. **Digital India Initiative:**
   - Supports high-speed internet connectivity, e-governance in education, and smart classroom setups.
   - Provides financial assistance to state governments and educational institutions for ICT deployment.

3. **Rashtriya Madhyamik Shiksha Abhiyan (RMSA) and Samagra Shiksha:**
    - These schemes provide funding for ICT labs, computer-assisted learning, and teacher training in government schools.
    - Emphasize bridging the digital divide in rural and remote areas.
4. **Higher Education Funding:**
    - University Grants Commission (UGC) allocates funds to universities for EdTech initiatives, digital libraries, e-learning platforms, and research in educational technology.

2. Public-Private Partnerships (PPP)

Public-private partnerships play a vital role in strengthening EdTech initiatives by leveraging private expertise, technology, and resources:

1. **Collaboration with EdTech Startups:**
    - Startups provide innovative solutions, such as adaptive learning platforms, gamified content, AI-driven assessments, and mobile learning apps.
    - Examples include BYJU'S, Vedantu, Toppr, and Labster, which collaborate with government schools and universities.
2. **Corporate Social Responsibility (CSR) Funding:**
    - Private companies invest in digital infrastructure, teacher training, and educational content development under CSR initiatives.
    - This funding helps enhance ICT access in underserved regions.

3. **EdTech Grants and Competitions:**
    - Corporates and foundations provide grants, awards, and seed funding to innovative EdTech solutions that address challenges in accessibility, engagement, and learning outcomes.

3. Institutional Support and Capacity Building

1. **Universities and Colleges:**
    - Higher education institutions support EdTech initiatives by establishing **ICT cells, digital libraries, and e-learning centers**.
    - Promote research and development in educational technology through dedicated departments and research grants.
2. **Teacher Training Institutions:**
    - Provide continuous professional development programs for educators to integrate technology into pedagogy effectively.
    - Funded workshops, online courses, and digital literacy programs improve teacher capacity in ICT use.
3. **State Education Departments:**
    - Offer technical support, resources, and funding to implement ICT-based initiatives at the school level.
    - Monitor the effective use of grants for digital infrastructure and EdTech content.

4. International and Multilateral Support

India also benefits from international agencies and multilateral organizations for EdTech development:

1. **UNESCO and UNICEF:**
   - Provide funding, technical guidance, and resources for digital education initiatives, particularly for marginalized students.
2. **World Bank and Asian Development Bank (ADB):**
   - Finance large-scale ICT projects, online education platforms, and teacher training programs across Indian states.
3. **Global EdTech Collaborations:**
   - Partnerships with universities and organizations abroad facilitate exchange programs, digital content development, and capacity building.

5. Challenges in Funding and Support

1. **Resource Allocation Gaps:**
   - Limited funds in certain states and rural regions affect equitable implementation.
2. **Sustainability Issues:**
   - Short-term grants may not ensure long-term maintenance of ICT infrastructure.
3. **Monitoring and Accountability:**
   - Effective utilization of funds requires proper oversight and transparent reporting mechanisms.
4. **Digital Divide:**
   - Even with funding, lack of internet access, devices, and digital literacy can hinder ICT adoption.

Chapter 16

Technological Innovations in Higher Education

16.1 MOOCs and Open Educational Resources (OER)

Introduction

Massive Open Online Courses (**MOOCs**) and Open Educational Resources (**OER**) have emerged as transformative tools in global education. They provide accessible, flexible, and high-quality learning opportunities to students, educators, and lifelong learners. MOOCs enable learners to access structured online courses offered by renowned institutions, while OERs provide free digital resources such as textbooks, lecture notes, videos, and interactive modules. Both initiatives align with the growing emphasis on technology-driven education and lifelong learning, making knowledge more inclusive and democratized.

1. MOOCs (Massive Open Online Courses)

Definition:
MOOCs are online courses designed for unlimited participation, accessible through the internet, and typically offered by universities or educational platforms.

Key Features:

1. **Scalability:**
    - MOOCs can serve thousands of learners worldwide simultaneously.
2. **Accessibility:**

  - Learners can access courses anytime, anywhere, using laptops, tablets, or smartphones.
3. **Variety of Subjects:**
  - Courses cover multiple disciplines, including science, technology, arts, humanities, management, and social sciences.
4. **Flexible Learning:**
  - Students can pace their learning according to individual schedules and progress.
5. **Interactive Tools:**
  - Forums, quizzes, peer assessments, and video lectures promote active engagement.

Popular Platforms:

- **Coursera, edX, FutureLearn, NPTEL, SWAYAM** (India)
- Provide certificates, specialization tracks, and professional credentials.

Benefits of MOOCs:

1. **Democratization of Education:**
  - Learners from remote and underprivileged areas can access quality content.
2. **Professional Development:**
  - Teachers, professionals, and students can upgrade skills and gain certifications.
3. **Global Exposure:**
  - Learners interact with peers and instructors from different countries, broadening perspectives.
4. **Cost-Effectiveness:**
  - Many MOOCs are free or low-cost, reducing financial barriers to education.

Challenges of MOOCs:

1. **Completion Rates:**
    - Many learners start but do not complete courses due to lack of motivation or guidance.
2. **Digital Literacy Requirements:**
    - Learners need basic digital skills to navigate platforms effectively.
3. **Limited Personal Interaction:**
    - Large-scale courses may restrict one-on-one interaction with instructors.

2. Open Educational Resources (OER)

Definition:
OER are freely accessible, openly licensed educational materials that can be used, adapted, and shared by educators and learners.

Key Features:

1. **Free Access:**
    - Resources are available online without subscription fees.
2. **Adaptability:**
    - Teachers can customize content to suit local contexts and learner needs.
3. **Variety of Formats:**
    - Includes textbooks, lecture slides, videos, simulations, quizzes, and interactive modules.
4. **Collaboration and Sharing:**
    - Facilitates peer-to-peer sharing and global collaboration among educators.

Global Examples:

- **Khan Academy, MIT OpenCourseWare, OER Commons, OpenLearn**
- In India: **DIKSHA, e-PG Pathshala, NROER**

Benefits of OER:

1. **Equity in Education:**
    - Reduces disparities by providing resources to students and teachers regardless of geography or income.
2. **Teacher Empowerment:**
    - Enables educators to innovate, remix, and improve teaching content.
3. **Encourages Lifelong Learning:**
    - Learners can access materials beyond formal education for self-paced study.
4. **Cost Reduction:**
    - Reduces expenditure on textbooks and learning materials for institutions and students.

Challenges of OER:

1. **Quality Control:**
    - Ensuring accuracy, relevance, and credibility of open resources can be challenging.
2. **Awareness and Training:**
    - Teachers and students need awareness and training to effectively use OER.
3. **Sustainability:**
    - Requires consistent updating and maintenance of resources.

3. Integration of MOOCs and OER in India

1. **Government Initiatives:**
   - **SWAYAM** and **NPTEL** provide MOOCs and OER for school, college, and university students.
   - **DIKSHA** offers OER for school curricula, teacher training, and skill development.
2. **Blended Learning Models:**
   - MOOCs and OER are integrated into classroom teaching to complement face-to-face instruction.
3. **Teacher Professional Development:**
   - Educators use MOOCs and OER to enhance pedagogical skills and stay updated with technological and subject knowledge.
4. **Student-Centric Learning:**
   - Learners use online resources for exam preparation, skill enhancement, and self-paced study.

16.2 Research Trends in Educational Technology (EdTech)

Introduction

Educational Technology (EdTech) has evolved rapidly in the 21st century, transforming teaching, learning, and educational research. The proliferation of digital tools, online platforms, artificial intelligence, and data-driven technologies has created new avenues for educational research. Research in EdTech focuses not only on the effectiveness of technology-mediated learning but also on pedagogical innovations, learner engagement, accessibility, and policy implementation. Understanding research trends helps educators, policymakers, and institutions adopt evidence-based practices and improve educational outcomes.

1. Technology-Enhanced Learning (TEL)

Overview:
Technology-Enhanced Learning refers to the use of digital tools to facilitate, support, and improve learning processes.

Research Focus:

1. **Effectiveness of Digital Tools:**
   - Studies explore how digital simulations, virtual labs, multimedia content, and interactive platforms improve comprehension, retention, and critical thinking.
2. **Student Engagement:**
   - Research evaluates how gamification, adaptive learning, and interactive activities affect motivation, participation, and learning outcomes.
3. **Personalized Learning:**
   - AI-driven adaptive learning systems are studied for their capacity to tailor content to individual learner needs and learning styles.

Examples:

- Use of virtual reality (VR) for immersive science experiments.
- Gamified apps for mathematics and language learning.

2. Online Learning and MOOCs

Overview:
Research in online learning and MOOCs focuses on understanding learner behavior, engagement, and outcomes in virtual environments.

Key Trends:

1. **Learner Analytics:**
    - Studies analyze interaction patterns, completion rates, and assessment performance to optimize course design.
2. **MOOC Effectiveness:**
    - Research investigates how MOOCs contribute to knowledge acquisition, skill development, and employability.
3. **Blended Learning Impact:**
    - Studies compare blended learning models with traditional classrooms to determine effectiveness, retention, and engagement.

Examples:

- Impact of discussion forums on collaborative learning.
- Predictive analytics for identifying at-risk learners in online courses.

3. Mobile Learning (m-Learning)

Overview:
Mobile learning leverages smartphones, tablets, and educational apps to provide anytime, anywhere learning.

Research Focus:

1. **Accessibility and Inclusivity:**
   - Studies explore how mobile learning addresses the needs of learners in remote or underprivileged regions.
2. **Microlearning:**
   - Research examines the effectiveness of short, focused learning modules delivered via mobile platforms.
3. **Engagement Strategies:**
   - Studies evaluate notifications, gamification, and interactive apps to enhance motivation and sustained learning.

Examples:

- Language learning apps like Duolingo and their impact on proficiency.
- Mobile-based quizzes for formative assessment in schools.

4. Artificial Intelligence and Adaptive Learning

Overview:
AI is increasingly being integrated into EdTech to provide personalized learning experiences and automated assessment.

Research Trends:

1. **Adaptive Learning Systems:**
   - Studies explore algorithms that adjust content difficulty, pace, and instructional strategies based on learner performance.
2. **Intelligent Tutoring Systems:**

    - Research investigates AI tutors' ability to guide learners individually and provide immediate feedback.
3. **Predictive Analytics:**
    - Research uses data to predict student outcomes and suggest interventions for improving learning success.

Examples:

- AI-driven math problem solvers.
- Systems predicting student dropout in MOOCs or online courses.

5. Gamification and Game-Based Learning

Overview:
Gamification integrates game elements such as points, badges, and leaderboards into learning environments, while game-based learning uses actual educational games.

Research Focus:

1. **Motivation and Engagement:**
    - Studies assess how gamified elements increase learner participation and intrinsic motivation.
2. **Learning Outcomes:**
    - Research evaluates cognitive gains, skill development, and retention achieved through games.
3. **Design Strategies:**
    - Effective integration of narrative, challenges, and feedback in learning games is a key research area.

Examples:

- Interactive simulations for science experiments.
- History-based adventure games to teach critical thinking and decision-making.

6. Data Analytics in Education (Learning Analytics)

Overview:
Learning analytics uses data from digital platforms to analyze learning behavior and outcomes.

Research Trends:

1. **Student Progress Monitoring:**
   - Studies track performance patterns, engagement, and learning trajectories.
2. **Intervention Strategies:**
   - Research investigates early identification of struggling students and personalized interventions.
3. **Feedback Mechanisms:**
   - Effective feedback loops using analytics to guide learners are increasingly studied.

Examples:

- Dashboards that provide teachers with real-time performance insights.
- Predictive modeling for dropout prevention.

7. Emerging Research Areas

1. **Virtual Reality (VR) and Augmented Reality (AR):**
   - Investigating immersive learning environments for enhanced engagement and experiential learning.

2. **Inclusive Technology:**
   - Research on assistive technologies for differently-abled learners.
3. **Ethics in EdTech:**
   - Data privacy, AI ethics, and equitable access are becoming critical research areas.

16.3 Industry-Academia Collaborations in Educational Technology

Introduction

Industry-academia collaborations have become a critical component in the development and adoption of Educational Technology (EdTech). By linking educational institutions with technology companies, startups, and research organizations, these collaborations bridge the gap between academic research, practical applications, and real-world workforce requirements. They enable innovation, skill development, and the creation of cutting-edge tools that enhance teaching, learning, and assessment.

1. Importance of Industry-Academia Collaborations

1. **Bridging Skill Gaps:**
   - Collaborations ensure that students acquire skills that align with current industry needs, particularly in digital literacy, coding, AI, and data analytics.
   - Industry partners provide insights into emerging trends, ensuring curriculum relevance.
2. **Innovation and Research:**
   - Joint research projects between universities and tech companies lead to the development of innovative

EdTech tools, adaptive learning systems, VR/AR applications, and AI-driven platforms.
   - Universities gain access to resources, labs, and expertise to test and refine educational technologies.
3. **Enhanced Employability:**
   - Exposure to industry tools and projects prepares students for the workforce.
   - Internship and mentorship programs provide practical experience alongside theoretical knowledge.
4. **Teacher Professional Development:**
   - Educators gain training in the latest technologies, software, and pedagogical approaches, which can then be implemented in classrooms.

2. Forms of Collaboration

1. **Joint Research and Development (R&D):**
   - Universities and EdTech companies collaborate to design innovative digital learning resources.
   - Examples include developing AI-driven adaptive learning platforms, VR laboratories, and interactive simulations.
2. **Curriculum Co-Design:**
   - Industry experts assist in designing courses that integrate current technological trends, such as AI, coding, data analytics, and gamification.
   - Co-created syllabi ensure alignment between educational objectives and workplace competencies.
3. **Internships and Experiential Learning:**
   - Industry partners provide internships, project-based learning, and hands-on workshops.

    - Students gain practical exposure to EdTech tools and real-world problem-solving.
4. **Funding and Grants:**
    - Companies often provide financial support for research projects, EdTech labs, and pilot implementations in educational institutions.
    - Grants encourage innovation in adaptive learning, gamification, and online learning platforms.
5. **Professional Development and Workshops:**
    - Industry experts conduct workshops, training sessions, and webinars for educators on emerging EdTech tools and methodologies.

3. Global Examples of Successful Collaborations

1. **United States:**
    - MIT and Harvard collaborate with EdTech startups to develop MOOCs (e.g., edX platform) and AI-driven personalized learning systems.
    - Google for Education partners with universities for professional development programs and digital skill training.
2. **Finland:**
    - EdTech companies collaborate with schools to implement interactive digital curricula, promoting student-centered and project-based learning.
3. **Singapore:**
    - Industry-academia collaborations drive national EdTech innovation, providing VR/AR labs and AI-enabled learning analytics platforms in schools and universities.
4. **India:**

- **SWAYAM and NPTEL**: Universities partner with tech companies to develop and host MOOCs.
- EdTech startups such as BYJU'S, Toppr, and Vedantu collaborate with educational institutions to provide content, tools, and teacher training.
- Industry-sponsored labs and incubation centers in universities promote EdTech research and entrepreneurship.

4. Benefits to Students and Institutions

1. **Enhanced Learning Experiences:**
   - Access to state-of-the-art EdTech tools, VR/AR labs, and simulation environments.
   - Exposure to project-based learning and real-world applications.
2. **Research and Innovation Opportunities:**
   - Students and faculty engage in research that drives technological innovation in education.
   - Institutions gain recognition for pioneering EdTech solutions.
3. **Skill Development and Employability:**
   - Students acquire industry-relevant skills, improving employability in technology-driven sectors.
4. **Sustainability and Resource Sharing:**
   - Collaborations enable cost-effective implementation of digital infrastructure and EdTech resources through shared expertise and funding.

5. Challenges in Industry-Academia Collaborations

1. **Alignment of Goals:**

   - Academic objectives and industry priorities may differ, requiring careful negotiation to balance innovation with pedagogical relevance.
2. **Data Privacy and Ethics:**
   - Student data usage in EdTech platforms must comply with legal and ethical standards.
3. **Sustainability of Partnerships:**
   - Long-term collaborations need consistent engagement, funding, and strategic planning.
4. **Digital Divide:**
   - Ensuring equitable access to technology for all students, particularly in rural and marginalized areas, remains a challenge.

16.4 Case Studies from Universities in Educational Technology

Introduction

Educational technology (EdTech) has become a cornerstone in modern higher education, facilitating personalized learning, expanding access, and enhancing teaching methodologies. Universities worldwide have implemented various EdTech initiatives, yielding valuable insights into the integration of technology in academic settings. This section explores several case studies from diverse institutions, highlighting their approaches, challenges, and outcomes in adopting educational technologies.

1. University of Chicago – Personalised Adaptive Learning (PAL) Program

Overview:

The University of Chicago's Development Innovation Lab evaluated Andhra Pradesh's PAL program, which utilized adaptive learning technologies to personalize education for students in government schools.

Implementation:

- **Technology Used:** Adaptive learning platforms tailored to individual student needs.
- **Scale:** Initiated in 60 schools in 2018, expanded to 1,224 schools across all 26 districts.
- **Partnerships:** Collaboration with the Central Square Foundation and ConveGenius for content and technology delivery.

Outcomes:

- **Learning Gains:** Students in PAL schools achieved learning gains equivalent to 1.9 additional years within 17 months.
- **Equity:** Improvements were consistent across all grade levels, with younger students showing especially notable progress.

Lessons Learned:

- Combining evidence-based technology with effective governance can significantly enhance educational outcomes.
- Scalability of EdTech initiatives is feasible with proper planning and support.

2. Arizona State University – Adaptive Courseware Implementation

Overview:

Arizona State University (ASU) integrated adaptive courseware to improve student engagement and success in gateway courses.

Implementation:

- **Technology Used:** Adaptive learning platforms providing personalized learning pathways.
- **Faculty Involvement:** Intensive coaching and professional development for instructors.
- **Support Structures:** Collaborative learning and networking opportunities for institutional teams.

Outcomes:

- **Student Success:** Increased pass rates and reduced achievement gaps in targeted courses.
- **Faculty Feedback:** Positive reception towards adaptive learning tools, with reports of enhanced teaching effectiveness.

Lessons Learned:

- Faculty development is crucial for the successful adoption of adaptive learning technologies.
- Institutional support and collaboration are key to scaling EdTech initiatives effectively.

3. Stanford University – Mobile Inquiry-Based Learning Environment (SMILE)

Overview:

Stanford University developed the SMILE platform to promote inquiry-based learning through mobile technology.

Implementation:

- **Technology Used:** Mobile application facilitating student-generated questions and peer evaluations.
- **Pedagogical Approach:** Encouraged higher-order thinking skills such as analysis, evaluation, and creation.
- **Data Analytics:** Real-time learning analytics provided insights into student engagement and understanding.

Outcomes:

- **Student Engagement:** Increased active participation and critical thinking among students.
- **Teacher Insights:** Enhanced ability to identify learning gaps and provide timely interventions.

Lessons Learned:

- Mobile technology can effectively support inquiry-based learning models.
- Real-time analytics are valuable for adaptive teaching strategies.

4. University of Helsinki – Digital Pedagogy and Learning Analytics

Overview:

The University of Helsinki implemented digital pedagogy strategies supported by learning analytics to improve teaching and learning outcomes.

Implementation:

- **Technology Used:** Learning management systems integrated with analytics tools.
- **Faculty Training:** Professional development programs focused on data-driven teaching practices.
- **Student Support:** Personalized feedback mechanisms based on analytics data.

Outcomes:

- **Teaching Effectiveness:** Improved instructional strategies through data-informed decisions.
- **Student Performance:** Enhanced student outcomes due to targeted interventions.

Lessons Learned:

- Learning analytics can inform and improve pedagogical practices.
- Ongoing faculty development is essential for maximizing the potential of digital pedagogy.

5. University of Melbourne – Blended Learning Model

Overview:

The University of Melbourne adopted a blended learning approach to integrate online and face-to-face learning experiences.

Implementation:

- **Technology Used:** Online platforms for content delivery and collaboration.
- **Course Design:** Courses structured to combine in-person lectures with online discussions and activities.
- **Assessment Methods:** Incorporation of both online quizzes and traditional examinations.

Outcomes:

- **Student Satisfaction:** High levels of student engagement and satisfaction with the blended model.
- **Learning Outcomes:** Improved academic performance and deeper learning experiences.

Lessons Learned:

- Blended learning can offer flexibility and enhance learning experiences.
- Effective integration requires careful planning and alignment of online and offline components.

6. Indian Institute of Technology (IIT) Bombay – SWAYAM and NPTEL Courses

Overview:

IIT Bombay contributed to the development of SWAYAM and NPTEL platforms to provide online education to a broader audience.

Implementation:

- **Technology Used:** Online course platforms offering video lectures, assignments, and certifications.
- **Course Offerings:** Wide range of courses in engineering, sciences, and humanities.
- **Collaborations:** Partnerships with other IITs and institutions to create diverse content.

Outcomes:

- **Access to Education:** Increased access to quality education for learners across India.
- **Recognition:** Enhanced reputation of IIT Bombay as a leader in online education.

Lessons Learned:

- Online platforms can democratize access to education.
- Collaborative efforts enhance the quality and reach of online courses.

7. Community College of Qatar – Hybrid Learning with Technology-Rich Instructional Tools

Overview:

The Community College of Qatar (CCQ) implemented a hybrid learning model integrating technology-rich instructional tools.

Implementation:

- **Technology Used:** Interactive tools and platforms to support both in-person and online learning.

- **Course Delivery:** Combination of traditional lectures and digital content.
- **Feedback Mechanisms:** Use of technology to gather student feedback and adjust teaching methods.

Outcomes:

- **Student Engagement:** Increased student interaction and participation.
- **Teaching Adaptability:** Enhanced ability to adapt teaching strategies based on feedback.

Lessons Learned:

- Hybrid learning models can be effective when supported by appropriate technologies.
- Continuous feedback is crucial for improving teaching and learning experiences.

16.5 Preparing Students for Future Careers through Educational Technology

Introduction

The rapid technological advancements in the 21st century have transformed the landscape of work. Careers now demand digital literacy, critical thinking, adaptability, and problem-solving skills. Educational Technology (EdTech) plays a pivotal role in preparing students to meet these evolving requirements. By integrating technology into teaching and learning, institutions can equip learners with the skills, competencies, and mindset needed for future careers across industries.

1. Enhancing Digital Literacy and 21st-Century Skills

Overview:

Digital literacy is the foundational skill for future-ready careers. EdTech tools enable students to develop competencies in technology use, data handling, communication, and collaboration.

Applications:

1. **Coding and Computational Thinking:**
   - Platforms like Code.org, Scratch, and GitHub Learning Lab allow students to develop programming skills and problem-solving abilities.
2. **Digital Communication and Collaboration:**
   - Tools such as Microsoft Teams, Zoom, and Google Workspace enhance collaboration in real-time, preparing students for virtual work environments.
3. **Critical Thinking and Problem-Solving:**
   - Gamified learning and simulation tools promote analytical thinking and decision-making skills.

Impact:

- Students gain confidence in using technology effectively.
- Skills acquired align with industry requirements, enhancing employability.

2. Career-Oriented Learning through Online Platforms

Overview:

Online learning platforms, MOOCs, and certification courses bridge the gap between academic learning and industry expectations.

Applications:

1. **MOOCs and Skill-Based Courses:**
    - Platforms such as Coursera, edX, and Udemy offer specialized courses in AI, data analytics, digital marketing, and entrepreneurship.
2. **Certification Programs:**
    - Industry-recognized certificates validate skills, making students more competitive in job markets.
3. **Microlearning Modules:**
    - Short, focused lessons enable learners to acquire specific skills in a time-efficient manner.

Impact:

- Students can tailor learning pathways based on career interests.
- Enhances lifelong learning habits and professional adaptability.

3. Internship and Industry Collaboration Opportunities

Overview:
Hands-on experience in real-world settings is critical for career readiness. EdTech facilitates internships, virtual labs, and industry projects.

Applications:

1. **Virtual Internships and Simulations:**
    - Platforms like Forage and virtual labs allow students to practice real-world tasks in a controlled environment.

2. **Project-Based Learning:**
    - Industry-linked projects foster application of knowledge and problem-solving in professional contexts.
3. **Mentorship Programs:**
    - EdTech platforms connect students with industry experts for guidance, feedback, and networking opportunities.

Impact:

- Students develop practical skills and professional competencies.
- Exposure to workplace culture and expectations enhances career preparedness.

4. Leveraging Artificial Intelligence and Adaptive Learning

Overview:
AI-driven tools provide personalized learning experiences, helping students focus on skill gaps and strengths.

Applications:

1. **Adaptive Learning Platforms:**
    - Systems like Smart Sparrow or ALEKS tailor content based on individual performance.
2. **AI Career Guidance:**
    - AI-powered platforms provide recommendations for skill development, suitable courses, and career pathways.

3. **Predictive Analytics:**
    - Analytics help identify students' strengths and weaknesses, enabling targeted support for career readiness.

Impact:

- Personalized learning pathways improve skill acquisition efficiency.
- Students make informed decisions about career trajectories based on data-driven insights.

5. Developing Soft Skills through Technology

Overview:
Beyond technical knowledge, soft skills like communication, teamwork, adaptability, and emotional intelligence are vital for future careers. EdTech supports development of these competencies.

Applications:

1. **Collaborative Platforms:**
    - Tools like Trello, Slack, and Miro enhance teamwork and project management skills.
2. **Virtual Role-Playing and Simulations:**
    - Platforms simulate workplace scenarios to practice negotiation, conflict resolution, and decision-making.
3. **Online Workshops and Webinars:**
    - Interactive sessions improve presentation, communication, and leadership skills.

Impact:

- Students acquire transferable skills valued in all industries.
- Increases employability and professional adaptability.

6. Promoting Lifelong Learning and Career Adaptability

Overview:
The dynamic nature of the job market requires continuous learning. EdTech encourages self-directed and lifelong learning habits.

Applications:

1. **Continuous Learning Platforms:**
   - LinkedIn Learning and Khan Academy provide ongoing skill enhancement opportunities.
2. **Digital Portfolios:**
   - Platforms like Portfolium allow students to showcase skills, projects, and achievements to prospective employers.
3. **Micro-credentialing:**
   - Badges and short-term credentials validate new skills acquired in emerging fields.

Impact:

- Students remain adaptable to changing industry demands.
- Supports career mobility and professional growth.

7. Case Examples

1. **Stanford University:**
   - Integrates AI, coding, and entrepreneurship courses with industry mentorship, preparing students for technology-driven careers.

2. **Indian Institute of Technology (IIT), Bombay:**
   - Offers SWAYAM/NPTEL courses combined with internships, projects, and industry collaborations for practical exposure.
3. **Massachusetts Institute of Technology (MIT):**
   - Emphasizes problem-solving through open-access resources, virtual labs, and collaborative learning platforms.

Chapter 17

Technology for Administrative Support in Education

17.1 School and College Management Systems

Introduction

In today's educational landscape, managing schools and colleges efficiently has become increasingly complex due to growing student populations, diverse curricula, regulatory requirements, and the need for seamless communication among stakeholders. School and College Management Systems (SCMS) leverage technology to streamline administrative tasks, enhance academic planning, improve communication, and ensure transparency. These systems play a critical role in ensuring that educational institutions operate effectively while providing better experiences for students, teachers, and administrators alike.

1. What are School and College Management Systems (SCMS)?

A School and College Management System is a comprehensive software platform designed to automate and manage various administrative, academic, and communication tasks within educational institutions. These systems integrate functionalities related to student records, attendance tracking, timetable creation, fee management, examination processing, communication, and reporting.

SCMS can be cloud-based or installed locally and often feature dashboards that allow users to access relevant information easily.

These platforms are scalable and can be customized according to the needs of schools, colleges, or universities.

2. Key Features of School and College Management Systems

1. **Student Information Management:**
    - Maintains a centralized database of student profiles, including personal details, academic records, attendance, health information, and extracurricular achievements.
    - Enables easy access and updates while ensuring data security.
2. **Attendance Tracking:**
    - Automates attendance monitoring using biometric devices, RFID cards, or manual entries through apps and portals.
    - Generates attendance reports for teachers, students, and parents.
3. **Timetable and Scheduling:**
    - Helps create and manage class schedules, exam timetables, and faculty workloads.
    - Alerts users to conflicts and enables optimization based on available resources.
4. **Fee Management:**
    - Streamlines fee collection, invoicing, and financial reporting.
    - Supports online payments, auto reminders, and installment planning.
5. **Examination and Assessment Management:**
    - Facilitates the creation of question papers, exam scheduling, evaluation, and result generation.

- Provides analytics to track student performance over time.

6. **Communication Tools:**
   - Integrates messaging systems for announcements, notices, event calendars, and parent-teacher communication.
   - Supports mobile apps, SMS alerts, and emails for effective communication.
7. **Library and Resource Management:**
   - Manages book inventories, issue/return logs, and online catalogues.
   - Provides access to e-books, journals, and other learning resources.
8. **Human Resource and Payroll:**
   - Tracks faculty records, attendance, leaves, and payroll processing.
   - Integrates with other administrative tasks to enhance efficiency.
9. **Analytics and Reporting:**
   - Provides dashboards and reports on academic performance, attendance patterns, financial health, and other key metrics.
   - Supports informed decision-making by administrators.

3. Benefits of Implementing SCMS

1. **Enhanced Efficiency:**
   - Automating repetitive administrative tasks saves time and reduces manual errors.
2. **Improved Academic Planning:**

- Timetable management and real-time attendance tracking help optimize teaching schedules.

3. **Better Communication:**
   - Integrated communication tools ensure timely information flow among students, parents, teachers, and administrators.
4. **Transparency and Accountability:**
   - Centralized data management allows institutions to maintain records securely and audit processes when needed.
5. **Cost and Resource Management:**
   - Digital fee collection and resource tracking help control expenses and streamline budgeting.
6. **Student-Centric Approach:**
   - Personalized dashboards, progress tracking, and parent notifications enhance the learning experience.

4. Popular School and College Management Systems

1. **Fedena:**
   - A user-friendly platform widely used in schools and colleges for attendance, exams, fee management, and communications.
2. **Educomp:**
   - Offers cloud-based management solutions that integrate learning content, assessments, and administration.
3. **OpenSIS:**
   - Open-source platform designed for schools and higher education institutions with customizable modules.
4. **Talisma:**

- Provides CRM solutions along with academic and administrative management tools.

5. **ThinkWave:**
   - Offers grading, attendance, and parent communication tools aimed at K-12 schools.

5. Challenges in Implementing SCMS

1. **Cost of Implementation:**
   - Advanced systems may be expensive, requiring investment in hardware, software, and training.
2. **Data Security and Privacy:**
   - Managing sensitive information like student records and financial data requires robust security measures.
3. **Resistance to Change:**
   - Teachers and administrators accustomed to manual processes may be hesitant to adopt new technology.
4. **Internet and Infrastructure Issues:**
   - Schools and colleges in remote areas may struggle with connectivity or access to digital devices.

6. Best Practices for Successful SCMS Implementation

1. **Training and Support:**
   - Conduct workshops and provide technical support to help users navigate the system.
2. **Phased Implementation:**
   - Start with core modules like attendance and fee management before expanding to other functionalities.
3. **Data Backup and Security:**

- Implement secure servers, encryption, and periodic backups to protect sensitive information.

4. **Feedback Mechanisms:**
   - Regularly gather feedback from teachers, students, and parents to improve usability.

17.2 Attendance Tracking and Scheduling

Introduction

Efficient attendance tracking and scheduling are critical components of school and college management. These systems help ensure that students are present for classes, allow teachers to monitor participation, and facilitate academic planning. Technology-driven solutions for attendance and scheduling have revolutionized administrative processes by making them more accurate, automated, and accessible. By reducing manual tasks, improving transparency, and enabling real-time updates, these systems enhance teaching effectiveness and student engagement while ensuring compliance with regulatory standards.

1. Importance of Attendance Tracking

Attendance is more than just a record of presence. It is an important indicator of student engagement, discipline, and academic performance. Irregular attendance can be linked to poor academic outcomes, low motivation, and other underlying issues such as health concerns or socio-economic challenges.

Key reasons attendance tracking is essential:

1. **Monitoring Student Participation:**

   - Helps teachers and administrators identify patterns in absenteeism.
2. **Enhancing Academic Performance:**
   - Regular attendance correlates with better comprehension and learning outcomes.
3. **Ensuring Compliance:**
   - Helps institutions maintain records required by educational boards and accreditation bodies.
4. **Supporting Student Welfare:**
   - Early identification of attendance gaps can prompt counseling or interventions.

2. Technology-Driven Attendance Systems

Modern attendance tracking systems use a combination of hardware and software to automate attendance recording. These systems are scalable, secure, and adaptable to different institutional needs.

A. Biometric Attendance Systems

- **How It Works:** Students and staff use fingerprint or facial recognition devices to mark attendance.
- **Benefits:**
  - Eliminates proxy attendance.
  - Ensures accuracy.
  - Provides real-time attendance data.
- **Challenges:**
  - Requires investment in hardware.
  - May face privacy concerns if data protection measures are not robust.

B. RFID and Smart Cards

- **How It Works:** Students carry RFID cards that are scanned upon entry and exit.
- **Benefits:**
  - Quick and non-intrusive.
  - Integrates with other campus facilities such as libraries and laboratories.
- **Challenges:**
  - Risk of card misuse if lost or stolen.

C. Mobile App Attendance

- **How It Works:** Students mark attendance through mobile applications using GPS verification or QR codes.
- **Benefits:**
  - Convenient and flexible.
  - Supports remote or hybrid learning scenarios.
- **Challenges:**
  - Depends on smartphone availability and internet connectivity.

D. Web Portals and Learning Management Systems (LMS)

- **How It Works:** Attendance is tracked within LMS platforms where students check in during virtual classes.
- **Benefits:**
  - Useful for online or blended learning environments.
  - Offers integrated academic reports.
- **Challenges:**
  - Requires reliable internet access and student discipline.

3. Features of an Ideal Attendance Tracking System

1. **Real-Time Monitoring:**
   - Immediate updates on attendance status.
2. **Automated Reports:**
   - Generates daily, weekly, or monthly attendance summaries for teachers and administrators.
3. **Alerts and Notifications:**
   - Sends reminders to students with low attendance.
   - Informs parents or guardians about absenteeism.
4. **Integration with Academic Systems:**
   - Links attendance data to gradebooks and learning analytics for holistic monitoring.
5. **Data Security and Privacy:**
   - Ensures encryption and secure storage of sensitive information.

4. Scheduling in Educational Institutions

Scheduling involves planning class times, examination schedules, faculty allocation, and student timetables. It ensures that academic and extracurricular activities are structured efficiently, avoiding conflicts and maximizing the use of available resources.

Key aspects of scheduling:

1. **Timetable Creation:**
   - Defines when classes, labs, and exams will be held.
2. **Faculty Assignment:**
   - Matches teachers to courses based on expertise and availability.
3. **Resource Allocation:**

- Ensures classrooms, laboratories, and other facilities are appropriately assigned.

4. **Flexibility:**
   - Provides options for hybrid classes, elective courses, and personalized learning paths.

5. Technology Solutions for Scheduling

A. Automated Timetable Software

- Uses algorithms to generate optimized schedules based on constraints such as teacher availability, student electives, and classroom capacity.

B. Cloud-Based Scheduling Tools

- Enables real-time sharing of schedules with students and faculty.
- Supports dynamic changes in case of emergencies or adjustments.

C. Integration with Attendance Systems

- Ensures that schedules are aligned with attendance monitoring, making it easier to track absences and follow-up interventions.

6. Benefits of Technology-Based Scheduling

1. **Efficient Use of Resources:**
   - Reduces idle time and optimizes classroom usage.
2. **Improved Academic Planning:**

- Helps teachers align content delivery with available periods and learning objectives.

3. **Transparency:**
   - Students and faculty can access updated schedules anytime, reducing confusion.
4. **Support for Hybrid Models:**
   - Allows institutions to design flexible schedules that accommodate both in-person and online learning.

7. Challenges in Attendance and Scheduling Systems

1. **Infrastructure Constraints:**
   - Schools and colleges in remote areas may lack reliable internet access or devices.
2. **Privacy Concerns:**
   - Handling biometric data or location tracking requires strict adherence to data protection laws.
3. **Resistance to Adoption:**
   - Teachers and administrators may be hesitant to replace traditional methods with technology-driven systems.
4. **Integration Issues:**
   - Different platforms may not communicate seamlessly, requiring technical expertise.

8. Best Practices for Implementation

1. **Pilot Testing:**
   - Start with a small group before full-scale implementation.
2. **User Training:**

    - Provide workshops and support for teachers, students, and administrative staff.
3. **Data Protection:**
    - Implement secure storage and encryption protocols.
4. **Feedback Loops:**
    - Regularly collect user feedback and make adjustments to the system.
5. **Compliance:**
    - Ensure that the system adheres to regional and international data protection regulations.

17.3 Digital Libraries and Resource Repositories

Introduction

Digital libraries and resource repositories have become essential tools in modern educational ecosystems. With advancements in information and communication technology (ICT), these platforms provide seamless access to a vast collection of academic resources, e-books, journals, research papers, multimedia content, and learning materials. By offering anytime, anywhere access, they enhance the learning experience, promote self-directed learning, and support educators in designing more effective instructional strategies. These systems are particularly beneficial in schools and colleges, where students and faculty require reliable, updated, and curated academic resources.

1. What are Digital Libraries and Resource Repositories?

A **digital library** is an online collection of digital resources such as books, research articles, journals, audio-visual material, and databases that can be accessed electronically. A **resource**

repository refers to a structured digital archive that stores and manages educational content, instructional tools, and supplementary learning materials.

These platforms are accessible via computers, tablets, and smartphones and are designed to be user-friendly, searchable, and interactive. Many educational institutions partner with national or international digital library services to expand access and ensure quality.

2. Key Features of Digital Libraries and Resource Repositories

1. **Search and Retrieval Tools:**
   - Advanced search filters help users locate resources by topic, author, publication date, and keywords.
2. **Curated Collections:**
   - Organized into categories such as subject-specific content, research papers, case studies, and learning modules.
3. **Multimedia Integration:**
   - Includes videos, audio recordings, interactive simulations, and visual diagrams alongside text-based resources.
4. **Access Controls and Permissions:**
   - Secure login credentials ensure that only authorized users can access certain materials, while public resources are freely available.
5. **User-Friendly Interfaces:**
   - Designed with intuitive navigation, bookmarking, and annotation tools for personalized learning experiences.

6. **Offline Access and Download Options:**
    - Some platforms offer downloadable content, enabling access even without internet connectivity.

3. Benefits of Digital Libraries and Resource Repositories

1. **Improved Accessibility:**
    - Students and teachers can access a wide range of academic materials anytime and from any location.
2. **Enhanced Learning Opportunities:**
    - Facilitates self-paced learning by providing diverse formats such as videos, lectures, and interactive exercises.
3. **Cost-Effective:**
    - Reduces the need for expensive textbooks and print resources, making education more affordable.
4. **Promotes Research and Collaboration:**
    - Offers access to scholarly articles and datasets, encouraging research-oriented learning and peer collaboration.
5. **Supports Inclusive Learning:**
    - Helps students with different learning styles through multimedia resources and assistive technologies.

4. Examples of Digital Libraries and Repositories

1. **National Digital Library of India (NDLI):**
    - A comprehensive platform providing access to millions of academic resources from primary school to postgraduate levels, covering subjects such as science, engineering, humanities, and social sciences.
2. **Directory of Open Access Journals (DOAJ):**

- A global repository of peer-reviewed open-access journals available for research and reference.

3. **Project Gutenberg:**
   - Offers over 60,000 free e-books, including classical literature, reference works, and historical texts.
4. **JSTOR and IEEE Xplore:**
   - Provide access to scholarly articles and technical research papers, particularly useful for higher education and research-oriented learning.
5. **Institutional Repositories:**
   - Many universities host their own digital libraries where theses, dissertations, faculty research, and teaching materials are archived.

5. Role of Digital Libraries in Teaching and Learning

1. **Supplementing Curriculum:**
   - Educators can enrich classroom lessons by referencing additional material available in digital libraries.
2. **Encouraging Independent Learning:**
   - Students can explore topics of interest beyond the syllabus, promoting curiosity and critical thinking.
3. **Supporting Assessment and Assignments:**
   - Provides credible sources for essays, projects, and research assignments.
4. **Fostering Interdisciplinary Learning:**
   - Access to resources from diverse fields encourages cross-disciplinary exploration and innovation.

6. Challenges in Implementing Digital Libraries

1. **Digital Divide:**
    - Students in remote areas or underprivileged communities may lack internet access or digital devices.
2. **Copyright and Licensing Issues:**
    - Ensuring that digital content is legally accessible while respecting intellectual property rights remains a concern.
3. **Technical Literacy:**
    - Some users may require training to effectively navigate digital libraries.
4. **Content Curation and Quality Control:**
    - Institutions must ensure that the available resources are accurate, relevant, and up to date.

7. Best Practices for Effective Use of Digital Libraries

1. **Training Programs:**
    - Conduct workshops to familiarize students and teachers with search tools, navigation, and academic referencing.
2. **Integration with Learning Management Systems (LMS):**
    - Embedding digital libraries within LMS platforms allows seamless access to resources linked with course content.
3. **Regular Updates:**
    - Continuously update and expand the library's collections to include new research, journals, and textbooks.
4. **Collaboration with Academic Networks:**
    - Partner with other institutions and global repositories to enhance resource sharing and exchange.

5. **Ensuring Accessibility:**
    - Provide options such as text-to-speech tools, adjustable fonts, and translation features for students with special needs.

8. Future Trends

1. **AI-Powered Search:**
    - Artificial intelligence will further refine search capabilities, recommending personalized resources based on user preferences.
2. **Integration with Virtual and Augmented Reality:**
    - Immersive learning environments will make accessing and interacting with content more engaging.
3. **Data Analytics for Resource Utilization:**
    - Insights from user interactions will help educators understand how resources are being used and which materials are most effective.
4. **Global Educational Networks:**
    - Universities and schools are increasingly collaborating on global platforms, ensuring knowledge sharing and resource accessibility worldwide.

17.4 Communication Tools for Educational Institutions

Introduction

Effective communication is the backbone of any educational institution. Whether it's sharing academic information, coordinating administrative tasks, engaging with parents, or supporting students, seamless communication plays a vital role in ensuring the smooth functioning of schools and colleges. Technological advancements have revolutionized communication by offering diverse digital tools that enable instant, transparent, and efficient interactions. Communication tools not only facilitate academic and administrative processes but also foster a collaborative learning environment and strengthen relationships among all stakeholders—students, teachers, parents, and administrators.

1. Importance of Communication in Educational Institutions

1. **Enhancing Academic Collaboration:**
   - Facilitates coordination between teachers, students, and departments for lesson planning, projects, and assessments.
2. **Administrative Efficiency:**
   - Improves workflow by streamlining tasks like attendance updates, scheduling, notices, and fee management.
3. **Parental Involvement:**
   - Keeps parents informed about student performance, school activities, and upcoming events, thus promoting accountability.
4. **Student Support:**
   - Provides avenues for mentoring, counseling, and academic assistance through digital channels.
5. **Crisis Management:**
   - Enables quick dissemination of information during emergencies, health advisories, or schedule changes.

2. Types of Communication Tools

A. Email Platforms

- **Usage:**
  - Used for formal communication, sharing academic documents, reports, circulars, and announcements.
- **Benefits:**
  - Provides a written record, supports attachments, and allows mass communication.

B. Learning Management Systems (LMS)

- **Usage:**
  - Tools like Google Classroom, Moodle, and Canvas provide integrated communication features such as forums, message boards, announcements, and notifications.
- **Benefits:**
  - Centralizes communication and connects academic activities with resources.

C. Instant Messaging Apps

- **Usage:**
  - Platforms like WhatsApp, Telegram, and Microsoft Teams enable informal or quick communication for class updates, reminders, and group discussions.
- **Benefits:**
  - Supports real-time interaction and multimedia sharing (images, videos, documents).

D. Video Conferencing Tools

- **Usage:**

- Tools like Zoom, Google Meet, and Microsoft Teams allow virtual classes, webinars, faculty meetings, and parent-teacher conferences.

- **Benefits:**
    - Overcomes geographical barriers, supports remote learning, and encourages interactive participation.

E. Notice Boards and Portals

- **Usage:**
    - Digital notice boards and portals display schedules, exam dates, academic achievements, and administrative notices.
- **Benefits:**
    - Offers consistent access to important information without manual intervention.

F. Feedback and Survey Tools

- **Usage:**
    - Google Forms, SurveyMonkey, and Typeform are used to collect feedback from students, parents, and staff regarding academic quality, infrastructure, or events.
- **Benefits:**
    - Encourages open dialogue and helps institutions gather insights for improvement.

3. Features of Effective Communication Tools

1. **User-Friendly Interfaces:**
    - Tools should be intuitive and easy to navigate for users of all ages and tech proficiency levels.

2. **Integration with Academic Systems:**
    - Communication tools work best when linked with attendance records, grading systems, and scheduling platforms.
3. **Multilingual Support:**
    - Offering communication in multiple languages ensures inclusivity and better understanding.
4. **Real-Time Updates:**
    - Immediate notifications and alerts keep students and staff informed.
5. **Data Privacy and Security:**
    - Secure login credentials, encryption, and access controls protect sensitive information.
6. **Collaboration Features:**
    - Forums, discussion boards, and chatrooms support academic dialogue and teamwork.

4. Benefits of Using Communication Tools

1. **Improved Engagement:**
    - Students are more likely to participate when they receive regular updates and reminders.
2. **Streamlined Processes:**
    - Scheduling, assessments, and announcements can be automated, reducing administrative workload.
3. **Enhanced Transparency:**
    - Academic and administrative information is accessible to all stakeholders, promoting trust and accountability.
4. **Better Decision Making:**

  - Feedback tools enable institutions to make data-driven decisions for improving teaching, learning, and infrastructure.
5. **Support for Remote and Hybrid Learning:**
  - Communication tools ensure that students and teachers remain connected, even outside the physical classroom.

5. Challenges in Communication Tools Implementation

1. **Digital Literacy Gaps:**
  - Not all users may be comfortable navigating new tools, requiring training and support.
2. **Connectivity Issues:**
  - Poor internet access in certain regions can hinder real-time communication.
3. **Data Security Risks:**
  - Mishandling of personal information can lead to breaches and privacy concerns.
4. **Overload of Information:**
  - Excessive notifications or messages can overwhelm students and teachers.

6. Best Practices for Effective Communication

1. **Training and Orientation:**
  - Conduct sessions to teach users how to utilize communication tools effectively.
2. **Clear Communication Policies:**
  - Define protocols on how and when information should be shared to avoid confusion.
3. **Feedback Mechanisms:**

- Encourage users to share their experiences and suggestions for tool improvement.

4. **Balanced Usage:**
   - Avoid sending unnecessary alerts while ensuring that important information reaches everyone.
5. **Data Protection Measures:**
   - Implement strict security guidelines to protect sensitive student and staff information.

7. Future Trends in Educational Communication Tools

1. **Artificial Intelligence (AI) Integration:**
   - AI can automate responses, schedule updates, and predict communication needs based on usage patterns.
2. **Voice-Enabled Interfaces:**
   - Voice assistants will simplify navigation and enhance accessibility for users with disabilities.
3. **Collaborative Learning Networks:**
   - Educational communities across institutions will use shared platforms for joint projects and research discussions.
4. **Enhanced Analytics:**
   - Insights from communication patterns will guide better academic planning and student support.

17.5 Improving Efficiency with Technology

Introduction

In educational institutions, efficiency plays a vital role in ensuring that academic activities, administrative tasks, and communication processes are conducted smoothly and effectively. With increasing student populations, expanding curricula, and growing administrative complexities, traditional methods are often unable to meet modern educational demands. Technology offers powerful solutions to enhance efficiency across all aspects of education. By automating repetitive tasks, streamlining workflows, and providing real-time access to information, technology helps institutions optimize their operations, improve teaching and learning outcomes, and foster better stakeholder collaboration.

1. Areas Where Technology Improves Efficiency

A. Administrative Processes

1. **Automated Record Keeping:**
   - Student attendance, academic records, and financial data are managed digitally, reducing paperwork and minimizing errors.
2. **Fee Collection and Accounting:**
   - Online payment gateways and automated invoicing systems ensure timely fee collection and generate transparent financial reports.
3. **Exam Management:**
   - Digital scheduling, question paper generation, and automated evaluation processes save time and reduce manual efforts.
4. **Timetable Scheduling:**
   - Software tools create conflict-free timetables based on available faculty, classrooms, and student groups.

B. Academic Operations

1. **Resource Access:**

   - Digital libraries and repositories allow instant access to study material, enhancing academic planning and research capabilities.
2. **Learning Analytics:**
   - Data-driven insights from learning management systems help identify students' strengths, weaknesses, and learning patterns for targeted interventions.
3. **Personalized Learning:**
   - Adaptive learning platforms adjust content delivery according to students' performance, making learning more efficient and engaging.

C. Communication and Collaboration

1. **Instant Messaging:**
   - Enables quick dissemination of announcements, reducing delays in reaching students or staff.
2. **Virtual Meetings:**
   - Video conferencing tools support remote learning, faculty discussions, and parent-teacher interactions without physical constraints.
3. **Feedback Systems:**
   - Online surveys and forms allow institutions to gather feedback instantly and implement improvements swiftly.

2. Technology Tools That Drive Efficiency

1. **Learning Management Systems (LMS):**

    - Centralized platforms like Google Classroom, Moodle, or Canvas integrate content sharing, grading, attendance, and communication.
2. **Cloud Storage Solutions:**
    - Platforms like Google Drive or Microsoft OneDrive facilitate collaborative document editing, instant sharing, and secure backups.
3. **Data Analytics Platforms:**
    - Tools such as Tableau or Microsoft Power BI provide graphical insights into student performance, attendance trends, and operational metrics.
4. **Scheduling Software:**
    - Automated tools like Fedena or OpenSIS generate optimized schedules and ensure effective allocation of resources.
5. **Communication Apps:**
    - WhatsApp, Telegram, or Microsoft Teams help create discussion groups, share updates, and resolve queries instantly.
6. **Artificial Intelligence Tools:**
    - AI chatbots assist with routine queries, appointment scheduling, and learning suggestions, freeing up human resources for more strategic tasks.

3. Benefits of Improving Efficiency with Technology

1. **Time-Saving:**
    - Automating repetitive tasks like attendance tracking, report generation, and fee collection allows educators to focus more on teaching and student development.
2. **Cost Reduction:**

- Digital solutions reduce the need for physical infrastructure, paperwork, and manual labor, resulting in long-term savings.

3. **Accuracy and Consistency:**
   - Automated systems minimize human errors and ensure that data is consistent across departments.
4. **Enhanced Student Support:**
   - Real-time data allows teachers to monitor student progress and provide interventions when needed.
5. **Better Planning and Forecasting:**
   - Analytics tools help institutions anticipate trends, manage resources, and plan future academic activities efficiently.
6. **Scalability:**
   - Technology-driven solutions can accommodate growing student numbers and expanding curriculum needs without significantly increasing operational burdens.

4. Challenges in Adopting Technology for Efficiency

1. **Infrastructure Gaps:**
   - Some institutions, especially in rural or underdeveloped areas, lack the necessary hardware, software, and internet access.
2. **Resistance to Change:**
   - Educators and administrators may be reluctant to adopt new systems due to a lack of familiarity or fear of redundancy.
3. **Data Privacy Concerns:**
   - Handling sensitive information like student records and financial data requires robust security protocols.

4. **Training Requirements:**
   - Effective use of technology depends on adequate training and continuous support for users.

5. Strategies for Successful Implementation

1. **Phased Rollout:**
   - Begin with critical areas like attendance and communication before expanding to more complex modules like analytics and scheduling.
2. **User Training Programs:**
   - Conduct workshops to ensure teachers, students, and staff are comfortable with new tools.
3. **Secure Data Management:**
   - Implement encryption, multi-factor authentication, and regular backups to protect institutional data.
4. **Feedback and Iteration:**
   - Encourage users to share their experiences and suggestions to refine technology solutions.
5. **Collaboration with Tech Providers:**
   - Partner with trusted technology vendors for tailored solutions and ongoing technical support.

6. Case Examples

1. **A University Using LMS:**
   - A major university integrated an LMS that automated assignment submission, grading, and class schedules, improving student engagement by 40%.
2. **A Rural School Using Mobile Learning Apps:**

- A school in a remote area provided offline educational apps on tablets, enabling students to access lessons without consistent internet access.

3. **A College Using AI Chatbots:**
    - A college implemented AI-based chatbots to answer FAQs, significantly reducing the administrative workload during admission periods.

Chapter 18

Impact of Technology on Social and Emotional Learning (SEL)

18.1 Managing Screen Time and Stress

Introduction

With the growing use of digital devices in education, managing screen time and stress has become an important aspect of student and teacher well-being. Online classes, virtual meetings, assignments, and research work demand prolonged hours in front of screens, which can lead to physical discomfort, mental fatigue, and even anxiety. While technology enhances learning opportunities, it also poses challenges that need careful management. Balancing screen time and stress is essential to ensure that students remain healthy, focused, and motivated. Educational institutions must adopt strategies to help users develop healthy digital habits while leveraging technology for academic excellence.

1. Understanding the Impact of Excessive Screen Time

1. **Physical Effects:**
    - Eye strain, headaches, blurred vision, and sleep disturbances are common problems associated with prolonged screen exposure.
    - Poor posture during screen use can result in neck and back pain.
2. **Mental and Emotional Effects:**
    - Continuous screen use may lead to stress, anxiety, irritability, and attention fatigue.

   - Over-dependence on digital platforms can reduce social interaction, affecting emotional well-being.
3. **Cognitive Impacts:**
   - Long hours in front of screens without breaks can lower concentration levels and impair memory retention.
   - Multitasking across devices often leads to distraction and reduced academic performance.

2. Recommended Daily Screen Time Limits

Experts recommend that educational screen time should be regulated based on age and purpose:

- **For school-age children (6–18 years):**
  - A maximum of 2–4 hours per day for academic work, with breaks every 30–40 minutes.
- **For higher education students:**
  - Up to 6–8 hours daily may be required but should be interspersed with rest periods, physical activity, and offline tasks.

Screen time should also be balanced with offline learning methods, recreational activities, and adequate sleep.

3. Strategies to Manage Screen Time

A. Structured Learning Schedules

- Plan study hours with dedicated offline time to read textbooks, solve problems, or reflect on learning.
- Include breaks between sessions to stretch, hydrate, and rest eyes.

B. Use of Screen-Time Monitoring Tools

- Applications like "Digital Wellbeing" or "Screen Time" (available on smartphones and laptops) can track usage patterns and set usage limits.
- Alerts and reminders encourage users to take regular breaks.

C. Implementing the "20-20-20 Rule"

- Every 20 minutes, look at something 20 feet away for at least 20 seconds to reduce eye strain and improve focus.

D. Setting Up Ergonomic Workspaces

- Use chairs with proper back support, adjustable desks, and appropriate lighting to prevent physical discomfort.
- Maintain correct posture to avoid musculoskeletal strain.

E. Encouraging Offline Activities

- Promote hobbies like reading, gardening, arts, sports, or yoga to reduce screen dependency.
- Organize outdoor activities or group discussions that allow students to socialize beyond screens.

4. Stress Management Techniques

1. **Mindfulness and Meditation:**
   - Incorporating short breathing exercises, guided meditation, or mindfulness sessions can help students stay calm and centered.
2. **Time Management:**

   - Breaking tasks into smaller, manageable parts prevents feeling overwhelmed and reduces anxiety.
3. **Seeking Support:**
   - Counseling services, peer support groups, and mentorship programs can provide emotional assistance.
4. **Healthy Sleep Habits:**
   - Avoid screens at least an hour before bedtime to ensure restful sleep, which is crucial for mental health.
5. **Physical Exercise:**
   - Regular exercise not only improves physical fitness but also helps in relieving stress and enhancing mood.
6. **Healthy Nutrition:**
   - Balanced meals rich in vitamins, minerals, and hydration support overall well-being and resilience against stress.

5. Role of Educators and Institutions

1. **Awareness Campaigns:**
   - Conduct workshops to educate students and teachers about the risks of excessive screen time and methods to manage it.
2. **Flexible Academic Planning:**
   - Design assignments that encourage offline learning and group projects instead of continuous online interaction.
3. **Mental Health Resources:**
   - Provide access to counseling services, wellness programs, and peer mentoring networks.

4. **Technology Use Policies:**
    - Set guidelines for appropriate use of devices during classes and promote responsible screen habits.
5. **Encouraging Social Interaction:**
    - Create opportunities for face-to-face group discussions, study circles, and extracurricular activities.

6. Challenges in Managing Screen Time and Stress

1. **Academic Pressure:**
    - Students may feel compelled to stay connected for longer hours to complete assignments or participate in virtual classes.
2. **Lack of Awareness:**
    - Many students and teachers are unaware of the long-term effects of screen overuse.
3. **Technological Dependence:**
    - Educational platforms, communication tools, and digital resources have become integral parts of learning, making it hard to reduce screen usage.
4. **Parental Expectations:**
    - In some cases, parents may push students to achieve more, inadvertently encouraging extended screen time.

7. Best Practices for Sustainable Digital Habits

1. **Set Clear Boundaries:**
    - Define screen usage windows and encourage breaks for meals, exercise, and relaxation.
2. **Encourage Self-Regulation:**

- Teach students to self-monitor their habits and make conscious choices about when and how to use devices.

3. **Promote Digital Detox Periods:**
   - Designate specific times during the day or week for device-free learning and interaction.
4. **Lead by Example:**
   - Teachers and administrators should model healthy screen habits to reinforce positive behaviors.

18.2 Building Empathy in Digital Classrooms

Introduction

As education increasingly shifts to digital platforms, fostering empathy within online classrooms has become essential. Unlike traditional classrooms, where face-to-face interactions naturally support understanding and compassion, virtual learning environments often lack personal connection. Without non-verbal cues, eye contact, or spontaneous conversations, students and teachers may feel isolated or misunderstood. Building empathy in digital classrooms helps create supportive, inclusive, and collaborative learning spaces where students feel valued, understood, and motivated. Empathy is not only critical for mental well-being but also for academic success, group interactions, and social-emotional learning.

1. Understanding Empathy in Educational Contexts

Empathy is the ability to understand and share the feelings, perspectives, and experiences of others. In classrooms, empathetic relationships between students and teachers encourage trust, open communication, and collaborative learning. It helps:

1. **Reduce Anxiety and Stress:**
    - Students feel safer expressing their struggles, questions, and concerns when they believe their teachers and peers genuinely care.
2. **Promote Active Engagement:**
    - Empathy fosters a sense of belonging, which motivates students to participate more actively in discussions and learning activities.
3. **Enhance Social and Emotional Development:**
    - Students learn to recognize emotions, respect diversity, and practice compassion, improving their interpersonal skills.

2. Challenges to Empathy in Digital Classrooms

1. **Lack of Physical Presence:**
    - Absence of body language, facial expressions, and spontaneous interactions can make communication feel distant or impersonal.
2. **Technical Barriers:**
    - Poor internet connectivity, inadequate devices, or lack of digital literacy may prevent some students from participating fully, making them feel excluded.
3. **Increased Screen Fatigue:**
    - Continuous virtual interactions can lead to burnout, reducing patience and attentiveness.
4. **Anonymity and Miscommunication:**

- Online platforms may encourage impersonal behavior, where students are less likely to consider how their words affect others.

3. Strategies for Building Empathy in Digital Classrooms

A. Create a Safe and Inclusive Environment

- Begin online sessions with check-ins where students share how they feel, their challenges, or their expectations.
- Encourage students to use their names when speaking or posting messages to humanize interactions.
- Promote respect and kindness in all discussions, setting clear guidelines for behavior.

B. Practice Active Listening

- Pay close attention to students' verbal cues and emotional expressions, even through chats or video feeds.
- Acknowledge contributions and concerns, responding with validation rather than judgment.

C. Encourage Peer Support

- Use breakout rooms for small group discussions where students can share experiences and collaborate in a more personal setting.
- Assign group projects that require teamwork, emphasizing roles, responsibilities, and empathy-based interactions.

D. Share Stories and Experiences

- Teachers and students can share personal stories related to academic challenges, achievements, or mental health, fostering mutual understanding.
- Storytelling helps create empathy by allowing students to see beyond academic roles.

E. Integrate Social-Emotional Learning (SEL)

- Introduce activities that focus on emotional intelligence, conflict resolution, and self-awareness.
- Offer mindfulness exercises and reflection tasks to help students connect with their emotions and those of others.

F. Use Technology to Humanize Interaction

- Encourage video participation where possible, helping students see facial expressions and gestures.
- Use polls, emoji reactions, and discussion forums to express feelings and opinions.

4. Role of Teachers in Empathy Building

1. **Model Compassionate Behavior**
    - Teachers should demonstrate patience, active listening, and supportive communication. Their behavior sets the tone for how students interact with one another.
2. **Be Approachable and Supportive**
    - Offer virtual office hours where students can ask questions, seek help, or talk about personal issues in a judgment-free space.

3. **Provide Constructive Feedback**
   - Feedback should be encouraging and solution-oriented, emphasizing effort and learning progress rather than mistakes.
4. **Recognize Individual Needs**
   - Acknowledge differences in learning styles, cultural backgrounds, and personal circumstances, adjusting teaching methods to accommodate them.

5. Role of Students in Building Empathy

1. **Practice Compassionate Communication**
   - Students should avoid judgmental or dismissive language and instead offer encouragement and constructive suggestions.
2. **Support Peers**
   - Engage in peer mentoring, answer questions, and assist classmates who are struggling with technology or coursework.
3. **Respect Diversity**
   - Embrace cultural, linguistic, and personal differences, recognizing that each student's experience is unique.
4. **Reflect on Emotional Responses**
   - Encourage students to pause and consider how their words or actions may impact others.

6. Case Examples

1. **Virtual Peer Mentoring Programs**
   - Some colleges have implemented peer support groups where senior students assist juniors with

academic and emotional challenges, building a sense of community.

2. **Check-In Routines in Online Classes**
   - Teachers begin each session with a "one-word check-in," where students share how they feel, allowing space for empathy-driven discussions.
3. **Mindfulness Integration**
   - Schools have introduced weekly mindfulness exercises, helping students manage stress and foster patience in online learning environments.

7. Best Practices for Sustaining Empathy

1. **Encourage Open Dialogue**
   - Regularly invite students to share feedback on the learning environment and emotional well-being.
2. **Celebrate Achievements Together**
   - Recognize academic, creative, or personal accomplishments to boost confidence and create a sense of belonging.
3. **Promote Reflection and Journaling**
   - Assign tasks where students reflect on their feelings, interactions, and learning journey to cultivate empathy and self-awareness.
4. **Foster Collaboration Beyond Academics**
   - Organize virtual social events, group projects, and creative challenges that encourage peer interaction beyond classroom tasks.

18.3 Emotional Well-Being and Mental Health

Introduction

With the increasing integration of technology in education, attention to emotional well-being and mental health has become more important than ever. Students and teachers are spending extended periods online, attending virtual classes, completing assignments, and engaging in digital communication. While technology offers educational benefits, it also exposes users to stress, isolation, anxiety, and burnout. Emotional well-being is not just about managing stress—it involves maintaining a healthy balance between academic responsibilities, personal life, and mental health. Educational institutions have a responsibility to create environments where students feel emotionally supported, empowered, and resilient while using technology.

1. Understanding Emotional Well-Being and Mental Health

1. **Emotional Well-Being:**
   - It refers to the ability to cope with everyday stresses, express emotions appropriately, and build healthy relationships with peers and educators.
2. **Mental Health:**
   - It encompasses psychological, emotional, and social functioning. Good mental health enables individuals to perform academically, handle pressures, and recover from setbacks.
3. **The Impact of Technology:**
   - While technology facilitates learning, overuse, dependence, or lack of boundaries can lead to anxiety, sleep disturbances, and reduced social interactions, affecting mental health.

2. Common Emotional and Mental Health Challenges in Digital Learning Environments

1. **Screen Fatigue and Eye Strain:**
    - Prolonged exposure to screens without breaks can cause headaches, blurred vision, and irritability.
2. **Social Isolation:**
    - Reduced face-to-face interactions with friends and family can lead to loneliness and depression.
3. **Performance Pressure:**
    - Constant availability and comparison with peers can lead to anxiety and fear of failure.
4. **Sleep Disturbances:**
    - Late-night screen use, irregular schedules, and excessive workload disrupt sleep patterns, impacting mental health.
5. **Digital Distractions:**
    - Social media, gaming, and non-academic content can increase procrastination and distract from studies, leading to guilt and stress.

3. Signs of Emotional Distress

Students may exhibit emotional strain in various ways, including:

- Lack of motivation or engagement in academic activities.
- Withdrawal from peers or social interactions.
- Increased irritability or mood swings.
- Sleep problems or fatigue.
- Feelings of hopelessness, anxiety, or sadness.
- Difficulty focusing or retaining information.

Recognizing these signs early can help educators and peers provide timely support.

4. Strategies for Promoting Emotional Well-Being

A. Regular Mental Health Check-Ins

- Begin online classes with brief wellness check-ins where students share how they feel.
- Use anonymous surveys or feedback forms to assess emotional challenges and provide support.

B. Balanced Academic Schedules

- Design assignments with realistic deadlines and encourage time management techniques.
- Include buffer time to avoid burnout during exams or heavy coursework periods.

C. Encouraging Self-Care Practices

- Promote activities such as journaling, meditation, exercise, and relaxation techniques to manage stress.
- Provide resources and workshops on nutrition, sleep hygiene, and mindfulness.

D. Creating Support Systems

- Establish peer mentoring groups where students can share challenges and offer advice.
- Provide access to professional counseling services, helplines, and mental health resources.

E. Reducing Stigma Around Mental Health

- Normalize conversations around mental health to encourage students to seek help.
- Share stories of resilience and coping strategies from fellow students or faculty members.

5. Role of Educators and Institutions

1. **Modeling Healthy Behaviors**
    - Teachers can demonstrate work-life balance, stress management, and compassionate communication.
2. **Providing Accessible Resources**
    - Institutions should offer digital libraries, wellness programs, and self-help tools that support emotional well-being.
3. **Promoting Inclusivity**
    - Address diverse mental health needs by acknowledging cultural backgrounds, personal experiences, and learning styles.
4. **Encouraging Breaks and Offline Activities**
    - Integrate short breaks during online sessions and assign non-screen-based learning tasks.
5. **Monitoring and Responding with Care**
    - Educators should be trained to identify signs of emotional distress and offer empathetic support or refer students to appropriate services.

6. Mental Health Tools and Technologies

1. **Mental Health Apps**

- Applications like Headspace, Calm, and MindShift provide guided meditations, breathing exercises, and mood tracking.

2. **Tele-Counseling Platforms**
   - Virtual counseling platforms offer confidential therapy sessions with mental health professionals.
3. **Digital Wellness Dashboards**
   - Tools that track screen time, sleep patterns, and activity levels help students self-monitor and make informed lifestyle choices.
4. **Peer Support Forums**
   - Online communities where students share coping strategies, provide encouragement, and reduce feelings of isolation.

7. Building Resilience in Students

1. **Empowerment Through Self-Awareness**
   - Encourage students to identify stress triggers and learn adaptive coping strategies.
2. **Setting Realistic Expectations**
   - Teach students to set achievable goals and celebrate small successes.
3. **Developing Problem-Solving Skills**
   - Provide structured exercises that teach students how to break down challenges and seek solutions.
4. **Fostering a Positive Learning Environment**
   - Recognize effort, creativity, and collaboration rather than focusing solely on grades or performance metrics.

8. Case Examples

1. **University Wellness Programs**
   - Some universities offer integrated wellness platforms with counseling, meditation guides, and 24/7 support lines, leading to a noticeable reduction in student anxiety.
2. **School-Led Mindfulness Initiatives**
   - Schools incorporating short daily mindfulness sessions have reported improved concentration and reduced behavioral issues.
3. **Peer-Led Emotional Support Groups**
   - Student-led support groups offer confidential sharing spaces, empowering peers to support one another and reduce stigma.

18.4 Digital Etiquette and Social Skills

Introduction

As education increasingly takes place in virtual environments, digital etiquette and social skills have become essential components of a healthy learning experience. Unlike face-to-face interactions, online communication can be misinterpreted, misunderstood, or even become a source of conflict if not handled with care. Proper digital behavior helps maintain respect, professionalism, and collaboration while minimizing stress and distractions. Teaching students and educators how to communicate thoughtfully and responsibly in online settings is key to building constructive relationships, fostering trust, and enhancing academic success.

1. What is Digital Etiquette?

Digital etiquette, or "netiquette," refers to the set of guidelines and behaviors that govern respectful, responsible, and effective communication in digital spaces. It includes how students interact in virtual classrooms, how they present themselves through text or video, and how they collaborate in group settings.

Good digital etiquette involves:

1. Being polite, patient, and empathetic.
2. Using appropriate language and tone.
3. Respecting others' privacy and space.
4. Avoiding distractions and multitasking during sessions.
5. Giving constructive feedback and encouragement.

2. Importance of Social Skills in Digital Learning

1. **Building Trust and Connection**
   - Online platforms can feel impersonal, making it harder to build relationships. Social skills like empathy, active listening, and positive reinforcement help foster trust.
2. **Improving Collaboration**
   - Group projects, peer discussions, and problem-solving tasks require effective communication, teamwork, and conflict resolution.
3. **Enhancing Engagement**
   - Students who feel connected and supported are more likely to participate actively, ask questions, and contribute ideas.
4. **Preventing Miscommunication**

- Misunderstandings in text-based communication are common. Social skills help clarify intent and promote respectful dialogue.

3. Core Elements of Digital Etiquette

A. Communication

- Speak clearly and respectfully, whether in video calls, discussion forums, or email.
- Avoid typing in all caps, as it may be perceived as shouting.
- Use emojis or punctuation thoughtfully to express emotions without causing confusion.

B. Respecting Time and Attention

- Join virtual sessions on time.
- Mute microphones when not speaking to avoid background noise.
- Avoid multitasking during class to stay engaged.

C. Privacy and Safety

- Do not share others' personal information or recordings without permission.
- Protect passwords and login credentials.
- Report suspicious activity or harmful behavior.

D. Inclusive Language

- Use gender-neutral or culturally sensitive language.
- Avoid humor or sarcasm that may be misinterpreted.

E. Feedback and Interaction

- Offer constructive feedback rather than criticism.
- Ask clarifying questions when unsure.
- Encourage peers by acknowledging their efforts and contributions.

4. Developing Social Skills in Virtual Classrooms

1. **Active Listening**
    - Focus on the speaker, avoid interrupting, and respond thoughtfully.
2. **Expressing Thoughts Clearly**
    - Use simple, structured sentences to convey ideas.
3. **Empathy and Understanding**
    - Recognize that classmates may be dealing with challenges outside the classroom.
4. **Conflict Resolution**
    - Approach disagreements calmly, seek clarification, and offer solutions rather than escalating issues.
5. **Building Rapport**
    - Engage in casual conversations, celebrate achievements, and share positive feedback.

5. Tools and Techniques for Enhancing Digital Etiquette

1. **Online Orientation Programs**
    - Educate students about proper conduct, communication strategies, and safe use of digital platforms at the beginning of the course.
2. **Interactive Workshops**

- Conduct sessions focused on empathy, team-building, and responsible communication.

3. **Discussion Guidelines**
   - Provide clear rules for posting messages, responding to classmates, and handling disagreements.
4. **Role-Playing Activities**
   - Use simulated scenarios where students practice handling disagreements, offering feedback, and participating in discussions.
5. **Peer Mentoring**
   - Pair students with peers who can model good etiquette and help navigate virtual interactions.

6. Common Mistakes in Digital Communication

1. **Over-sharing or Under-sharing**
   - Some students may share too much personal information, while others may avoid engaging altogether.
2. **Ignoring Tone and Context**
   - Text messages lack facial expressions, making it easier to misinterpret sarcasm or humor.
3. **Interrupting Others**
   - Speaking over classmates in video calls or dominating discussions can discourage participation.
4. **Neglecting Privacy**
   - Sharing screenshots or personal details without consent can breach trust.
5. **Using Disrespectful Language**
   - Harsh criticism, slang, or insensitive remarks can lead to emotional distress.

7. Encouraging Positive Digital Behavior

1. **Recognize and Reward Good Practices**
   - Highlight examples of respectful communication and collaboration during sessions.
2. **Promote Self-Reflection**
   - Encourage students to evaluate their communication style and set goals for improvement.
3. **Encourage Regular Check-Ins**
   - Periodic discussions about emotional health and group dynamics help maintain a positive learning environment.
4. **Provide Support for Conflict Resolution**
   - Offer structured approaches for resolving disagreements, including mediation or peer-led discussions.
5. **Create Safe Spaces**
   - Ensure that students feel comfortable expressing concerns without fear of judgment or exclusion.

8. Case Examples

1. **University Discussion Forums**
   - A university implemented structured discussion boards where students are required to follow guidelines, leading to more thoughtful and constructive exchanges.
2. **Online Group Projects**
   - Students assigned roles like "discussion facilitator" and "feedback provider" to ensure balanced participation and respectful communication.
3. **Digital Etiquette Training**

- Schools conducted workshops on online safety, empathy, and effective communication, resulting in a noticeable improvement in classroom interactions.

18.5 Supporting Teachers and Students

Introduction

The growing reliance on technology in education has brought both opportunities and challenges for teachers and students. While digital tools enhance learning experiences, they also present issues like screen fatigue, stress, isolation, and difficulties in communication. Supporting teachers and students in navigating these challenges is essential to ensure that technology serves as a helpful tool rather than a source of frustration. Emotional well-being, social interaction, and mental health support play a crucial role in helping learners and educators adapt to new digital environments. A supportive atmosphere encourages resilience, motivation, and healthy learning habits.

1. Why Support Matters

1. **For Students**
    - Students face academic pressure, uncertainty, and distractions when learning online. Support helps them cope with anxiety, build confidence, and stay engaged.
    - Emotional and social assistance fosters a sense of belonging and encourages collaboration.
2. **For Teachers**

- Teachers may struggle with technology management, instructional adjustments, and maintaining student engagement.
- Providing professional development, peer networks, and mental health resources enables teachers to deliver quality education while balancing personal well-being.

2. Types of Support Needed

A. Emotional Support

- Addressing stress, anxiety, and feelings of isolation through counseling, peer interactions, and wellness programs.
- Encouraging open dialogue where students and teachers feel safe expressing their concerns.

B. Academic Support

- Offering tutorials, guides, and mentorship to assist with learning challenges or technology-related difficulties.
- Providing feedback that is constructive, timely, and encouraging.

C. Technological Support

- Training teachers and students on how to use learning platforms effectively.
- Ensuring access to reliable internet connections and user-friendly tools.

D. Social Support

- Creating opportunities for group interactions, discussion forums, and collaborative learning tasks.
- Promoting inclusion by respecting diverse backgrounds, learning styles, and abilities.

3. Strategies to Support Students

1. **Wellness Check-Ins**
    - Begin classes by asking students how they are doing emotionally and academically.
    - Anonymous feedback forms can help students share challenges without fear of judgment.
2. **Counseling Services and Helplines**
    - Provide virtual counseling sessions with trained professionals.
    - Share contact information for mental health resources.
3. **Mentorship Programs**
    - Pair students with peers or senior students who can guide them through academic and personal challenges.
4. **Encouraging Healthy Digital Habits**
    - Teach students how to manage screen time, set realistic goals, and practice self-care.
5. **Flexible Learning Plans**
    - Offer recorded lectures, alternative assignments, and extended deadlines for students facing difficulties.

4. Strategies to Support Teachers

1. **Professional Development Workshops**
    - Organize training sessions on using digital tools, creating engaging content, and managing virtual classrooms.
2. **Peer Support Groups**
    - Encourage teachers to share best practices, troubleshoot issues together, and exchange experiences.
3. **Access to Resources**
    - Provide guides, templates, and instructional material libraries to simplify lesson planning.
4. **Emotional and Psychological Support**
    - Offer wellness programs, counseling, and stress management resources tailored to teachers' needs.
5. **Recognition and Appreciation**
    - Celebrate teachers' efforts and achievements to boost morale and create a supportive environment.

5. Role of Educational Institutions

1. **Creating a Culture of Care**
    - Integrate well-being initiatives into the curriculum and overall learning experience.
2. **Providing Technology Access**
    - Ensure that students and teachers have access to necessary devices and internet connectivity.
3. **Offering Training and Guidance**
    - Make learning platforms easier to use through tutorials, helplines, and user-friendly interfaces.
4. **Encouraging Collaboration**

- Promote teamwork, cross-disciplinary projects, and discussion forums where teachers and students support each other.

5. **Monitoring Well-Being**
   - Use periodic surveys and feedback forms to assess emotional and academic needs and implement supportive policies accordingly.

6. Case Examples

1. **Student Support Programs**
   - Some universities have launched "Student Wellness Weeks" where workshops on stress management, mindfulness, and time planning are offered alongside academic tutorials.
2. **Teacher Support Networks**
   - Schools have established teacher support groups that meet weekly to share challenges, discuss teaching strategies, and exchange resources.
3. **Tech-Enabled Assistance**
   - Educational platforms are incorporating AI-driven tools to monitor student engagement and suggest interventions for those at risk of burnout or falling behind.

7. Best Practices for Sustainable Support

1. **Foster Open Communication**
   - Encourage students and teachers to speak openly about their challenges and seek assistance without hesitation.
2. **Normalize Mental Health Conversations**

- Regularly discuss emotional well-being, making it a routine topic rather than a sign of weakness.

3. **Encourage Peer Learning**
    - Promote peer-to-peer support networks that enable sharing of strategies and experiences.
4. **Personalize Support Systems**
    - Tailor interventions based on individual needs, learning styles, and personal circumstances.
5. **Monitor and Adjust**
    - Continuously assess the effectiveness of support programs and make adjustments as needed.

Chapter 19

Case Studies and Best Practices

19.1 Rural Education through Technology

Introduction

Rural education has long faced barriers that hinder students from accessing quality learning opportunities. Geographic isolation, poor infrastructure, shortage of trained teachers, and financial constraints are among the major challenges affecting rural schools. However, advances in technology offer innovative solutions to bridge these gaps. By leveraging digital tools, internet connectivity, mobile learning, and virtual classrooms, rural communities can access educational resources, improve teaching practices, and enhance learning outcomes. Technology in rural education not only empowers students academically but also supports social and economic development by creating opportunities for lifelong learning and skill-building.

1. Challenges in Rural Education

1. **Limited School Infrastructure**
   - Many rural schools lack proper classrooms, libraries, laboratories, and internet access, making it difficult for students to learn effectively.
2. **Teacher Shortages**
   - Recruiting and retaining qualified teachers in remote areas remains a persistent problem, resulting in multi-grade classrooms and reduced instructional support.
3. **Connectivity Issues**

   - Poor or inconsistent internet access limits the use of digital tools and platforms, especially for video lessons or interactive content.
4. **Financial Constraints**
   - Many families in rural areas cannot afford devices such as smartphones, tablets, or laptops, restricting students' access to online education.
5. **Language and Cultural Barriers**
   - Educational content often does not cater to local languages or the cultural context of rural students, making it harder for them to engage.

2. How Technology Can Support Rural Education

A. Access to Learning Resources

- **Digital Libraries and e-Content**
  - Platforms like e-Pathshala and National Repository of Open Educational Resources (NROER) provide textbooks, videos, and interactive content in multiple languages, available for free or at low cost.
- **Mobile Learning**
  - Offline apps and downloadable content allow students to access lessons even in areas with limited connectivity.

B. Virtual Classrooms and Distance Learning

- **Online Lessons**
  - Students can attend live or recorded classes, enabling learning beyond school hours and geographical boundaries.
- **Interactive Sessions**

    - Video conferencing tools allow rural students to interact with teachers and peers, participate in discussions, and clarify doubts.

C. Teacher Training and Support

- **Webinars and Online Courses**
    - Digital platforms offer professional development programs to train rural teachers in pedagogy, classroom management, and technology use.
- **Peer Support Networks**
    - Messaging apps and forums help teachers exchange ideas, share resources, and support one another.

D. Skill Development

- **Vocational Training**
    - Online platforms offer courses in digital literacy, agriculture, healthcare, entrepreneurship, and more, providing rural students with skills for employment and self-reliance.
- **Certification Programs**
    - Virtual assessments and certification enhance credibility and open pathways to higher education and career opportunities.

3. Government and Institutional Initiatives

1. **Digital India Mission**
    - Works to enhance internet infrastructure and provide affordable access to digital tools in rural areas.
2. **PM eVidya**

   - Aims to unify online education platforms and broadcast educational content through television and radio for students without internet access.
3. **BharatNet Project**
   - Expands broadband connectivity to rural communities, laying the foundation for digital education.
4. **CSR and NGO Partnerships**
   - Many organizations collaborate with schools to provide devices, training, and offline learning centers in underserved regions.

4. Best Practices for Implementing Technology in Rural Schools

1. **Blended Learning Approach**
   - Combining digital content with in-person teaching ensures continuity of learning even when connectivity is an issue.
2. **Local Content Development**
   - Creating educational material in regional languages and contextual examples helps students relate to the subject matter.
3. **Community Learning Centers**
   - Shared spaces equipped with computers, tablets, and internet access allow students to learn together and support one another.
4. **Parental Engagement**
   - Educating parents on digital safety, screen time management, and the benefits of technology helps ensure students' sustained participation.
5. **Monitoring and Evaluation**

- Regular feedback from students and teachers helps assess the effectiveness of digital tools and identify areas for improvement.

5. Real-Life Case Examples

1. **e-Pathshala's Impact**
    - In several states, e-Pathshala's free educational content has enabled thousands of rural students to access lessons remotely, improving learning outcomes.
2. **Community Radio Projects**
    - Schools in remote areas have adopted community radio broadcasts to share lessons and learning tips, reaching students without internet access.
3. **Mobile Learning Vans**
    - Some initiatives have introduced technology-equipped vehicles that travel to villages, offering workshops and access to digital content.
4. **Teacher Empowerment Programs**
    - Online teacher training programs have helped educators in rural schools gain confidence in using technology and improve classroom management.

6. Challenges and Recommendations

1. **Device and Internet Access**
    - Governments and private sectors should collaborate to provide affordable devices and expand connectivity in rural areas.
2. **Training and Digital Literacy**

- Continuous training for teachers and students is necessary to build competence and comfort in using technology.

3. **Sustainability**
    - Efforts should focus on long-term solutions rather than one-time interventions, ensuring technology integration is maintained and supported.
4. **Inclusion and Equity**
    - Special attention should be given to marginalized groups, including girls, children with disabilities, and economically disadvantaged families.

19.2 Smart Classrooms in Urban Areas

Introduction

Urban education environments have seen significant transformations due to technological advancements. Smart classrooms—learning spaces equipped with digital tools and interactive platforms—have emerged as powerful solutions to enhance student engagement, improve teaching methods, and create dynamic learning experiences. With better infrastructure, faster internet, and access to modern devices, urban schools and colleges are increasingly adopting smart classroom technologies to prepare students for the demands of a globalized, knowledge-driven world. These classrooms not only support academic learning but also foster creativity, collaboration, and critical thinking.

1. What are Smart Classrooms?

A smart classroom is a technology-enhanced learning environment where digital tools are integrated into everyday teaching and learning processes. These classrooms typically include:

1. **Interactive Whiteboards**
   - Used for dynamic presentations, annotations, and real-time explanations.
2. **High-Speed Internet Connectivity**
   - Ensures access to online content, cloud-based platforms, and video conferencing.
3. **Learning Management Systems (LMS)**
   - Allow teachers to upload course material, track progress, and communicate with students.
4. **Audio-Visual Equipment**
   - Projectors, microphones, and speakers improve content delivery and ensure that all students can participate actively.
5. **Smart Devices**
   - Tablets, laptops, and mobile apps that support personalized learning and instant feedback.
6. **Virtual and Augmented Reality Tools**
   - Enhance understanding by offering immersive learning experiences in subjects like science, history, and arts.

2. Features of Smart Classrooms in Urban Schools

1. **Personalized Learning Paths**
   - Students can learn at their own pace, with access to recorded lectures and adaptive content tailored to their strengths and weaknesses.
2. **Collaborative Learning Spaces**

  - Digital tools encourage group discussions, peer-to-peer learning, and project-based activities.
3. **Instant Feedback and Assessment**
   - Teachers can conduct quizzes, polls, and assessments online, offering immediate results to help students improve.
4. **Access to Global Resources**
   - Urban classrooms benefit from seamless access to educational content from around the world, including simulations, videos, and expert lectures.
5. **Environmentally Friendly Practices**
   - Digital content reduces reliance on printed materials, contributing to sustainability efforts.

3. Benefits of Smart Classrooms

1. **Enhanced Engagement**
   - Interactive tools make learning more interesting, helping students stay focused and motivated.
2. **Improved Academic Performance**
   - Technology-supported teaching methods cater to different learning styles, resulting in better understanding and retention.
3. **Skill Development**
   - Smart classrooms help students acquire technical skills such as data analysis, digital communication, and problem-solving.
4. **Teacher Efficiency**
   - Automated grading, lesson planning tools, and content libraries allow teachers to save time and focus on student interaction.
5. **Inclusivity and Accessibility**

   - Tools like text-to-speech, subtitles, and adaptive learning platforms support students with diverse learning needs.

4. Implementation Strategies for Urban Schools

1. **Infrastructure Development**
   - Schools must ensure reliable internet, power supply, and appropriate classroom layouts to support technology-based learning.
2. **Training and Capacity Building**
   - Teachers should receive continuous training to effectively integrate technology into lesson plans and address challenges.
3. **Curriculum Integration**
   - Technology should be embedded within the curriculum rather than treated as an add-on, ensuring that digital tools complement learning objectives.
4. **Data-Driven Approaches**
   - Schools can use learning analytics to monitor student progress and tailor instruction accordingly.
5. **Community and Parent Engagement**
   - Encouraging families to understand and support technology use helps students practice responsible and balanced use of digital tools at home.

5. Challenges in Urban Smart Classrooms

1. **Digital Divide**
   - Even within cities, socio-economic disparities can prevent equal access to devices and internet services.
2. **Over-Reliance on Technology**

   - Excessive screen time or dependence on digital tools may hinder the development of soft skills and critical thinking.
3. **Cybersecurity Risks**
   - Increased connectivity exposes students and schools to data breaches and online threats, requiring robust security measures.
4. **Teacher Preparedness**
   - Some teachers may struggle to adapt to new technologies without adequate training and support.
5. **Maintenance and Costs**
   - Keeping equipment up-to-date and functional requires significant financial investment and technical expertise.

6. Case Examples of Urban Smart Classrooms

1. **Delhi Government Schools**
   - Several schools have implemented interactive boards and LMS platforms, improving student participation and academic tracking.
2. **Private International Schools in Mumbai**
   - These schools use virtual labs, AI-driven analytics, and digital assessment tools to create personalized learning experiences.
3. **Blended Learning Models in Bengaluru**
   - Urban institutions combine in-person classes with online platforms, providing students with flexible access to course materials.
4. **Collaborations with EdTech Startups**

- Schools are partnering with startups to offer affordable learning solutions, ensuring wider access to smart classroom tools.

7. Best Practices for Effective Smart Classrooms

1. **Balanced Use of Technology**
    - Integrate digital tools thoughtfully without overwhelming students, encouraging creativity and discussion.
2. **Continuous Teacher Development**
    - Offer refresher courses and peer mentoring to ensure teachers stay confident and updated in using technology.
3. **Student-Centered Learning**
    - Design activities that encourage students to explore, experiment, and engage with real-world problems.
4. **Focus on Cyber Hygiene**
    - Teach students about safe internet practices, data privacy, and responsible communication.
5. **Regular Feedback and Improvement**
    - Conduct surveys and feedback sessions to continuously assess the effectiveness of smart classroom strategies.

19.3 Teacher Experiences and Reflections

Introduction

The integration of technology into classrooms has significantly reshaped the roles of teachers, influencing their teaching styles, interactions with students, and professional growth. While educational technologies such as smart classrooms, online platforms, and digital resources have brought new opportunities, they have also presented challenges that require adjustments and learning. Teachers' experiences and reflections are critical to understanding the practical impact of technology in education, especially in urban schools where access to tools and infrastructure is more prevalent. Their insights offer valuable lessons for improving implementation strategies, supporting training programs, and fostering positive learning environments.

1. Positive Experiences with Technology

A. Enhanced Teaching Methods

Many teachers have found that technology enriches their instructional approaches:

- Interactive tools like smart boards and multimedia presentations make lessons more engaging.
- Visual aids help explain complex concepts, especially in subjects like science, mathematics, and geography.
- Digital quizzes and assessments provide instant feedback, allowing teachers to track student progress effectively.

One teacher from a metropolitan school shared:

“With technology, I can now create interactive lessons that keep students involved throughout the class. They ask more questions and participate actively, which wasn’t as easy in the traditional classroom setup.”

B. Access to Educational Resources

Teachers appreciate the convenience of digital libraries, online courses, and global educational networks:

- They can download teaching materials, worksheets, and research papers anytime.
- Online forums and webinars expose teachers to new pedagogical methods and subject matter updates.

A senior educator reflected:

"Earlier, we relied on textbooks and printed notes, but now I have access to thousands of resources at my fingertips. It has made lesson planning easier and more efficient."

C. Personalized Learning Support

Technology has helped teachers cater to diverse learning needs:

- Adaptive learning platforms allow teachers to assign tasks based on student performance.
- Students with learning disabilities can benefit from assistive tools like text-to-speech and screen readers.

A teacher remarked:

"I now create assignments that match each student's pace and style of learning, which has improved their confidence and classroom participation."

2. Challenges Faced by Teachers

A. Technical Difficulties

Teachers often encounter problems with software glitches, internet disruptions, and outdated devices:

- A common concern is the lack of technical support during lessons.
- Teachers sometimes spend valuable class time troubleshooting devices instead of teaching.

One teacher shared:

"Technology is helpful, but it's frustrating when the system crashes or the internet stops working during a session. It disrupts the flow of teaching and affects students' concentration."

B. Increased Workload

Integrating technology requires additional planning and training:

- Preparing digital content, monitoring online assignments, and responding to student queries add to teachers' responsibilities.
- Some teachers feel the need to constantly update their skills, leading to stress and burnout.

A teacher reflected:

"Adapting to technology has been challenging. The workload has increased, and balancing administrative tasks with teaching has become tougher."

C. Student Distraction

While technology engages students, it can also become a source of distraction:

- Students may stray to non-educational websites or social media during online sessions.
- Managing attention and maintaining discipline becomes more complex in virtual environments.

A teacher explained:

"I find that students sometimes multitask or lose focus during online classes. Keeping them engaged requires constant effort."

3. Reflections on Professional Growth

Despite challenges, teachers acknowledge that technology has helped them grow professionally:

- Many teachers now experiment with innovative teaching methods and digital tools.
- Peer collaboration through online communities has improved their problem-solving abilities.
- The need to stay updated with technology has encouraged lifelong learning and adaptability.

One teacher's reflection:

"Technology has made me more resourceful. I am learning new skills daily and experimenting with creative ways to teach. It's a continuous journey."

4. Emotional and Social Impact

Teachers' reflections also highlight how technology affects their emotional well-being and relationships with students:

- Technology has encouraged empathy, as teachers must be patient and supportive when students face difficulties using devices or understanding concepts.
- Virtual interactions have reshaped teacher-student relationships, requiring more communication and trust-building efforts.
- Teachers appreciate being seen as facilitators rather than traditional authority figures, fostering a collaborative classroom culture.

A teacher noted:

"I have learned to connect with students on a deeper level. They now feel comfortable sharing their struggles and asking for help, which has strengthened our bond."

5. Lessons Learned and Recommendations

A. Importance of Training and Support

- Continuous professional development helps teachers adapt to new tools.
- Technical support teams should be available during online sessions.

B. Balanced Use of Technology

- Teachers need to integrate technology thoughtfully without overwhelming students or creating dependencies.

C. Encouraging Peer Learning

- Teachers benefit from sharing experiences, strategies, and resources with colleagues.

D. Promoting Digital Citizenship

- Teaching students responsible use of technology, time management, and ethical behavior is essential.

19.4 Student-Centered Technological Approaches

Introduction

Student-centered learning focuses on the individual needs, interests, and learning styles of students, empowering them to take ownership of their educational journey. In urban classrooms, where access to technology is more widespread, student-centered technological approaches have revolutionized the way teachers engage with learners. These approaches shift the emphasis from teacher-led instruction to interactive, participatory learning environments where students actively shape their learning experiences. Technology plays a crucial role in providing personalized content, encouraging collaboration, and fostering creativity, ensuring that education is relevant, meaningful, and inclusive.

1. Understanding Student-Centered Technological Approaches

Student-centered technological approaches are designed to adapt to the preferences, pace, and abilities of learners rather than enforcing a uniform teaching method. The key principles include:

1. **Personalization**
    - Tailoring content, assignments, and assessments according to individual learning needs.
2. **Active Engagement**
    - Encouraging learners to participate in discussions, projects, and problem-solving activities.
3. **Collaboration**
    - Facilitating group activities where students learn from and with their peers.
4. **Autonomy**
    - Allowing students to make decisions about what, when, and how they learn.
5. **Reflection and Feedback**
    - Providing regular feedback that helps learners evaluate their progress and set goals.

2. Technologies that Support Student-Centered Learning

A. Learning Management Systems (LMS)

- LMS platforms like Google Classroom, Moodle, and Canvas allow teachers to upload customized content, assign tasks, and track student progress.
- Students can access learning material at their convenience and work at their own pace.

B. Adaptive Learning Software

- Programs like DreamBox or Smart Sparrow adjust content difficulty based on student performance.
- Real-time feedback helps learners identify gaps and work on areas requiring improvement.

C. Multimedia Tools

- Videos, animations, and simulations offer alternative ways to understand complex concepts.
- Interactive diagrams and virtual labs allow learners to experiment and explore in a risk-free environment.

D. Mobile Learning Apps

- Educational apps provide bite-sized learning modules, quizzes, and games that keep students engaged outside the classroom.
- Apps can integrate gamification elements like badges and rewards to motivate learners.

E. Communication Platforms

- Tools like Zoom, Microsoft Teams, or Google Meet enable students to collaborate on projects, participate in group discussions, and connect with experts.

3. Benefits of Student-Centered Technological Approaches

1. **Enhanced Motivation**

   - Students feel empowered when they have control over their learning path, increasing their motivation and participation.
2. **Improved Learning Outcomes**
   - Personalized content ensures that learners are neither bored nor overwhelmed, leading to better comprehension and retention.
3. **Development of Critical Thinking and Problem-Solving Skills**
   - Interactive activities encourage students to analyze, reflect, and apply knowledge creatively.
4. **Inclusivity**
   - Students with diverse learning styles, including those with disabilities, benefit from customized learning tools and multiple content formats.
5. **Preparation for Real-World Challenges**
   - Exposure to technology fosters skills like collaboration, digital literacy, and time management—essential for future careers.

4. Examples of Student-Centered Technological Approaches

A. Project-Based Learning Using Digital Tools

In many urban schools, students are assigned projects where they explore real-life problems, conduct research using online databases, and present their findings through videos or presentations. For example, a project on environmental sustainability may include interactive models, online surveys, and video interviews.

B. Flipped Classrooms

Teachers provide pre-recorded video lessons for students to watch at home, allowing classroom time to be used for discussions, activities, and problem-solving exercises. This approach promotes active learning and better utilization of classroom interaction.

C. Peer Learning Networks

Students form virtual study groups where they share notes, solve problems together, and conduct peer reviews. Platforms like Edmodo or Discord provide spaces for collaborative learning, promoting community engagement.

D. Self-Assessment Tools

Digital quizzes, polls, and surveys help students assess their understanding. Tools like Kahoot or Quizizz allow learners to compete in a fun and interactive environment, reinforcing learning through repetition and feedback.

5. Challenges in Implementing Student-Centered Technological Approaches

1. **Digital Literacy Gaps**
   - Not all students are equally comfortable navigating digital platforms, requiring additional guidance and support.
2. **Over-Reliance on Technology**
   - Excessive dependence on digital tools may reduce interpersonal communication and affect social learning.
3. **Equity and Access Issues**

- Even in urban areas, some students lack access to devices or stable internet connections, creating disparities in participation.

4. **Need for Teacher Training**
    - Teachers must be equipped with strategies to effectively integrate technology without compromising pedagogical objectives.
5. **Monitoring and Data Privacy**
    - Collecting student data for personalization must be handled carefully to protect privacy and ensure ethical use.

6. Teachers' Reflections on Student-Centered Technology

Teachers in urban schools often share that student-centered approaches have helped them build deeper relationships with learners. They observe:

- Students becoming more confident in expressing their ideas and asking questions.
- A shift from passive listening to active engagement and discussion.
- Improvement in critical thinking and creativity as students are encouraged to explore topics independently.

One teacher commented:

"Allowing students to take charge of their learning has transformed the classroom environment. Students are more curious, and I've seen a genuine interest in learning."

Another teacher reflected:

"Technology has opened doors for students who struggled with traditional methods. Now they learn through formats that suit them best, and they are thriving."

7. Recommendations for Effective Implementation

1. **Focus on Student Needs First**
    - Technology should enhance—not dictate—learning experiences.
2. **Promote Balanced Use**
    - Encourage offline activities and discussions alongside digital tools.
3. **Train Students and Teachers**
    - Provide ongoing workshops and tutorials to build digital confidence.
4. **Incorporate Feedback Loops**
    - Regular reflection sessions help teachers fine-tune their approaches based on student experiences.
5. **Ensure Accessibility and Inclusivity**
    - Work towards providing devices, connectivity, and tailored content for all students.

19.5 Lessons Learned and Recommendations

Introduction

The integration of technology into education, especially in urban classrooms, has brought about significant changes in teaching and learning processes. However, these changes have not come without challenges. Through the experiences of teachers, students, and administrators, valuable lessons have been learned that can guide the future implementation of technology in education. This section summarizes the key lessons learned and offers practical recommendations for creating more effective, inclusive, and sustainable educational environments through technology.

1. Lessons Learned from Implementing Technology in Urban Classrooms

A. Technology is a Tool, Not a Solution by Itself

One of the most important lessons is that technology alone cannot solve educational challenges. It is a tool that must be integrated thoughtfully into pedagogy and classroom management. Effective teaching practices, strong relationships between teachers and students, and supportive administrative policies are essential components that technology can enhance but not replace.

B. Personalized Learning Enhances Student Engagement

Teachers have observed that when students are allowed to learn at their own pace using digital resources, their engagement and motivation improve. Personalized content helps students feel empowered and fosters a sense of ownership over their learning journey.

C. Teacher Training is Crucial

Implementing technology effectively depends largely on teachers' comfort and familiarity with digital tools. Schools that invest in professional development and continuous learning for teachers have seen better outcomes and smoother integration.

D. Infrastructure Must Be Reliable and Accessible

The effectiveness of technological approaches is often compromised by unreliable internet connections, outdated devices, or lack of access to necessary tools. Schools that proactively address these issues create more equitable learning environments.

E. Collaboration and Communication Enrich Learning

Platforms that encourage peer interaction, group projects, and discussions have been shown to enhance student learning. Students benefit from sharing perspectives and learning from their peers in a supportive environment.

F. Balanced Use Prevents Over-Reliance

Teachers have realized that while technology can make learning exciting, excessive screen time or dependence on digital tools can hinder social interactions and critical thinking. Balanced approaches that combine online and offline activities yield better educational experiences.

G. Ethical and Privacy Concerns Must Be Addressed

With the increasing use of digital platforms comes the responsibility to protect student data and privacy. Teachers and schools must be vigilant in adopting ethical practices and ensuring that students are aware of how their information is being used.

2. Recommendations for Future Implementation

A. Prioritize Training and Support for Teachers

- Conduct workshops and seminars that help teachers learn how to effectively integrate technology into their curriculum.
- Offer mentorship programs where experienced teachers support peers in overcoming challenges.
- Provide technical support during classes to resolve issues promptly.

B. Design Student-Centered Learning Experiences

- Incorporate tools that allow students to choose how and when they learn, catering to individual learning styles.
- Create opportunities for interactive learning through group projects, virtual labs, and gamified quizzes.
- Encourage reflection by prompting students to set learning goals and evaluate their progress.

C. Ensure Inclusive Access to Technology

- Work with government agencies and non-profits to provide devices and internet access to economically disadvantaged students.
- Develop multilingual content and accessible formats to cater to diverse student populations, including those with disabilities.
- Implement offline learning solutions where connectivity is limited.

D. Promote Responsible Use of Technology

- Educate students about cyber safety, digital etiquette, and ethical behavior online.

- Encourage mindful use of technology by setting screen-time limits and promoting offline learning activities.
- Regularly assess how students are using technology and guide them toward healthy digital habits.

E. Foster Collaboration Between Stakeholders

- Create partnerships between schools, technology providers, and community organizations to share resources and expertise.
- Involve parents and guardians in workshops and discussions about the benefits and challenges of technology in education.
- Encourage teachers to exchange best practices through online forums and local networks.

F. Develop Monitoring and Feedback Systems

- Implement tools that track student progress and provide actionable feedback to teachers.
- Conduct surveys and feedback sessions to gather student and teacher perspectives, using this information to refine learning strategies.
- Use data analytics responsibly to inform teaching practices while ensuring students' privacy.

G. Integrate Technology Thoughtfully into Curriculum Design

- Align technology tools with learning objectives to ensure that digital resources support rather than distract from educational goals.
- Design lessons that incorporate both digital and hands-on activities to provide a well-rounded learning experience.

- Regularly review and update teaching methods to keep pace with technological advancements.

3. The Way Forward

The lessons learned from integrating technology into urban classrooms demonstrate that success requires more than the availability of digital tools. It demands a holistic approach that considers teacher training, infrastructure, student engagement, and ethical concerns. Moving forward, schools should focus on:

- Building resilient and adaptable learning environments.
- Promoting equity and inclusivity in access to technology.
- Encouraging collaborative learning and innovation.
- Embedding technology into pedagogical practices rather than using it as an add-on.

When thoughtfully implemented, technology can enrich education, empower learners, and create opportunities for lifelong learning. By learning from past experiences and following the recommendations outlined above, schools can create meaningful and sustainable student-centered educational experiences that prepare learners for the challenges and opportunities of the future.

Appendices

A. Glossary of Technical Terms

This glossary provides definitions of key technical terms frequently used in discussions about educational technology. It is designed to help students, teachers, and researchers better understand concepts and tools used in modern learning environments.

1. Adaptive Learning

A method of learning that uses technology to personalize educational content based on the learner's performance and needs. It adjusts the difficulty and type of material in real time.

2. Artificial Intelligence (AI)

The simulation of human intelligence processes by computers and software, enabling systems to perform tasks such as learning, reasoning, and decision-making.

3. Assistive Technologies

Tools and devices that help students with disabilities access learning materials, such as screen readers, speech-to-text programs, and hearing aids.

4. Augmented Reality (AR)

A technology that overlays digital content (images, sounds, text) onto the real-world environment, often through smartphones, tablets, or AR glasses.

5. Blended Learning

An educational approach that combines traditional classroom teaching with online learning, allowing students to benefit from both methods.

6. Cloud Computing

The use of remote servers hosted on the internet to store, manage, and process data, enabling access to educational resources from anywhere at any time.

7. Cybersecurity

Measures and protocols designed to protect digital devices, networks, and data from unauthorized access, threats, or cyberattacks.

8. Data Analytics

The process of collecting, organizing, and analyzing data to help educators understand student performance and improve learning strategies.

9. Digital Divide

The gap between individuals or communities that have access to modern information and communication technologies and those that do not.

10. Digital Literacy

The ability to effectively and safely use digital tools, platforms, and devices to access, evaluate, create, and communicate information.

11. E-Learning (Electronic Learning)

A form of education that uses digital platforms, such as websites, apps, or software, to deliver instructional content outside of traditional classrooms.

12. Flipped Classroom

A learning model where students study instructional material, such as video lectures, at home and use classroom time for interactive activities, discussions, and problem-solving.

13. Gamification

The application of game-design elements such as points, badges, and leaderboards in educational settings to increase motivation and engagement.

14. Interactive Whiteboard

A digital board that allows teachers to display content, annotate, and interact with multimedia during lessons, often using a touch-sensitive surface.

15. Learning Management System (LMS)

Software platforms like Google Classroom or Moodle that help educators organize courses, distribute content, track student progress, and communicate with learners.

16. Microlearning

A method of delivering learning content in small, easily digestible segments, allowing students to learn in short bursts suited to their schedules.

17. Mobile Learning (M-Learning)

Learning conducted via mobile devices like smartphones and tablets, which provides flexible access to educational content anytime, anywhere.

18. Open Educational Resources (OER)

Teaching and learning materials that are freely available online for anyone to use, adapt, and share, such as textbooks, videos, and exercises.

19. Online Assessment Tools

Digital tools that allow educators to create quizzes, assignments, and tests that students can complete remotely, often with instant feedback.

20. Plagiarism

The act of copying or presenting someone else's work, ideas, or content as one's own without proper acknowledgment, often considered unethical and punishable in academic settings.

21. Smart Classroom

A classroom equipped with advanced technological tools, such as interactive whiteboards, high-speed internet, and multimedia resources, to support interactive and personalized learning.

22. Social Learning

A learning process that emphasizes collaboration, communication, and shared experiences among peers to enhance understanding and problem-solving.

23. Virtual Laboratory

A simulated online environment where students can conduct experiments and explore scientific concepts without the need for physical equipment.

24. Virtual Reality (VR)

A computer-generated simulation that immerses users in a fully digital environment, often used in education to create realistic scenarios for learning.

25. Webinars

Online seminars or workshops that provide interactive sessions between educators and students or experts, allowing real-time communication and collaboration.

B. Useful Websites, Apps, and Online Platforms

☐ Websites

1. **National Repository of Open Educational Resources (NROER)**
   https://nroer.gov.in
   A government platform offering free and open educational resources in multiple languages. Includes videos, images, e-books, and lesson plans.
2. **SWAYAM**
   https://swayam.gov.in
   An initiative by the Government of India providing free online courses from school to higher education levels, along with assessments and certifications.
3. **Khan Academy**
   https://www.khanacademy.org
   A widely used platform offering interactive exercises, instructional videos, and practice lessons for math, science, economics, and more.
4. **Coursera**
   https://www.coursera.org
   Offers online courses, specializations, and degrees from leading universities worldwide. Includes certification options and professional learning paths.
5. **edX**
   https://www.edx.org
   Provides free and paid courses from universities like Harvard, MIT, and Berkeley. Includes interactive assignments, quizzes, and discussion forums.
6. **OpenStax**
   https://openstax.org

A nonprofit offering peer-reviewed, openly licensed textbooks for students and educators across various subjects.

7. **Google Scholar**
   https://scholar.google.com
   A research tool that helps students and teachers find scholarly articles, theses, books, and conference papers.

Apps for Teaching and Learning

1. **Google Classroom**
   An integrated platform for managing assignments, sharing resources, and providing feedback in a structured way. Works with Google Docs, Sheets, Slides, and Drive.
2. **Quizizz**
   https://quizizz.com
   A gamified platform where teachers can create quizzes, assignments, and surveys that engage students in learning through fun, interactive formats.
3. **Kahoot!**
   https://kahoot.com
   Allows teachers to create quizzes, polls, and learning games that students can participate in real-time using smartphones or computers.
4. **Microsoft Teams**
   https://www.microsoft.com/en/microsoft-teams/group-chat-software
   A collaboration tool offering video conferencing, chat, file sharing, and assignment management for schools and universities.
5. **Edmodo**
   https://new.edmodo.com
   A secure social learning platform where teachers can post

lessons, assign homework, and encourage student collaboration.

6. **Nearpod**
   https://nearpod.com
   Allows teachers to create interactive lessons with quizzes, polls, and videos, encouraging student engagement and formative assessment.
7. **Remind**
   https://www.remind.com
   A communication tool that helps teachers send reminders, updates, and assignments to students and parents via text or app notifications.

□ Online Platforms for Researchand Collaboration

1. **ResearchGate**
   https://www.researchgate.net
   A professional network for researchers and scientists to share papers, ask questions, and collaborate.
2. **Academia.edu**
   https://www.academia.edu
   Allows academics to share research papers and connect with others in their field.
3. **TED-Ed**
   https://ed.ted.com
   Provides educational videos and lesson plans designed to spark curiosity and enhance critical thinking.
4. **Padlet**
   https://padlet.com
   A virtual board where teachers and students can post notes, images, videos, and documents, encouraging collaborative learning.

5. **Canva for Education**
   https://www.canva.com/education/
   Offers design templates for presentations, posters, infographics, and worksheets that can be easily customized.

□ Learning Management Systems (LMS)

1. **Moodle**
   https://moodle.org
   A popular open-source LMS that supports course management, assignment tracking, and interactive forums.
2. **Blackboard**
   https://www.blackboard.com
   Provides a secure platform for course content delivery, assessments, grading, and student collaboration.
3. **Schoology**
   https://www.schoology.com
   An LMS offering tools for creating assignments, fostering discussions, and assessing student performance.

□ Digital Libraries and Open Resources

1. **Project Gutenberg**
   https://www.gutenberg.org
   Provides over 60,000 free e-books, including classic literature and academic texts.
2. **ERIC (Education Resources Information Center)**
   https://eric.ed.gov
   A comprehensive database of educational research articles, reports, and papers for educators and policymakers.
3. **Internet Archive**
   https://archive.org

Offers access to millions of books, audio files, videos, and web archives for educational use.

- **Platforms for Professional Development**

1. **LinkedIn Learning**
   https://www.linkedin.com/learning/
   Offers video courses in teaching techniques, digital tools, leadership, and more for continuous professional growth.
2. **FutureLearn**
   https://www.futurelearn.com
   Provides online courses from global universities focusing on education, technology, and other fields.

C. Recommended Tools and Software

This section provides a curated list of tools and software that enhance teaching, learning, assessment, collaboration, and classroom management. These resources are suitable for educators, students, and institutions seeking to effectively integrate technology into education.

- **Learning Management Systems (LMS)**

1. **Google Classroom**
   A free and easy-to-use platform that integrates with other Google tools like Docs, Sheets, Slides, and Drive. It helps in creating, sharing, and grading assignments efficiently.
2. **Moodle**
   A flexible, open-source LMS that supports course management, online discussions, and assessments, widely used by schools and universities.

3. **Canvas**
   A modern LMS that offers interactive course designs, analytics, and mobile-friendly access for teachers and students.
4. **Blackboard**
   Provides tools for course content management, assessments, grading, and communication with learners in a secure digital environment.

□ Content Creation Tools

1. **Canva for Education**
   An intuitive design tool offering templates for presentations, posters, infographics, and worksheets, suitable for visually engaging educational content.
2. **Powtoon**
   A platform for creating animated videos and presentations, making learning more interactive and easier to understand.
3. **Edpuzzle**
   Enables teachers to turn video lessons into interactive sessions by adding quizzes, notes, and voiceovers.
4. **Screencast-O-Matic**
   A screen recording tool useful for creating tutorials, lectures, and demonstrations.

□ Assessment and Feedback Tools

1. **Quizizz**
   A gamified assessment tool that allows teachers to create fun quizzes and polls for students, with real-time feedback.

2. **Kahoot!**
   Encourages learning through games and quizzes, making assessment engaging and interactive.
3. **Google Forms**
   A versatile tool for creating surveys, quizzes, and feedback forms, with automatic grading and data collection.
4. **Socrative**
   Helps teachers conduct instant quizzes and polls to assess student understanding in real time.

□ Collaboration and Communication Tools

1. **Microsoft Teams**
   A collaboration platform offering video conferencing, file sharing, chat, and classroom scheduling, making it ideal for blended learning environments.
2. **Slack**
   Enables structured communication among students and teachers through channels and direct messaging.
3. **Padlet**
   A virtual bulletin board where users can post notes, images, and videos, encouraging collaborative learning.
4. **Zoom**
   Offers reliable video conferencing with screen sharing, breakout rooms, and interactive sessions.

□ Multimedia and Interactive Tools

1. **Nearpod**
   Allows teachers to create interactive lessons with quizzes, polls, 3D objects, and collaborative activities.

2. **ThingLink**
   Lets teachers add multimedia tags to images and videos, transforming static content into interactive learning experiences.
3. **Flipgrid**
   A video discussion platform that encourages student participation by enabling them to record and share short video responses.

Mobile Learning Apps

1. **Duolingo**
   A gamified app for language learning, offering bite-sized lessons and personalized feedback.
2. **Quizlet**
   Allows students to create and share flashcards, study sets, and practice tests for efficient memorization and learning.
3. **Khan Academy App**
   Provides access to a vast library of video lessons, practice exercises, and progress tracking across subjects.
4. **Brainscape**
   Offers adaptive flashcards for improving memory retention and self-paced learning.

Research and Reference Tools

1. **Google Scholar**
   A search engine for finding academic articles, research papers, and theses across various disciplines.
2. **Zotero**
   A reference management tool that helps students and researchers organize sources and create citations easily.

3. **Mendeley**
   A free tool for managing, sharing, and citing research papers, fostering academic collaboration.

□ Specialized Educational Tools

1. **Tinkercad**
   An easy-to-use 3D design and modeling tool for STEM projects, promoting hands-on learning.
2. **Labster**
   Offers virtual labs with interactive simulations, enabling students to experiment safely in a digital environment.
3. **Edmodo**
   A learning platform that connects students and teachers, allowing assignment sharing, feedback, and discussion.
4. **ClassDojo**
   Focuses on classroom behavior management and parent communication, helping create a positive learning environment.

□ Security and Privacy Tools

1. **Norton Security**
   Protects devices from malware, viruses, and phishing attempts, ensuring secure access to educational resources.
2. **LastPass**
   A password manager that helps users store and manage passwords securely, reducing the risk of unauthorized access.
3. **Google Workspace for Education**
   Offers enterprise-level security and data protection for schools using Google's suite of educational tools.

D. Teacher Training Modules

This section outlines structured training modules designed to equip teachers with the knowledge, skills, and confidence needed to effectively integrate educational technology into their teaching practices. These modules can be delivered through workshops, online courses, or blended formats and are aligned with modern pedagogical approaches and classroom needs.

Module 1: Introduction to Educational Technology

Duration: 4 hours
Objectives:

- Understand the role of technology in education
- Explore different types of educational technologies and tools
- Reflect on how technology can enhance teaching and learning

Topics Covered:

- Definition and scope of educational technology
- Overview of ICT tools and platforms
- Trends in digital learning
- Case studies of successful technology integration

Activities:

- Group discussion on technology experiences
- Interactive quizzes on tech tools
- Video demonstrations of learning platforms

Assessment:

- Reflective journal entry on how technology can be applied in their own classrooms

Module 2: Using Learning Management Systems (LMS)

Duration: 6 hours
Objectives:

- Learn how to set up and use LMS platforms for classroom management
- Create and share assignments, resources, and assessments
- Track student progress and provide timely feedback

Topics Covered:

- Introduction to platforms like Google Classroom, Moodle, and Canvas
- Setting up classes and user profiles
- Designing courses and uploading materials
- Managing student submissions and grading

Activities:

- Hands-on training on creating an LMS class
- Simulation exercises for setting assignments and quizzes
- Peer reviews of course structures

Assessment:

- Submission of a sample lesson plan using LMS

Module 3: Designing Digital Content and Interactive Lessons

Duration: 5 hours

Objectives:

- Understand instructional design principles for online and blended learning
- Create engaging content using multimedia tools
- Use gamification and interactive elements to enhance student participation

Topics Covered:

- Principles of instructional design (ADDIE, Kemp, etc.)
- Tools like Canva, Powtoon, Nearpod, and Edpuzzle
- Incorporating videos, quizzes, and discussion boards

Activities:

- Designing a digital lesson plan
- Creating an interactive quiz or activity
- Presenting lesson designs for feedback

Assessment:

- Uploading and sharing a sample interactive lesson with peers

Module 4: Assessment and Feedback through Technology

Duration: 4 hours

Objectives:

- Learn how to create and administer digital assessments
- Use tools for automated grading and personalized feedback

- Analyze data to improve learning outcomes

Topics Covered:

- Online test platforms (Quizizz, Kahoot!, Google Forms)
- Providing formative and summative assessments
- Using analytics dashboards to track progress

Activities:

- Creating an online test with feedback
- Exploring real-time data tracking tools
- Role-playing feedback sessions

Assessment:

- Designing an assessment plan aligned with learning objectives

Module 5: Promoting Inclusive and Assistive Learning

Duration: 4 hours
Objectives:

- Explore tools and strategies for supporting diverse learners
- Learn how to make digital content accessible
- Understand the ethical considerations involved in technology use

Topics Covered:

- Assistive technologies for students with disabilities
- Accessibility guidelines (WCAG standards)

- Case studies in inclusive classrooms

Activities:

- Demonstration of screen readers, text-to-speech, and subtitles
- Group discussions on classroom challenges
- Creating accessible content templates

Assessment:

- Developing an accessibility checklist for lesson plans

Module 6: Cybersecurity and Data Privacy

Duration: 3 hours
Objectives:

- Understand the importance of data protection in digital classrooms
- Learn how to safeguard student information and prevent breaches
- Implement policies for ethical use of technology

Topics Covered:

- Basics of cybersecurity and safe internet practices
- Data privacy laws and regulations (like GDPR, local guidelines)
- Preventing plagiarism and ensuring academic integrity

Activities:

- Identifying potential security threats in simulated scenarios
- Creating classroom rules for ethical use of technology
- Group brainstorming for cybersecurity protocols

Assessment:

- Drafting a data protection policy for school use

Module 7: Professional Growth and Networking

Duration: 3 hours
Objectives:

- Explore opportunities for continuous professional development using technology
- Join online communities for resource sharing and mentoring
- Use digital tools to build a personal learning network

Topics Covered:

- Online certifications, webinars, and workshops
- Participating in forums and peer networks
- Tools like LinkedIn Learning, ResearchGate, and academic platforms

Activities:

- Creating a personal professional development plan
- Networking simulation exercises
- Setting goals for long-term learning

Assessment:

- Submission of a professional learning roadmap

Module 8: Managing Screen Time and Digital Wellbeing

Duration: 3 hours
Objectives:

- Balance the use of technology to prevent burnout
- Promote healthy screen time habits for teachers and students
- Address stress and mental health concerns associated with digital learning

Topics Covered:

- Strategies to manage screen fatigue
- Encouraging breaks and offline learning activities
- Tools for mental health support and counseling

Activities:

- Stress management exercises
- Role-playing student-teacher interactions
- Designing classroom schedules to include screen breaks

Assessment:

- Creating a weekly wellness plan integrating digital and offline activities

E. References and Further Reading

Books

1. Bates, A. W., & Poole, G. (2003). *Effective Teaching with Technology in Higher Education: Foundations for Success*. Jossey-Bass.
2. Clark, R. C., & Mayer, R. E. (2016). *E-Learning and the Science of Instruction: Proven Guidelines for Consumers and Designers of Multimedia Learning*. Wiley.
3. Kozma, R. B. (2003). *Technology and Classroom Practices: An International Study*. International Society for Technology in Education (ISTE).
4. Mishra, P., & Koehler, M. J. (2006). *Technological Pedagogical Content Knowledge: A Framework for Teacher Knowledge*. Teachers College Record, 108(6), 1017–1054.
5. Prensky, M. (2010). *Teaching Digital Natives: Partnering for Real Learning*. Corwin Press.
6. Roblyer, M. D., & Hughes, J. E. (2019). *Integrating Educational Technology into Teaching*. Pearson.
7. Selwyn, N. (2016). *Education and Technology: Key Issues and Debates*. Bloomsbury Academic.

Research Articles and Journals

1. Al-Fraihat, D., Joy, M., & Sinclair, J. (2020). *Evaluating E-learning Systems Success: An Empirical Study*. Computers in Human Behavior, 102, 67–86.
2. Means, B., Toyama, Y., Murphy, R., Bakia, M., & Jones, K. (2010). *Evaluation of Evidence-Based Practices in Online Learning*. U.S. Department of Education.
3. Sangrà, A., Vlachopoulos, D., & Cabrera, N. (2012). *Building an Inclusive Definition of E-Learning: An Approach to the Conceptual Framework*. International Review of Research in Open and Distributed Learning, 13(2), 145–159.

4. Teo, T. (2011). *Factors Influencing Teachers' Intention to Use Technology: Model Development and Test*. Computers & Education, 57(4), 2432–2440.

Reports and Policy Documents

1. Ministry of Education, Government of India. (2020). *National Education Policy (NEP) 2020*. https://www.education.gov.in
2. Digital India Initiative. (2015). *Transforming India through Technology*. https://www.digitalindia.gov.in
3. UNESCO. (2013). *Policy Guidelines for Mobile Learning*. UNESCO Publishing.
4. World Bank. (2018). *World Development Report: Learning to Realize Education's Promise*. World Bank Publications.

Websites and Online Resources

1. SWAYAM – https://swayam.gov.in
2. National Repository of Open Educational Resources (NROER) – https://nroer.gov.in
3. Khan Academy – https://www.khanacademy.org
4. Coursera – https://www.coursera.org
5. edX – https://www.edx.org
6. Google Scholar – https://scholar.google.com

Further Reading and Reference Guides

1. Instructional Design Central – https://www.instructionaldesigncentral.com
2. Edutopia – https://www.edutopia.org

3. ISTE (International Society for Technology in Education) – https://www.iste.org
4. TeachThought – https://www.teachthought.com

Notes

www.ingramcontent.com/pod-product-compliance
Ingram Content Group UK Ltd.
Pitfield, Milton Keynes, MK11 3LW, UK
UKHW021346190726
13845UKWH00027B/743

9 789334 401080